EVIDENCE

AUSTRALIA
Law Book Co.
Sydney

CANADA AND USA
Carswell
Toronto

HONG KONG
Sweet & Maxwell Asia

NEW ZEALAND
Brookers
Wellington

SINGAPORE and MALAYSIA
Sweet & Maxwell Asia
Singapore and Kuala Lumpur

EVIDENCE—THE FUNDAMENTALS

EVIDENCE

FIRST EDITION

By

PHIL HUXLEY

LL.B LL.M., Formerly Principal Lecturer in Law, Nottingham Law School

LONDON
SWEET & MAXWELL
2008

First edition 2008

Published in 2008 by
Sweet & Maxwell Limited of 100 Avenue Road,
http://www.sweetandmaxwell.co.uk
Typeset by LBJ Typesetting Ltd of Kingsclere
Printed and bound in Great Britain by
Ashford Colour Press, Hants

No natural forests were destroyed to make this product;
only farmed timber was used and re-planted.

British Library Cataloguing in Publication Data

A CIP catalogue record for this book
is available from the British Library

ISBN 978-1-84703-416-8

PREFACE

According to the Encyclopedia Britannica evidence 'in law' consists of:

> 'any of the material items or assertions of fact that may be submitted to a competent tribunal as a means of ascertaining the truth of any alleged matter of fact under investigation before it.'

As we shall see the key passage in the definition is 'as a means. . .' Mastering the law of Evidence means mastery of the rules of *how* a matter in issue between the parties may be proved. The law of Evidence is primarily process rather than outcome driven. In criminal proceedings a key part of this process has, historically, been protection of the defendant from conviction on evidence deemed overly prejudicial to a fair trial. The concept of a trial fair to both parties is now of overwhelming importance in the conduct of trials and appeals. It is enshrined in art.6 of the European Convention on Human Rights and Fundamental Freedoms and its beneficence is to be seen in both its express and implied rights. In even the most democratic states governments are sometimes tempted to play fast and loose with the laws of Evidence, usually by violating the presumption of innocence as a cheap alternative to deep thought. While it is possible to study the law of Evidence as a loose body of rules and thereby to satisfy the demands of examiners, it is hoped that this process will itself provoke the inquiring mind as to why the law is as it is, what objectives it seeks to promote and how it might be improved.

This book seeks to provide a good grounding in the key areas of evidence in criminal proceedings at undergraduate level. It is hoped that the provision of tables and charts will render a little clearer that which Parliament and the courts often leave as at best opaque. The law is stated as at March 31, 2008.

'. . . certainty generally is an illusion, and repose is not the destiny of man.'

Oliver Wendell Holmes (1841–1935)
The Path of the Law 10 Harward Law Review 457 (1897)

ACKNOWLEDGMENTS

Grateful acknowledgment is made for permission to reproduce from the undermentionned works:

INCORPORATED COUNCIL OF LAW REPORTING
Law Reports, Appeal Cases

LEXISNEXIS BUTTERWORTHS
The All England Law Reports

JUDICIAL STUDIES BOARD *www.jsboard.co.uk*
Specimen Direction

CONTENTS

List of Figures

ABBREVIATIONS

Statutes

C&YPA: Children and Young Persons Act 1933
CAA: Child Abduction Act 1984
CEA: Criminal Evidence Act 1898
CJA: Criminal Justice Act (various years)
CJPOA: Criminal Justice and Public Order Act 1994
CPA: Criminal Procedure Act 1865
HRA: Human Rights Act 1998
PACE: Police and Criminal Evidence Act 1984
SOA: Sexual Offences Act 2003
YJCEA: Youth Justice and Criminal Evidence Act 1999

Other

ECHR: European Convention on Human Rights & Fundamental Freedoms
ECtHR: European Court of Human Rights
JSB: Judicial Studies Board

Information

Criminal Justice Act 2003		
Part 11	Content	Sections
Chapter 1	Evidence of bad character	98–113
Chapter 2	Hearsay	114–136
Chapter 3	Miscellaneous & Supplemental	137–141

TABLE OF CASES

TABLE OF STATUTES

Introduction

0.1 Brief history

The law of evidence is of great antiquity and until the end of the nineteenth century was developed almost entirely by trial judges at common law. Until the creation in 1907 of the Court of Criminal Appeal (abolished in 1967 and replaced by the Court of Appeal (Criminal Division)), the system of appeal was haphazard and most of the learned judgments in the subject are, therefore, from twentieth and twenty-first century cases. The latter part of the last century saw immense statutory change to the law of evidence which has continued into the present. Much of the, 'reform' is incoherent, slapdash in drafting, and ineffective and under-resourced in practice owing everything to courting passing tabloid popularity.

A further factor militating against consistency in the law was that when judges decided cases—which for our purposes tends to mean deciding whether a particular item of evidence was admissible—they did it not so much by reference to hard and fast rules or principles but rather by the exigencies of the particular case. Hence there is, or at least was, considerable doubt as to the scope of many of the alleged 'rules' of evidence since everything tended to turn on the facts of the case. This also gave rise to (as well as being the consequence of) the principle that a trial judge has discretion not to admit evidence if its admission would be unduly prejudicial to the defendant (judges run their own courts). While this discretion is certainly not unfettered, appellate courts remain slow to over-ride a trial judge's discretion since the judge has seen the witnesses and is in the best position to consider admissibility of evidence.

The rules of admissibility referred to above were usually created in the context of indictable trial i.e. before judge and jury. Although the overwhelming majority of criminal proceedings are now heard summarily i.e. in a magistrates' court the rules of evidence apply equally to both summary and indictable proceedings, though cynics would assert that in magistrates' courts they are honoured more in the breach than in the observance. The common law rules often reflect the division of function between judge (issues of law) and jury (issues of fact) and they do not always transfer easily to summary trial where both functions are exercised by the magistrates. The division between law and fact continues even in the most recent reforms such as the CJA 2003 which reflects the circumstances of indictable, rather than summary procedure. Where it is in issue, admissibility of evidence remains in the hands of the judge.

However, we live in changing times. The CJA 2003 abolished the common law rules on the admissibility of hearsay evidence and evidence of bad character. Consequently the jury now hears evidence formerly kept from them. Admissibility is sometimes subject to judicial discretion but is very often not leave-dependent. Under s.78(1) of PACE there is overall discretion to exclude evidence on which the prosecution proposes to rely where its admission would have an adverse effect on the fairness of the proceedings. Judicial discretion to exclude evidence on which the defendant wishes to rely is very limited—in general the criterion in such circumstances is relevance. In addition we shall find there are a number of situations where the judge is required to give the jury a specific warning about the dangers of relying on particular evidence. Examples are in relation to visual identification (see Ch.10, para.10.3.2) and where the prosecution wishes to rely on lies told by the defendant (see Ch.8 para.8.2.5).

Historical tipping points

(i) The Criminal Evidence Act 1898

It was not until 1898 that a defendant was allowed to go into the witness box and give sworn evidence in criminal proceedings generally. This is known as being 'competent in his own behalf' and is a landmark in the development of the law of evidence as well as of criminal law. Prior to 1898, the defendant's story could be recounted only by cross-examination of prosecution witnesses or by calling his own witnesses. The defendant was the one person who was not able to give sworn evidence and though he could make an unsworn statement from the dock (abolished by the CJA 1982 s.72(1)), he could not be cross-examined on it and its status as evidence was always dubious. Since he was not a competent witness, his state of mind was related to what a reasonable man would have thought or considered and that is the origin of the reasonable man test in criminal law. Once the defendant became competent, perhaps the reasonable man should have disappeared, since the defendant could tell the court of his mens rea. However, as all students of criminal law are aware, the reasonable man proved too useful to be abolished and he continues to stalk the corridors of the criminal law almost 100 years on. The writing seems finally to be on the wall for him following the decision of the House of Lords in *B (A Minor) v DPP* [2000] 1 All E.R. 833.

(ii) The Human Rights Act 1998

Under s.3 of the Act the courts are required to interpret all primary and subordinate legislation in a way which is compatible with the ECHR. In practice, this has meant paying close attention not only to the decisions of the ECtHR but also the *approach* of that court to Convention rights. This includes the express rights in the articles as well as those rights which the Court has been willing to imply such as the right to silence during questioning from the police. In the context of the law of evidence, there has been significant use of the HRA in relation to reverse proof burdens (see Ch.1, para.1.2), the admission of hearsay evidence (see Ch.4 para.4.6.8) and inferences from silence under police questioning (see Ch.8, para.8.2) based on art.6—the right to a fair trial. English courts have been slow to make declarations of incompatibility (s.4) preferring to achieve compatibility by 'reading down' wherever possible even when it produces bizarre outcomes as in *Lambert* [2002] 2 A.C. 545. The result of that decision is to give two different meanings to the word 'prove' within the same subsection.

0.2 Admissibility of evidence

The first principle of the law of evidence is that only evidence which is sufficiently relevant to an issue before the court is admissible and that any evidence which is irrelevant or insufficiently relevant must be excluded. Historically the principle was subject to a number of exceptions which excluded relevant evidence usually on the ground either of unreliability or prejudice to the defendant.

The question 'is this evidence relevant?' may well explain many decisions relatively easily without the need to plunder vast areas of the law of evidence. In general appellate courts in England have adopted a pragmatic rather than esoteric approach to relevance. In *Randall* [2003] UKHL 69 Lord Steyn [20] had this to say:

> '. . . Article 1 of Stephen's Digest of the Law of Evidence, 12th ed (1936), explains relevance as follows:
>
> > "any two facts to which it is applied are so related to each other that according to the common course of events one either taken by itself or in connection with other facts proves or renders probable the past, present or future existence or non-existence of the other."
>
> In *DPP v Kilbourne* [1973] AC 729, Lord Simon of Glaisdale put the position more simply, at p.756 D–E:
>
> > "Evidence is relevant if it is logically probative or disprobative of some matter which requires proof . . . relevant . . . evidence is evidence which makes the matter which requires proof more or less probable."
>
> A judge ruling on a point of admissibility involving an issue of relevance has to decide whether the evidence is capable of increasing or diminishing the probability of the existence of a fact in issue. The question of relevance is typically a matter of degree to be determined, for the most part, by common sense and experience: *Keane, The Modern Law of Evidence,* 5th ed (2000), at 20.'

Judges often refer to an item of evidence having or not having 'probative value.' This means having some use in proving or disproving some matter or making a conclusion more or less likely. Where evidence has probative value (and it is a relative, not an all or nothing matter), but is shown also to have potential to prejudice the defendant the judge must balance 'prejudicial effect against probative value'—a phrase which is recurrent in the law of evidence. The courts are a 'public authority' within s.6(1) and (3) of the HRA so are required to act in a way which is compatible with Convention rights. The decision on admissibility of individual items of evidence must be taken in the light of the courts' HRA obligations.

The principle stated above is in two parts. The first is that only relevant evidence is admissible; the second is that irrelevant evidence must be excluded. The latter is no less important than the former, as the case of *Sandhu* [1997] Crim. L.R. 288 indicates. The defendant was charged with making unauthorised alterations to a listed building—an offence of strict liability. The prosecution was permitted to prove the defendant was aware that his builder's activities went beyond the alteration authorisation granted to him. His appeal that evidence of mens rea was inadmissible on a charge of strict liability succeeded. The Court of Appeal held that such evidence was not an 'optional extra'. Any evidence which went beyond what is necessary to prove the offences in question is inadmissible and, on the present facts, was simply prejudicial to the defendant.

0.3 Classification of evidence

Different categories of rules

The rules of evidence fall into one of two categories—they are either exclusionary or inclusionary. Evidence governed by an exclusionary rule is inadmissible unless there is an exception which allows it to be given. In the same way, evidence governed by an inclusionary rule is admissible unless there is an exception which prevents it from being given.

Different classifications of evidence

Here is an exercise to try from your general knowledge. Try it! You will find that this section of work explains the classifications and you can write your answers in.

Figure 1—Different classifications of evidence

Classifications of evidence	Definition or Description or Example
Direct	
Hearsay	
Circumstantial	
Original	
Real	

Direct

Direct evidence is evidence which is usually in the form of the oral testimony of a witness who perceived the facts in issue with his own unaided senses. So a witness might tell the court of the speed of a vehicle he followed or the fact that he saw a supermarket customer put an item into their pocket instead of the wire basket.

Hearsay

In its spoken form (known as oral) hearsay evidence is the testimony of a witness (W) who tells the court what someone else (S) told W in order to prove that what S said is true. Suppose S witnesses an accident. S tells a police officer (W) who did not see the accident the registration number of the vehicle involved. It would not be hearsay if W were called to say that S had told him the registration number of a vehicle (Q: 'did S say something to you?' A: 'Yes he told me the number of a car') because W could give direct evidence of that fact. The hearsay issue engages when W is asked 'What did S say to you?' W's testimony as to the actual number would be hearsay evidence of the number. You should note even at this early stage that all we are saying is that W's evidence as the registration number would be hearsay—we are not saying anything about admissibility. These are completely different issues and you must keep them separate.

Figure 2—Table illustrating hearsay evidence

Question to W	W's answer	Hearsay Y/N; reason
Did S speak to you?	Yes	No; W knows this for himself
What did S say to you?	He gave me a car registration number	No; again W knows whether it was a car number
What was the number?	ABC 123	Yes; W is giving the court information which he doesn't know to be true.

In its written form (known as documentary) hearsay evidence is some type of recording of a permanent nature (writing, video/audio tape, email etc.) of information which is given to the court by a person who cannot vouch for the truth of the contents. A tape-recorded or hand written confession by the defendant supplied to the court by the police officer to whom it was made would be hearsay. The officer does not know whether the confession is true. Confessions are not only an example of hearsay—they are also an example of a statutory exclusionary rule. If the prosecution wishes to rely on a disputed confession allegedly made by the defendant it is inadmissible unless the prosecution proves beyond reasonable doubt that it was not obtained by the oppression of the defendant or in circumstances which would cause it to be unreliable: PACE s.76(2).

Hearsay might also be found in a gesture. Suppose a witness (W) sees her friend (S) getting out of a car sporting a black eye. W makes an inquisitive gesture about the black eye and S responds with a nod towards the man in the car (D). The nod would be hearsay if the incident were narrated to the court by W as evidence that D was responsible for the injury. Its admissibility would depend on a number of factors which we shall explore in Ch.4.

The common law was highly suspicious of hearsay and excluded it subject to a mosaic of exceptions. So hearsay was the best known example of an exclusionary rule. This has changed under the CJA 2003 as we shall see in Ch.4.

Circumstantial evidence

In contrast with direct evidence circumstantial evidence is evidence from which the existence or non-existence of facts in issue may be inferred; direct evidence is evidence of those facts directly. So proof that the defendant owns a gun is indirect or circumstantial evidence of his involvement in a crime if it is shown that his gun was used to kill P. Traditionally, circumstantial evidence is treated with suspicion on the ground that it is easy to manufacture. It is also said that it suffers from two fallibilities—fallibility of assertion and fallibility of inference—whereas direct evidence suffers only from the former. So perhaps the suspicion of circumstantial evidence is not unreasonable. On the other hand a strong chain of circumstantial evidence may draw the defendant as tightly into an offence as a single piece of direct evidence and it has been said that 'circumstances do not lie'—a reference to their alleged strength in contrast to fabricated direct oral evidence.

> 'Even the clearest and most perfect circumstantial evidence is likely to be at fault, after all, and therefore ought to be received with great caution. Take the case of any pencil, sharpened by any woman; if you have witnesses, you will find she did it with a knife; but if you take simply the aspect of the pencil, you will say she did it with her teeth.' (Mark Twain, *Pudd'nhead Wilson*)

Original evidence

Original evidence is evidence that a statement was made ('did A then say something to you?') or to prove the length of the blade of a knife or the existence of a bloodstain on an item of clothing. 'When a witness is asked to narrate another's assertion for some purpose other than that of inducing the court to accept it as true his evidence is said to be original.' (Cross and Tapper, p.47.)

Real evidence

This 'usually takes the form of some material produced for inspection in order that the court may draw an inference from its own observation as to the existence, condition or value of the article in question.' (Keane, p.10.) It would include a scar or broken limb in the victim of an assault. In *Clarke* [1995] 2 Cr. App. R. 425, it was held that facial mapping by video superimposition was 'a species of real evidence to which no special rules apply.' (per Steyn L.J.) The technique consists of creating two videos out of two batches of still photographs, one batch from an automatic camera at a bank and the other from police photographs of the defendant. The videos were then run superimposed on each other for the jury's benefit.

In *Luttrell* [2004] EWCA Crim 1344 the Court of Appeal held that lip-reading evidence from a video is, like facial mapping, a species of real evidence capable of passing the ordinary tests of relevance and reliability; and therefore being potentially admissible in evidence.

Summary

The above definitions are neither discrete nor self-contained and can overlap. In addition, though some of the terms are little used in practice, the direct/original/hearsay area is commonly referred to and is one of the most difficult to penetrate.

Did you attempt the exercise at the start of this section? If you did, how do your answers measure up? If not, do it now!

0.4 Function of judge and jury

For trial purposes offences are classified as either indictable, summary or 'either-way.' Indictable offences are tried before a judge and jury in the Crown court. Summary offences are tried before a magistrates' court. Either-way offences may be tried either at Crown court or by magistrates. The decision about venue for either-way offences turns mainly on whether the magistrates believe their limited sentencing powers are sufficient to dispose of the case in the event of a plea or finding of guilt.

At trials on indictment questions of law are for the judge while issues of fact are for the jury. In summary proceedings magistrates take advice on law from the clerk, but in effect the distinct functions at indictable trial are rolled up.

The judge

The major functions are questions of what the law is, admissibility of evidence, competence of witnesses and directions to the jury on the legal and factual issues arising in the case. As we shall see in later chapters some of these functions are exercised in the absence of the jury. When this happens the proceedings are known as a voir dire ('to speak the truth') or 'a trial within a trial.' This process may involve the judge in decisions relating to the facts something which, as we have seen, is normally the province of the jury. Similarly judicial decisions about the admissibility of evidence, the competence of a witness to give evidence at all, or the meaning of words or phrases may mean the jury never gets to evaluate the credibility of a witness or the weight of some evidence. The line between the functions of judge and jury is not as clear as it might appear.

Occasionally the judge will decide to admit a piece of evidence on a provisional basis—when he is persuaded that its relevance will be demonstrated later in the proceedings. This is known as conditional admissibility. If its relevance is not demonstrated the jury will be instructed to ignore it in their deliberations.

The judge has no power to stop a case before it starts only because he thinks the defendant has a defence to the charge and that to proceed would be a waste of time: *Attorney General's Reference (No.2 of 2000), The Times*, November 23, 2000. This does not affect the powers of the court with regard to abuse of process (see Ch.7, para.7.2.3) or if the prosecution is oppressive and vexatious. In *Hook, The Times*, November 2, 1994, the Court of Appeal reiterated that, where evidence was clearly inadmissible, it was the duty of the judge to challenge it and rule it inadmissible; not to do so would be a misdirection. We saw how important this is in *Sandhu* (see para.0.2).

The judge must also rule on any submission of 'no case to answer'. This is covered in Ch.2, para.2.5. Apart from any such submission the judge is entitled to direct an acquittal at any stage of the trial if satisfied there is no evidence which would justify convicting the defendant: *DPP v Stonehouse* (1977) 65 Cr. App. R. 192.

There are no circumstances in which the judge can tell a jury that they must convict the defendant: *Wang* [2005] UKHL 9. Neither should the judge indicate to the jury what their decision should be, though in the past not all judges were so scrupulous. In a civil case *Horton v McCurty* (1860) 5 H&N 667, Pollock J. is reported as saying:

> 'Gentlemen, I believe it is for you to decide whether this was a proper ground for dismissal—but if it be a matter of law . . . my opinion is that it is a good ground of dismissal.'

Unsurprisingly the jury found for the defendant.

It is the judge's function to identify whatever defence is raised on the evidence whether or not it is expressly relied on by the defence and, 'fairly and conveniently' place the defence before the jury: *Curtin* unreported, May 24, 1996 approved in *Soames-Waring, The Times*, July 20, 1998. In the latter case, the defendant did not give evidence but the jury had a summary of the interview with the police. It was sufficient for the judge to draw the jury's attention to the relevant pages of the summary, while inviting them to read it as a whole. It has been repeatedly stated that the judge's direction does not need to be a rehearsal of all of the evidence. The judge should remind the jury of the uncontested issues and 'identify succinctly those pieces of evidence which are in conflict': *Farr* [1999] Crim. L.R. 506 (per Rose L.J.). In *Amado-Taylor* [2000] 2 Cr. App. R. 189 the judge left it to counsel to address the jury on matters of fact directing them only on the law. The Court of Appeal held that this did not amount to putting the defence fairly and adequately before the jury and was improper.

The judge is not merely a referee disinterested between the parties.

> 'It is the responsibility of the judge to ensure that the proceedings are conducted in an orderly and proper manner which is fair to both prosecution and defence.' (per Lord Steyn in *Randall v R* [2002] UKPC 19 [10].

For example it will sometimes be necessary for him to take a view about whether admitting a particular item of evidence would deprive the defendant of a fair trial while balancing this against the public interest in convicting the guilty. The case of *Percival, The Times*, July 20, 1998 is a good illustration. The defendant was convicted in September 1997 of sexual offences against boys between 1957 and 1969. Holland J. said there was growing awareness of unreported sexual abuse and that this:

> 'has served to encourage experienced judges to be more liberal in their concept of what is possible by way of a fair trial in the face of delay.'

On the facts a fair trial was possible but they called for a firm direction on the burden and standard of proof. While delay caused each side difficulties, the problems were different in nature and importance. Holland J. said that the judge had reiterated the submissions of each side but lacking was a:

> 'clear expression . . . as to where he stood as the person seized with the task of securing a fair trial, notwithstanding the delay.'

Reviewing the evidence gave the judge the opportunity to make the point about delay.

> 'If long delayed cases were to go before juries, judges had to play a prominent role in ensuring that any conviction reflected a full appreciation of the problem, delay and the solution, the burden and standard of proof.'

The Court of Appeal has stressed that counsel and the judge should discuss in advance any particular directions on the law which the judge was minded to give in his direction: *N* [1998] Crim. L.R. 886. In *Wright, The Times*, March 3, 2000 the Court of Appeal said that judges at all levels could derive 'enormous assistance from submissions made to them by responsible advocates.' In that case the judge has commented on the failure of the defence to call a witness in support of a defence of duress. The Court held that, standing alone, such a statement detracted from the direction on burden of proof and was improper.

The jury

The jury decides issues of the weight or value to be attached to admissible evidence. In *Adams* [1996] 2 Cr. App. R. 466 the defence submitted the jury should use the Bayes Theorem (a statistical probability theory) to assist them in weighing the value of the DNA profile on which the prosecution case depended. The prosecution accepted the validity of this approach, as did the judge, who instructed the jury accordingly. On appeal that the judge's explanation had been inadequate, the Court of Appeal said that it had grave doubts as to whether the Theorem was admissible.

> 'Jurors evaluate evidence and reach conclusions not by means of a formula, mathematical or otherwise, but by the joint application of their individual common sense and knowledge of the world to the evidence before them.'

In *Adams (No.2)* [1998] 2 Cr. App. R. 467, the Court of Appeal held the evidence was inadmissible in cases lacking any special features.

Whilst weight of evidence or credibility of witnesses is generally the province of the jury, there are occasions when they will be instructed about the use they may make of admissible evidence. For example the jury must be warned not to treat a defendant's proven lie inexorably as evidence of guilt—there is a special ('*Lucas*' direction—see Ch.8. A similar situation arises in relation to disputed evidence of visual identification—see Ch.10). Such situations represent a sort of half-way house between judicial exclusion of the evidence and allowing the jury free rein with it. The number of such situations is not great in the English law of evidence but they do represent a further blurring of the line between the judicial and fact-finding functions with which we have been concerned in this section of work.

Specimen Direction

This is part of the Specimen Direction from the JSB on jury direction. It neatly summarises many of the issues we have considered above.

> 'Throughout this trial the law has been my area of responsibility, and I must now give you directions as to the law which applies in this case. When I do so, you must accept those directions and follow them.

I must also remind you of the prominent features of the evidence. However, it has always been your responsibility to judge the evidence and decide all the relevant facts of this case, and when you come to consider your verdict you, and you alone, must do that.

The facts of this case are your responsibility. You will wish to take account of the arguments in the speeches you have heard, but you are not bound to accept them. Equally, if in the course of my review of the evidence, I appear to express any views concerning the facts, or emphasise a particular aspect of the evidence, do not adopt those views unless you agree with them; and if I do not mention something which you think is important, you should have regard to it, and give it such weight as you think fit. When it comes to the facts of this case, it is your judgment alone that counts.'

0.5 Matters not susceptible of proof

Some issues arising in court are not the subject of proof in the normal way or, possibly, at all. There are three areas to consider. These are:

- formal admissions;
- judicial notice; and
- presumptions.

0.5.1 Formal admissions

A party to criminal litigation may formally admit some or all of the facts in issue. Where that occurs, no proof of the issue admitted is needed. Admissions are made by virtue of s.10 of the CJA 1967 which is in effect 'a self-contained code' (Murphy, p.604). They may be made by either prosecution or defence. Under s.10(4) an admission may, with the leave of the court, be withdrawn. Otherwise, once made the admission 'shall as against that party be conclusive evidence in the proceedings.' (s.10(1)).

0.5.2 Judicial notice

Some issues are so well known ('notorious') that no proof of them is required, e.g. that December 25 is Christmas Day in England or that cats are kept for domestic purposes. What is notorious changes over time.

Where the matter is not notorious, the court may take notice of it after enquiry or reference to an authoritative source. This might occur, for example, where the issue is the beliefs of a particular religious or political sect and it also applies to the meaning of words in common usage. In these circumstances, the inquiry does not amount to the judge hearing evidence.

However, a court may take judicial notice following the reception of evidence. In the civil case of *McQuaker v Goddard* [1940] 1 K.B. 687, Branson J. took notice that a camel is a domestic animal. He did this following expert evidence on the subject and his own reading of books. The Court of Appeal upheld the judge, noting that the witnesses were not giving evidence in the normal sense but were assisting the judge in 'forming his view as to what the ordinary course of nature in this regard in fact is a matter of which he is supposed to have complete knowledge.' This creates a precedent on the issue.

The effect of taking judicial notice

If the court takes notice of a fact the jury will be directed to take that fact as found. In *Gibson v Wales* [1983] 1 All E.R. 869 the Divisional Court held that a flick knife is an offensive weapon for statutory purposes and in *DPP v Hynde* [1998] 1 All E.R. 649 a butterfly knife was treated in the same way. The consequence is that, although this remains a question of fact, the jury must accept it as proved. Any other rule would permit one tribunal to find such a weapon to be offensive while another tribunal could find that it was not. That would be an 'affront to justice' (per Henry L.J.).

0.5.3 **Presumptions**

At its simplest, presumptions may be classified as falling into one of three areas. The first area is factual presumptions which are no more than examples of frequently recurring circumstances. Examples are an inference of guilty knowledge from unexplained possession of stolen goods or attempting to destroy evidence, or from an attempt to flee the scene of a crime.

The second area comprises what are called irrebuttable presumptions of law such as the rule that a child less than ten years of age cannot be guilty of a criminal offence or those found in s.76(1) and (2) of the SOA 2003. Notwithstanding that certain matters should be 'conclusively presumed' they are not presumptions but a legal rules and are not part of the law of evidence.

The third area is rebuttable presumptions of law. It is usual to include the 'presumptions' of innocence and sanity in this group but these are essentially aspects of the burden of proof rather than presumptions in the true sense.

1 Burden of Proof

1.1 Introduction

This chapter is concerned with two apparently simple questions 'which party to criminal proceedings proves what?' and 'to what standard?' The answer to the first question determines inter alia

- who starts the proceedings in court;
- the judge's direction to the jury; and
- advice the legal practitioner gives a client on the chances of success.

We shall find that the language used to describe some of the concepts in this area is far from clear and that does not help our study. To set the scene, let us imagine a dispute about an issue such as which is the best movie of all time; which is the best restaurant in town; which was the best football team last season? Such disputes usually start with someone making a proposition with which others disagree. The proponent of the issue will feel compelled to provide some sort of support for their proposition and those who disagree will often provide an alternative view without necessarily feeling under any compulsion to do so.

This gives us a (rough) working model for the chapter. In criminal proceedings the proponent might be likened to the prosecution while those who disagree might be likened to the defendant. The prosecution asserts the defendant's guilt and must convince the court of the truth of what it alleges. The defendant may either dispute the prosecution's version of events, or introduce new facts of his own, or both.

We start with by attempting to explain the vocabulary associated with this part of the law of evidence.

1.2 The meaning of 'burden of proof'

The dictionary definition of 'burden' is 'something that is carried' or 'load'. It defines 'proof' as 'evidence which establishes the truth or validity of something'. Putting them together we see that 'burden of proof' means something like the load or obligation to establish the truth of a proposition.

However, in legal proceedings we need to identify two separate meanings of 'burden of proof' and then to distinguish them from the expression 'evidential burden' with which they are too often conflated.

1.2.1 The overall (also referred to as 'general' or 'legal') burden

The overall burden is the obligation on a party to prove what is alleged. If the prosecution alleges the defendant is guilty of rape or murder or theft that is what must be proved at the end of the day, i.e. when the jury returns its verdict.

1.2.2 The specific proof burdens

This phrase refers to the legal issues which *must* be proved for a party to win their case. In a prosecution under the SOA s.3 (sexual assault) the burdens are

- intentional touching of B by A;
- sexual touching;
- lack of consent by B to the touching; and
- A's lack of reasonable belief that B consents.

The overall burden (see para.1.2.1) consists of the sum of the specific burdens. The definition of the crime (whether statutory or common law) tells the prosecutor what must be proved before he can secure a conviction. The source of the specific proof burdens is the substantive (sometimes called the 'black-letter') law. In theory each specific burden needs to be proved against the defendant before he can be convicted. In practice, most contested proceedings focus on one or at most two issues.

1.2.3 The evidential burden

This is the obligation to adduce evidence to make some matter a live issue in the trial. This will often be in order to support a specific proof burden which in turn may be an element in the overall burden of proof. According to Clarke L.J. in *Sheldrake v DPP* [2003] EWHC 273 (Admin) [52] discharging the evidential burden means:

> '. . . demonstrating by evidence. As I see it the evidence can be given by the prosecution or the defence. It might take the form of something said to the police at the scene, or something said in interview or something said by the defendant or anyone else in the witness box provided in each case that it is put in evidence.'

1.2.4 Proof and evidential burdens distinguished

The overall and specific burdens are proof burdens but the evidential burden is not. Putting this another way, if a party has a specific proof burden on an issue (such as that the touching was sexual in the example above) an evidential burden is an integral part of it but (i) adducing evidence about an issue is not the same thing as proving it; and (ii) a party with an evidential burden does not necessarily hold a specific proof burden with regard to that issue. This can be explained by imagining a prosecution for theft from a shop.

The overall burden is to prove theft contrary to the Theft Act 1968 s.1. The specific proof burdens are located in s.1 in the same way that we saw them in the SOA s.3 above. Let us suppose the prosecution leads evidence of the facts by calling a member of in-store security who saw the defendant and the evidence would, absent any explanation from the defendant, be sufficient to support a conviction. Now let us suppose the defendant asserts he forgot to pay (taking the goods without payment was an oversight) or that he was drowsy from medication. This amounts to a denial of dishonesty within s.1. In this hypothetical, the prosecution has adduced sufficient evidence to make the issue of dishonesty live and the defendant has countered it by evidence in his behalf. The defendant does not have a proof burden about dishonesty but you can see that unless he says something or calls evidence he runs the risk of being convicted.

Figure 3—Table illustrating burdens in the law of theft

Overall burden	Specific burdens	Evidential burden	
To prove theft contrary to the Theft Act 1968 s.1.	Dishonesty and others.	On prosecution as part of specific and overall burdens of proof.	On defendant to make it live issue or counter prosecution evidence but *not* as matter of proof.

The hypothetical above shows that each side can have an evidential burden *in respect of the same issue* though only one of them can hold the proof burden in respect of that issue.

It is said that a prosecutor discharges the evidential burden when he adduces sufficient evidence to require the judge to leave the issue to the jury. The prosecutor must do this in respect of all the contentious issues—sometimes referred to as the burden of 'passing the judge' but more usually as a prima facie case. This obligation must be discharged by 'half time', i.e. the point in the case when the prosecutor has called all his witnesses and tells the court that 'that is the prosecution's case'. The prosecution is not normally permitted to call any further evidence once it has closed its case.

When all the evidence is in, whoever decides the case (sometimes a jury, more often the magistrates) must be convinced by the evidence of the party who has both the overall and specific proof burdens, to the requisite standard of proof. It follows that the overall burden is decided only once and that is at the end of the trial when all the evidence has been presented.

Figure 4—Illustration of burdens

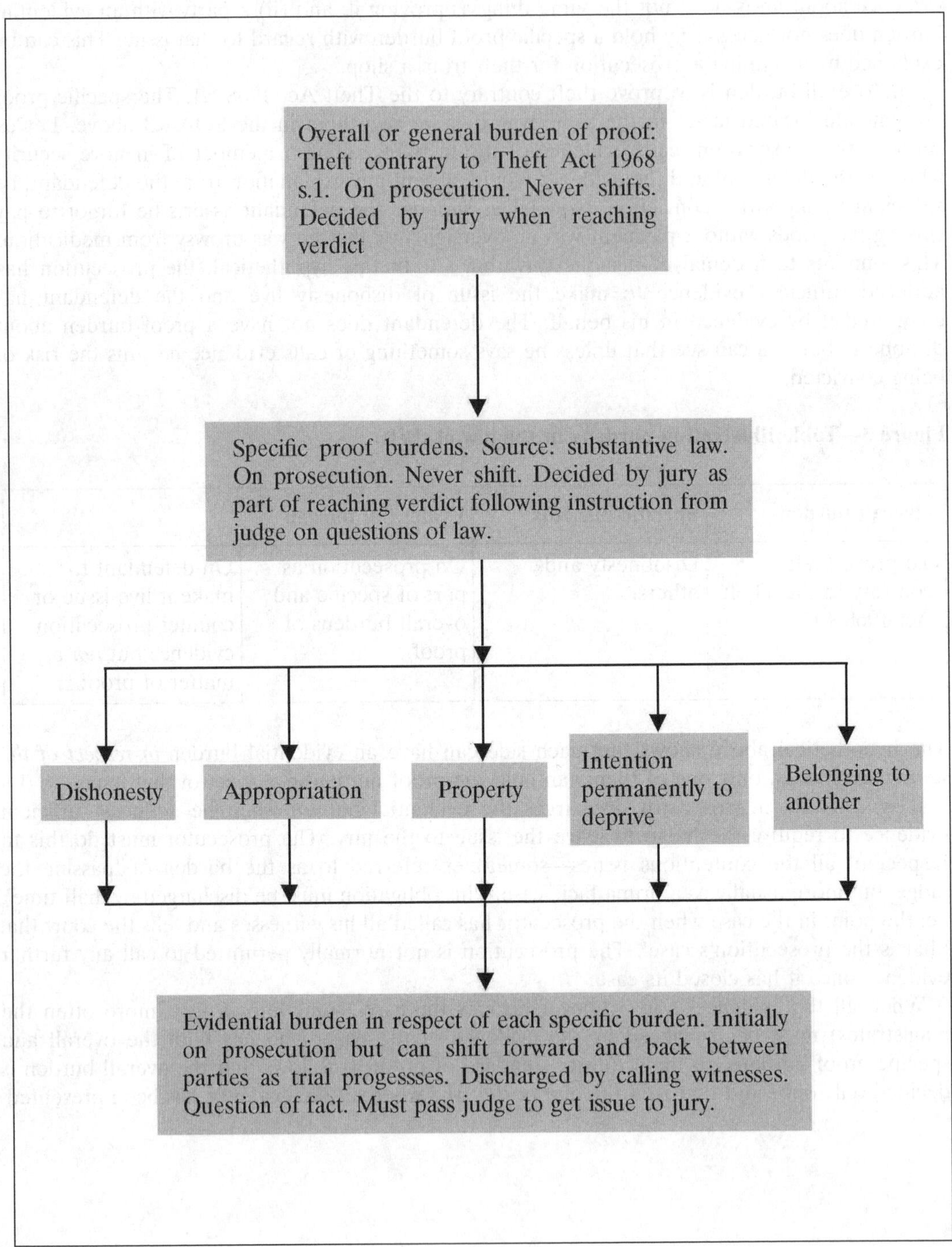

This chart represents what we have seen so far using the Theft Act 1968 s.1 as the model.

In considering this chart, remember that an evidential burden requires only that a party must adduce some evidence that what they say *could* be true—it can fall a long way short of proof. So the phrase 'evidential burden of proof' is a complete nonsense. In *Jayasena v R.* [1970] A.C. 618, 624 Lord Devlin said:

> 'Their Lordships do not understand what is meant by the phrase "evidential burden of proof." They understand, of course, that in trial by jury a party may be required to adduce some evidence in support of his case, whether on the general issue or on a particular issue, before that issue is left to the jury. How much evidence has to be adduced depends upon the nature of the requirement. It may be such evidence as, if believed and if left uncontradicted and unexplained, could be accepted by the jury as proof. Or it may be, as in English law when on a charge of murder the issue of provocation arises, enough evidence to suggest a reasonable possibility. It is doubtless permissible to describe the requirement as a burden, and it may be convenient to call it an evidential burden. But it is confusing to call it a burden of proof. Further, it is misleading to call it a burden of proof, whether described as legal or evidential or by any other adjective, when it can be discharged by the production of evidence that falls short of proof. The essence of the appellant's case is that he has not got to provide any sort of proof that he was acting in private defence. So it is a misnomer to call whatever it is that he has to provide a burden of proof . . .'

How much evidence discharges an evidential burden?

The answer is that everything depends on the issue in question. Sometimes a party can discharge an evidential burden by doing not much more than asserting the existence of a belief. So in a shoplifting case, the defendant may be able to put in doubt the issue of mens rea by doing not much more than asserting that he simply forgot to pay for the goods in question. The partial defence of provocation under the Homicide Act 1957 s.3 will be rendered live by almost any evidence that the defendant was provoked whether or not he is actually running provocation as his defence (see extract above per Lord Devlin). Such a low threshold is sometimes referred to as the 'scintilla' test.

There is, however, no general approach—much depends on the facts and something turns on the nature of the evidence in question. If the defendant asserts he was suffering from some relevant medical condition his own unsubstantiated testimony may fall well short of discharging the *evidential* (not proof) burden, i.e. making it a live issue in the case. When a judge decides that the volume and/or cogency of evidence adduced on behalf of the defendant falls below the required threshold, it narrows the possibilities for the defence with implications for a fair trial.

Evidence to make an issue live may arise during evidence in chief or during cross-examination. By way of example, evidence that the defendant was provoked could as easily arise from a witness called for the prosecution as one called for the defence. This could happen where a prosecution witness was asked what happened and replied, 'He (indicating the defendant) just went mad.' This underlines that there is no such thing as 'prosecution evidence' or 'defence evidence' but only evidence given by witnesses called for the prosecution or defence.

Figure 5—Summary table of proof and evidential burdens

Specific Proof Burden	Must have evidential burden too?	Yes.
	Must also have overall burden too?	No. D may have specific proof burden but never has overall burden.
Evidential burden	Always part of specific proof burden?	No. Consider position of D most of time in criminal proceedings.

1.3 *Woolmington v DPP* and defences

In *Woolmington v DPP* [1935] A.C. 462 the defendant was charged with murder of his wife by shooting. He said that the gun discharged accidentally. The trial judge (Swift J.) directed the jury:

> 'Once it is shown . . . that somebody has died through the act of another, that is presumed to be murder, unless the person who has been guilty of the act which causes the death can satisfy a jury that what happened was something less, something which might be alleviated, something which might be reduced to a charge of manslaughter, or something which was accidental, or something which could be justified.'

The House of Lords held the judge had misdirected the jury and had reversed the incidence of the burden of proof. Viscount Sankey said:

> '. . . where intent is an ingredient of a crime there is no onus on the defendant to prove that the act alleged was accidental. Throughout the web of the English Criminal Law one golden thread is always to be seen, that it is the duty of the prosecution to prove the prisoner's guilt subject to . . . the defence of insanity and subject also to any statutory exception . . . no matter what the charge or where the trial, the principle that the prosecution must prove the guilt of the prisoner is part of the common law of England and no attempt to whittle it down can be entertained.'

Many commentators have noted that the reference to the 'golden thread' as 'always' to be seen cannot be justified. Swift J. was an 'experienced judge' and there was abundant authority for the direction he gave even if, as Dennis (p.445) observes, his words seem 'thoroughly heretical to modern eyes'.

'Defences'

A text book on criminal law will deal with what are often called 'general defences.' These include duress, mistake, consent, non-insane automatism, drunkenness, necessity, self defence, etc. Where they are successfully pleaded they result in an outright acquittal of the defendant. Some 'defences' such as provocation and diminished responsibility are neither general, nor do they result in an outright acquittal. In addition some statutory defences such as provocation and diminished responsibility—which apply only to murder—are offence-specific.

In the context of the burden of proof, these defences have little in common with each other. Some of them e.g. consent are really no more than a denial of one of the prosecution's specific proof burdens. Others such as duress might be viewed as 'confession and avoidance'—the defendant seeks to excuse or justify his acts. In *Gill* [1963] 2 All E.R. 688, Edmund Davies J. said:

> 'The accused must raise the defence by sufficient evidence to go to the jury . . . the evidential burden is on him. The Crown are not called upon to anticipate such a defence and destroy it in advance. The defendant . . . must place before the court such material as makes duress a live issue fit and proper to be left to the jury.'

If there is a general rule with regard to defences and the burden of proof it rests on *Woolmington* (above). It follows that once a 'defence' is raised by evidence, the burden of (dis)proof is on the prosecution. We say that the defendant bears an evidential burden in respect of such defences though to the extent that the defence is really no more than a denial of an element of the offence, technically it may not be entirely accurate to say that the defendant bears an evidential burden at all. By way of example, if the defendant relies on an alibi the judge must direct that it is not for him to prove that he was elsewhere at the time but for the prosecution to prove his presence: *Preece* (1993) 96 Cr. App. R. 264. Presence at the time of the crime is one of the elements of the offence.

The law sometimes places the burden of proving a defence on the defendant. This is known as a reverse proof burden and where it happens, the defendant must prove the particular defence or lose in respect of it. We explore reverse proof burdens in detail below (see para.1.6), but the following issues should be noted now.

(i) Not all statutory offence-specific defences create reverse proof burdens. For example provocation is covered by the orthodox *Woolmington* principle: *Cascoe* [1970] 54 Cr. App. R. 401; *Cambridge* [1994] 99 Cr. App. R. 142.

(ii) The defendant does not bear the overall burden of proof.

(iii) The defendant has an evidential burden as part of his specific burden.

(iiii) Whenever the defendant has a specific proof burden, the *standard* of proof is the 'civil' standard, i.e. balance of probability, whereas the prosecution's proof standard is the 'criminal' standard, i.e. beyond reasonable doubt.

1.4 Shifting of burdens

We have identified three burdens—overall, specific and evidential—of which only the first two are proof burdens. In this section we are going to consider whether, depending on the volume and cogency of evidence produced by the parties, any of these burdens can shift from one party to the other. The alternative is that they are distributed between (in the sense of allocated to) the parties from the start and never move from them to the other side.

1.4.1 Evidential burdens

Suppose the defendant is charged with an offence. There is evidence from the prosecution of actus reus but the defendant says nothing. Is a conviction now inevitable? In early editions of his book, Professor Cross referred to 'tactical shifting' of the evidential burden. He illustrated it by imagining the position of a defendant at the close of the prosecution case which he described as 'in danger of conviction but not certain of it'. The defendant should, as a matter of tactics, now adduce evidence to rebut some element(s) of the prosecution case or raise some new issue. He could do this by any or all of the following

- cross-examining prosecution witnesses; or
- by now giving evidence himself; or
- calling his own witnesses.

If we imagine the defendant asserts he was coerced into committing the offence, he would need to adduce evidence of the coercion. The prosecution would seek to disprove the defence by *itself* adducing evidence in the same ways as the defendant had introduced evidence of the coercion. The evidential burden on the issue is thus seen to move between the parties. This is a consistent feature of criminal proceedings.

1.4.2 Specific proof burdens

Professor Cross stated that 'he who bears the risk of non-persuasion *on a particular issue* continues to do so until the tribunal has come to a decision' (emphasis supplied). The italicised words indicate that we are looking at specific proof burdens, not the overall burden.

As we have seen, the specific proof burdens are determined by the substantive law and represent, at least in theory, everything that must be proved to secure a conviction. The *Woolmington* principle together with its exceptions determines the incidence of the burdens—on whom they rest. Once laid on a particular party the specific proof burdens cannot move.

Quite incorrectly, some judges say that the specific proof burdens shift from the prosecution to the defendant as the result of the amount of evidence given by each side. This sounds almost like a game of football where, sometimes, one team is in possession of the ball whilst at other times the opposition has it. If this were a true analogy it would mean that sometimes the prosecution would hold the burden of proving (or disproving) some part of the crime, e.g. lack of consent in rape, while at other times the defendant would hold the burden of proving that same issue, i.e. that the victim *did* consent. There is an obvious logical difficulty here in that if one party can prove the affirmative of some proposition, the other party cannot disprove it.

In *Braithwaite* (1983) 77 Cr. App. R. 34 Lord Lane said:

> 'I then turn to s.2 of the 1916 (Prevention of Corruption) Act which deals with the presumption of corruption in certain cases. The effect of that is that when the matters in that

section have been fulfilled, *the burden of proof is lifted from the shoulders of the prosecution and descends upon the shoulders of the defence*. It then becomes necessary for the defendant to show, on a balance of probabilities, that what was going on was not reception corruptly as inducement or reward. In an appropriate case it is the judge's duty to direct the jury first of all that they must decide whether they are satisfied so as to feel sure that the defendant received money or gift or consideration, and then to go on to direct them that if they are so satisfied, then under s.2 of the 1916 Act *the burden of proof shifts*.

In the present case [the] judge, to put the matter shortly, upon the view that he took of the law, directed the jury that since ... there had admittedly been a receipt of goods or services, that amounted in law to consideration, and therefore, upon the very concessions made by the defence, *without further ado the burden of proof shifted*.' (emphases supplied)

This is nonsense. The specific burden of proving that he did not receive the gift corruptly *is and always was* on the defendant, although he did not have to discharge it until it was made to engage by the prosecution proving that the gift was in fact received. To quote Mustill L.J. in *Brady v Lotus Cars* [1987] 3 All E.R. 1050:

> 'thus, it may be said in one sense that the burden of proof shifts as the judge passes through the successive stages of his inquiry. In truth, however, this is an inaccurate use of language, for the dispute involves two separate issues, each with its own burden of proof, which remains unchanged throughout the course of the action.'

The conclusion is that the specific proof burdens cannot move during the trial.

1.4.3 The overall burden

This is always on the prosecution and cannot move. To assert otherwise would be to reverse the presumption of innocence enshrined in the common law and now found in art.6.2 of the ECHR.

1.5 Summary

Figure 6—Table summarising shifting of burdens

Type of burden	Can shift?	Reason
Overall burden	No	Always on prosecution: *Woolmington*
Specific Proof burdens	No	Fixed from outset on either prosecution or defendant
Evidential burden	Yes	Depending on quantum of evidence adduced by the parties in respect of specific proof burden in issue

1.6 Reverse proof burdens as exceptions to *Woolmington*

In *Woolmington* (see para.1.3) Lord Sankey said:

> 'throughout the web of English Criminal Law one golden thread is always to be seen, that it is the duty of the prosecution to prove the prisoner's guilt subject . . . to the defence of insanity and *subject also to any statutory exception*.' (emphasis supplied)

In *Mancini v DPP* [1942] A.C. 1 in which Lord Sankey also sat, Viscount Simon L.C. said the:

> 'only exceptions arise, as explained in *Woolmington's* case, in the defence of insanity and in offences where the onus of proof *is specially dealt with* in the statute.' (emphasis supplied)

There are three exceptions and they give rise to reverse proof burdens which are either 'express' or 'implied.' We shall see that the main problem with express reverse burdens is whether they violate the presumption of innocence (at common law and under art.6(2) of the ECHR). The same problem should also arise in principle in relation to implied reverse burdens but possibly a greater difficulty is discerning when such burdens arise in the first place.

1.7 The common law reverse proof burden

As we have seen, the defendant bears the burden of proving that he was insane at the time that he committed the act: *M'Naghten's* case.

1.8 Statutory express reverse proof burdens

Some statutory provisions expressly place the specific (not overall) proof burden on the defendant. Here are some examples.

Figure 7—Illustration of statutory express reverse proof burdens

1. Homicide Act 1957 s.2(2)	On a charge of murder it shall be a defence to prove . . .
2. Contempt of Court Act 1981 s.3	The burden of proving any fact tending to establish a defence afforded by this section to any person lies upon that person . . .

3. CJA 1988 s.139(4)	It shall be a defence for a person charged with an offence under this section to prove that he had good reason or lawful authority for having the article with him in a public place . . .
4. Trade Marks Act 1994 s.92(5)	It shall be a defence to show . . .

While it clear that examples 1–3 reverse the proof burden to the defendant, the fourth example uses the word 'show'. Should we distinguish 'show' from 'prove' the former leading to an evidential burden only while the latter imposes a proof burden on the defendant? The history of two cases shows the mess into which judges can get themselves. In *Johnstone* [2002] EWCA Crim 194 [82], Tuckey L.J. said 'show' was compatible with an evidential burden on the defendant. In *S* [2002] EWCA Crim 2558 Davis J. [25] held that 'show' created a legal burden on the defendant. The mess was deepened in the House of Lords in *Johnstone* [2003] UKHL 28, when Lord Nicholls, having shown clearly why it should create only an evidential burden, said that s.92(5) placed the proof burden of the defendant. This was clearly obiter.

1.8.1 **Express reverse proof burdens; compatibility with Article 6(2)**

Article 6(2) provides:

> 'Everyone charged with a criminal offence shall be presumed innocent until proved guilty according to law.'

To what extent if at all are express reverse proof burdens compatible with art.6(2)? We shall see there is no clear answer to this question but before exploring the reasons we need to consider issues surrounding the HRA 1998 as well as some of the jurisprudence of the ECtHR.

1.8.1.1 **The Human Rights Act 1998**

Reading down

Under s.3(1) if the court decides a statutory provision is incompatible with art.6(2) its primary duty is to 'read and give effect' to it in a way which makes it compatible. In context this means treating a provision which imposes a specific proof burden on the defendant as imposing only an evidential burden on him. The process is known as 'reading down'. It was held in *Ghaidan v Godin-Mendoza* [2004] UKHL 30 that s.3 has a remedial function and that there is no limit to the words that can be read in or out of a provision. This important statement of principle is applicable to all areas of law even though it may appear to run directly contrary to what Parliament 'intended': *Attorney General's Reference (No. 4 of 2002)* [2004] UKHL 43 per Lord Bingham [53]. While further consideration is outside the scope of this work we shall encounter reading down on a number of occasions.

In *Attorney General's Reference* (above), Lord Bingham said [31] that the function of the courts

> 'is never to decide whether a reverse burden should be imposed on a defendant, but always to assess whether a burden enacted by Parliament unjustifiably infringes the presumption of innocence.'

This statement is seen by many commentators as a corrective to the lamentable judgment of the Court of Appeal in *Attorney General's Reference (No. 1 of 2004)* [2004] 1 W.L.R. 2111 per Lord Woolf. Murphy (p.93) attributes the poverty of the judgment to 'the misconceived idea' that the outcomes of decisions on differing statutory provisions ought to be the same. Munday (p.108) reminds us that this is 'the wilderness of single instances', and that we should beware extrapolating too much from decisions which turn on the construction of specific statutory provisions.

> 'Mastering the lawless science of our law,
> That codeless myriad of precedent,
> That wilderness of single instances,
> Thro' which a few by wit or fortune lead,
> May beat a pathway out to wealth and fortune.'
> *Aylmer's Field*, Alfred Lord Tennyson (1793). Cited by Robert Stevens 'The Independence of the Judiciary: the case in England' Southern California Law Review, Vol.72, 597.

Declaration of incompatibility

If the provision cannot satisfactorily be read down, by virtue of the HRA s.4(1) and (2) a court may make a declaration of incompatibility described in *Ghaidan* (above) as 'an exceptional course of last resort.'

1.8.1.2 The jurisprudence of the European Court of Human Rights

The function of the ECtHR is to decide whether an applicant received a fair trial and not whether national legislation is valid.

1.9 Compatibility

In *Lambert* [2002] 2 A.C. 545 Lord Steyn said there are four issues to consider:

- The presumption of innocence;
- Does the provision make an inroad on art.6(2)?
- Justification; and
- Proportionality.

1.9.1 The presumption of innocence

As interpreted by the ECtHR art.6(2) is not absolute. Just as in *Woolmington* the House of Lords left the door open for exceptions, the European Commission said in *Lingens v Austria*

[1981] 26 DR 171 that neither reverse burdens, nor the imposition of strict liability, nor presumptions necessarily violate a fair trial. The limit is always what is reasonable in the circumstances.

In *Salabiaku v France* 13 E.H.R.R. 379 (1988) the Court held that:

> 'Presumptions of fact or of law operate in every legal system. Clearly the Convention does not prohibit such presumptions in principle. It does, however, require . . . States to remain within certain limits in this respect as regards criminal law.'

Some statutory provisions permit presumption of knowledge once primary facts are proved. By way of example in *Lambert* (above) the defendant was charged with possession of a controlled substance contrary to s.5(3) of the Misuse of Drugs Act 1971. He pleaded the defence under s.28(2) of the same Act, which so far as relevant reads:

> 'it shall be a defence for the (defendant) to prove he neither knew of nor suspected nor had any reason to suspect the existence of some fact . . . which is necessary for the prosecution to prove . . .'

Once the prosecution proves the primary facts of (i) possession and (ii) controlled substance the defendant will be guilty unless he brings himself within the ambit of s.28. However, not all the statutory provisions we shall encounter in this area of law involve presumptions of either fact or law.

1.9.2 An inroad into Article 6(2)?

Lord Steyn discussed this under a number of headings. It is important to remember that these are factors of which the court will take account. While one of them might on its own be sufficient to dispose of the case it would be unusual.

The prescribed punishment

Some offences carry only a disqualification, some a fine and others a prison sentence of varying length. The maximum penalty for an offence under the Misuse of Drugs Act 1971 s.5 (as in *Lambert*) is life imprisonment. Should we be looking at the prescribed maximum sentence (which is certainly what Lord Steyn referred to) or the standard tariff for the offence? Judicial ingenuity has marginalised the significance of the nominal maximum. In *S* [2002] EWCA Crim 2558 the Court of Appeal considered the likely *actual* penalty for an offence under s.1 of the Trade Marks Act 1994. While the maximum is ten years the commonest disposal was a fine or discharge. The court was informed that fewer that 10 per cent of convictions resulted in an immediate custodial sentence. Whether this what the Lord Steyn had in mind is open to question but if the point is whether the defendant received a fair trial, why is penalty relevant at all? Is there a sliding scale of fairness commensurate with penalty?

The moral dimension of the offence

In *Lambert* the charge was possession of a controlled drug 2 kilogrammes of cocaine at 76 per cent purity with intent to supply. The ratio of the case is that the Human Rights Act was not retrospective so the observations about proof and evidential burdens are obiter though of great significance. Lord Steyn referred to the extent to which the reversal was connected to the moral dimension of the offence through the mens rea requirement under s.28 of the Misuse of Drugs Act 1971 (see above). Placing disproof of mens rea on the defendant is significant when deciding whether a statutory provision violates art.6(2).

The same view was taken in *R. v DPP Ex p. Kebilene* [2000] 1 Cr. App. R. 275. The defendants were charged with offences under s.16A and s.16B of the Prevention of Terrorism (Temporary Provisions) Act 1989. (This statute has been repealed by the Terrorism Act 2000, but former ss.16A and 16B were substantially re-enacted in ss.57 and 58 of the later Act). The sections were concerned with the possession of articles and information not in themselves incriminating but which might be viewed as forming the accoutrements of terrorists. In the Divisional Court Lord Bingham C.J. referred to s.16A as a gross violation of the presumption of innocence—the prosecution did not need to prove anything to the criminal standard.

One problem is that there may well be no agreement about whether the provision requires mens rea. Section 92(1) of the Trade Marks Act 1994 creates an offence while subs.(5) provides a defence if the defendant can show he:

> 'believed on reasonable grounds that the use of the sign in the manner in which it was used . . . or was to be used, was not an infringement of the registered trade mark.'

It was held in *S* (above), that subs.(5) does not introduce a mental element into the definition of the offence. The prosecution is not required to prove any 'mens rea in the way that phrase is usually understood.' (per Davis J [28]) This was a major factor in the decision that subs.(5) (as a proof burden on the defendant) did not violate art.6(2).

In *Keogh* [2007] EWCA Crim 528 the Court of Appeal considered the effect of ss.2(1) and 3(1) of the Official Secrets Act 1989 holding that they created offences of intentional and damaging disclosure, without lawful authority, of a document relating to defence or international relations. By virtue of ss.2(3) and 3(4) it is a defence for the defendant 'to prove . . . he did not know, and had no reasonable cause to believe' disclosure would be damaging. Lord Phillips C.J. held 'assuming intentional disclosure' the offence was not 'committed regardless of any other aspect of the defendant's state of mind'. His Lordship held that attention had to be given to the defendant's state of mind when the intentional disclosure occurred and that involved whether he had reasonable cause to believe it would be damaging.

> 'In reality the offence will not be committed if the defendant did not know or have reasonable cause to believe in the existence of *the ingredients of the defence as defined in sections 2(3) and 3(4)*.' ([19] emphasis supplied)

It was a major breach of the presumption of innocence for the defendant to have to prove lack of mens rea. The judgment does not refer to the decision in *S*. Time will tell which of the two approaches to this type of offence-specific defence involving 'no mens rea' is preferred.

While most of the decisions about moral blameworthiness refer to mens rea, in *Attorney General's Reference (No.4 of 2002)* [2004] UKHL 43 [47] Lord Bingham described s.11(1) of the Terrorism Act 2000 as 'a provision of extraordinary breadth' which read on its own could result in the conviction and punishment 'for no conduct which could reasonably be regarded as blameworthy or such as should attract criminal sanctions'.

'Truly criminal' or just regulatory offence?

This issue was raised in *Lambert* (above) by Lord Clyde [174]. According to Tuckey L.J. in *Davies v Health & Safety Executive* [2002] EWCA Crim 2949 breaches of regulatory offences 'do not imply moral blameworthiness in the same manner as criminal fault'. While the distinction is commonly made it does not follow that regulatory offences are without a moral dimension. Nor does it follow that while 'truly criminal' offences are concerned with conduct, regulatory offences are concerned only with the consequences of conduct: *Wholesale Travel* (1991) 3 S.C.R. 154 (per Cory J.). In *Howe & Son (Engineers Ltd)* [1999] 2 All E.R. 249 the Court of Appeal indicated factors which would aggravate the seriousness of offences under Health and Safety legislation. They involve serious moral issues including causing death, neglect to heed warning and risks taken to save money.

The offence—defence dichotomy explained

It has been suggested that where a statutory provision creates an offence and a distinct defence placing the burden of proving the defence on the defendant is more easily justified. By way of example the Terrorism Act 2000 s.11 provides:

> (1) A person commits an offence if he belongs or professes to belong to a proscribed organization.
>
> (2) It is a defence for a person charged with an offence under subs.(1) to prove:
>
> (a) that the organisation was not proscribed on the last (or only) occasion on which he became a member or began to profess to be a member; and
>
> (b) that he has not taken part in the activities of the organisation at any time while it was proscribed.

In *Attorney General's Reference (No. 4 of 2002)* [2003] EWCA Crim 762 (Latham L.J.) held subs.(1) creates an offence and subs.(2):

> 'Expresses a very specific exception applicable to a limited class of defendants which does not affect, or infect, the criminal offence fully identified in s.11(1).'

Similarly, in the consolidated appeal *Lambert, Ali, Jordan* [2001] 1 Cr. App. R. 205 Lord Woolf C.J. (in the Court of Appeal) held that under s.2(2) of the Homicide Act 1957 if 'what the defendant was required to do was to establish a special defence or exception, that would be less objectionable'. In terms similar to those used by Latham L.J., Lord Woolf held that s.2(2) did not violate art.6(2). The defendant was not called upon *to prove an ingredient of the offence* and the subsection was of benefit to defendants who were in a position to take advantage of it. Where the prosecution is not required to prove all of the essential (definitional) elements of the offence (i.e. disproof of one or more of such elements lies with the defendant) there will always be an unacceptable violation of art.6(2). That was partly the problem in *Kebilene* as we saw above when we considered *Lambert* in relation to disproof of mens rea. It lies at the heart of the decision in *Keogh* (above). In *Attorney General's Reference (No. 4 of 2002)* [2004] UKHL 43 the House of Lords held that imposing a legal burden of proof on the defendant would violate art.6(2).

The offence—defence dichotomy criticised

In *Lambert*, Lord Steyn [35] accepted the appellant's argument that the 'defence' in s.28(2) is an ingredient of the offence under s.5(3). His Lordship doubted whether there is a principled distinction between offence and defence. He said that the distinction between constituent elements of the crime and 'defensive' issues can be unprincipled and arbitrary—it can often be a drafting issue. The focus must be not on technicalities but on substance. This echoes what was said by Lord Bingham in *Kebilene*. His Lordship cited the Canadian case of *Whyte* [1988] DLR 481 where Dickinson C.J. said that characterising a factor as an essential element, collateral issue, excuse or defence should not affect the status of the presumption of innocence.

Construction

The decision of the Court of Appeal in *Keogh* [31] (above) on the effect of ss.2(1) and 3(1) of the Official Secrets Act 1989 was partly informed by comparing the wording of the two subsections with that in s.5 where the burden of proving mens rea was 'undoubtedly' on the prosecution: per Phillips C.J.

Vague drafting

In *Attorney General's Reference (No. 4 of 2002)* [2004] UKHL 43 by a bare majority the House of Lords held that imposing a legal burden under the Terrorism Act 2000 s.11 would infringe art.6(2) and would have been prepared to read it down to impose an evidential burden only. We noted above Lord Bingham's view [47] that s.11(1) was 'a provision of extraordinary breadth' which read on its own could result in the conviction and punishment 'for no conduct which could reasonably be regarded as blameworthy or such as should attract criminal sanctions'.

1.9.3 Justification

In the words of Lord Hope in *Kebilene*: 'what is the nature of the threat faced by society which the provision is designed to combat?' In *Lambert*, Lord Steyn said that justification for legislative interference with the presumption of innocence could be found in the common defence to charges under s.5 of the Misuse of Drugs Act 1971—the defendant alleges he was unaware of the contents of the container. His Lordship said such defences (lack of knowledge of relevant facts or circumstances) pose real difficulties for the police and prosecuting authorities.

If there is no justification for the reverse burden, the court should immediately make a declaration of incompatibility under the HRA 1998 s.4. In general, however, it should not be too difficult for the prosecution to justify interference with the presumption. However, as Lord Steyn observed that is not the end of the matter.

1.9.4 Proportionality

The prosecution must demonstrate 'that the legislative means adopted were not greater than necessary': per Lord Steyn in *Lambert* [37]. The prosecution must show 'there was a pressing need to impose a legal rather than an evidential burden on the accused'. This is a key factor in the reasoning in *Lambert*. In *Sheldrake* (above) Clarke L.J. referred to it as 'the test of necessity' [61] and said [59] 'the question is then whether the prosecution have shown that it is necessary to impose a legal burden on the accused'. Later [84], reiterating the test of necessity, he said 'the test is not the lower test of whether it was reasonable to do so'.

It follows that decisions which do not require the prosecution to convince the court of the need to reverse the proof burden to the defendant must be regarded as suspect. The Court of Appeal descended to new levels of gullibility in *S* (above). Davis J. uncritically accepted that only by imposing a legal burden on the defendant under the Trade Marks Act 1994 s.92(5) could the British economy be saved £9 billion per annum and job losses of over 4,000 people. Similarly in *Johnstone* [2003] UKHL 28 Lord Nicholls [52 & 53] found compelling reasons of international pressure and the interests of consumers and traders alike as the basis for upholding a reverse proof burden under the same section.

Gullible jury syndrome

Some of their Lordships seem wedded to the notion that if a defendant merely asserts some fact(s) or state of affairs the fact finder will automatically believe. This underlies some of Lord Hutton's dissenting judgment in *Lambert*. If an evidential burden were imposed:

> 'all that a defendant would have to do to discharge such a burden would be to adduce some fact to raise the issue that he did not know that the article in the bag or the tablets on the table were a controlled drug, and the prosecution would then have to destroy that defence in such a manner as to leave in the jury's mind no reasonable doubt that it was a controlled drug in the bag or on the table.'

This is, of course, precisely what the prosecution has to do under *Woolmington* irrespective of the complexity of the offence or other difficulties of proof. Mere assertion by a defendant without supporting evidence is unlikely to persuade a jury to his point of view. Davis J. seems to have suffered the same lack of insight in *S* (above). The correct approach is, as Lord Steyn said *Lambert*:

> '. . . to bear in mind that it is not enough for the defence merely to allege the fact in question: the court decides whether there is a real issue on the matter.'

The outcome of Lambert

In *Lambert*, the House of Lords, while recognising the importance of the social objective of the legislation, read down s.28(2) to place an evidential, not proof, burden on the defendant. The imposition of an evidential burden was a proportionate response to the problems of drug dealing. Beyond that, the majority took different routes towards their conclusion.

Figure 8—Meaning of 'prove' in the Misuse of Drugs Act 1971 section 28(2) following *Lambert*

Misuse of Drugs Act 1971 s.28(2)	Meaning of 'prove'
(2) . . . in any proceedings for an offence to which this section applies it shall be a defence for the accused to *prove*	adduce evidence.
that he neither knew of nor suspected nor had reason to suspect the existence of some fact alleged by the prosecution which is necessary for the prosecution to *prove* if he is to be convicted of the offence charged.	convince the court beyond reasonable doubt.

Giving different meanings to the same word in a subsection seems a recipe for confusion and their Lordship's reluctance to make a declaration of incompatibility on these facts is incomprehensible.

The status of Lambert

In *Attorney General's Reference (No. 1 of 2004)* [2004] EWCA 1025 Lord Woolf C.J. asserted [38] the primacy of Lord Nicholls' approach in *Johnstone* over that of Lord Steyn in *Lambert*. He went as far as to discourage citation of any authority other than *Johnstone*. In a less unbalanced approach Lord Bingham [30] in *Attorney General's Reference (No. 4 of 2002)* [2004] UKHL 43 explained the differences of emphasis between Lords Steyn and Nicholls as 'explicable by the difference in the subject matter of the two cases'. *Lambert* 'should not be treated as superseded or implicitly overruled'. Lord Bingham explicitly refused to endorse points A–J of the Court of Appeal in *Attorney General's Reference (No. 1 of 2004)* [52] 'save to the extent that it is in accordance with the opinions of the House . . .'. His Lordship admonished the Court of Appeal for trying to pick and chose between decisions of the House reminding the lower court that the House must be regarded as the 'primary domestic authority on reverse burdens'.

Conclusion on Proportionality

It is very much a value judgment. Even when the judges agree on the justification for legislative interference with the presumption of innocence, the appealed cases reveal wide differences of opinion between them as to whether the imposition of a legal burden on the defendant is proportionate. By way of example in *Sheldrake* (above), the Court of Appeal held that imposing a proof burden under s.5(1) and (2) of the Road Traffic Act 1988 was not proportionate to the problem of being in charge of a motor vehicle with excess alcohol. The House of Lords [2004] UKHL 43 reversed the Court of Appeal holding that it is.

1.10 Other considerations about reverse proof burdens

1.10.1 Conviction even though the court has a doubt

Citing the 11th Report of the Criminal Law Revision Committee (CLRC) in *Lambert* Lord Steyn said:

> 'A transfer of a legal burden amounts to a far more drastic interference with the presumption of innocence than the creation of an evidential burden on the accused. The former requires the accused to establish his innocence. It necessarily involves the risk that, if the jury are faithful to the judge's direction, they may convict where the accused has not discharged the legal burden resting on him but left them unsure on the point. This risk is not present if only an evidential burden is created.'

This is a formidable objection to imposing a proof burden on the defendant, and it not susceptible to the 'offence—defence' dichotomy which we considered above. A criminal conviction may be a barrier to employment and is a bar to entry, even as a visitor, to some countries whatever the nature or circumstances of the conviction. The CLRC recommended [87–91] that all burdens on the defendant should be evidential unless expressly excluded by Parliament. In *Lambert* Lord Clyde said that the HRA 1998 'should encourage a reconsideration of a trend (in respect of reverse proof burdens) which has for over a decade been exposed to powerful criticism'.

1.10.2 The defendant's knowledge

The courts have used 'facts within the defendant's knowledge' as a justification for reversing the burden of proof. This is a blatant breach of the *Woolmington* principle amounting to an attempt to justify the unjustifiable. In the section below on Implied Reverse Proof burdens (see para.1.11), we shall see (*R. on the application of Grundy & Co Excavations Ltd v Halton Division Magistrates' Court* [2003] EWHC 272) that the Court of Appeal and House of Lords have expressly disclaimed such knowledge as the justification for impliedly reversing the proof burden to the defendant. It remains a mystery as to why it may justify reversal in cases of express burdens.

1.10.3 Citation of authority

Kebilene, Johnstone and *Lambert* cite the decisions of appellate courts in South Africa and Canada. In *Attorney General's Reference (No. 4 of 2002)* [2004] UKHL 43 Lord Bingham [33] acknowledged the 'valuable insights' gained from the reasoning of the judges in such cases but counselled caution. Such decisions are based on different enactments and 'the United Kingdom courts must take their lead from Strasbourg.' A similar view was expressed by Lord Roger [58] in the same Reference.

1.10.4 Footnote to *Kebilene*

When the Terrorism Act 2000 was passed, the draftsman took some account of the criticisms made in *Kebilene*. Although there has been substantial re-enactment of the old provisions, s.118 is new. Subsections (2) and (4) refer to offences in subs.(5). In so far as these offences expressly place a reverse proof burden on the defendant the effect of subss.(2) and (4) is that he can discharge the proof burden by adducing evidence to 'raise an issue' whereupon the court 'shall' assume the defence is satisfied unless the prosecution proves beyond reasonable doubt that it is not. A further and even more tortuous example of the same approach is found in the Regulation of Investigatory Powers Act 2000 s.53(3) which creates an offence of improper use of a key to protected information. The section provides that the defendant:

> 'shall be taken to have shown that he was not in possession of a key to protected information at a particular time if–
>
> i) sufficient evidence of that fact is adduced to raise an issue with respect to it; and
> ii) the contrary is not proved beyond a reasonable doubt.'

This places an evidential burden (only) on the defendant. Why governments instruct draftsmen to resort to such tortuous drafting is mystifying given the clean simplicity of the CLRC's proposal. After all, the outcome is precisely the same.

1.11 Statutory implied reverse proof burdens

There are two issues to consider. First, will the courts regard a statutory provision as impliedly placing a burden of proof on the defendant? Secondly, do such burdens give rise to problems in respect of art.6(2)?

1.11.1 Implied burden on the defendant?

Consider the similarities and differences in respect of the following hypothetical provisions with regard to the incidence of the proof and evidential burdens.

Statute One makes it an offence for a person unlawfully to be in possession of an offensive weapon in a public place.

Statute Two makes it an offence for a person to be in possession of an offensive weapon in a public place without lawful authority or excuse.

What the provisions have in common is that they criminalise possession of an offensive weapon in a public place. Where they differ is in the method by which they do this—the provisions are *constructed* in different ways.

In *Edwards* [1974] 2 All E.R. 1085 the defendant was convicted on indictment of selling intoxicating liquor without a justices' licence. The prosecution proved he sold the liquor but did not adduce any evidence that he did not have a licence. On appeal, Edwards argued that because the clerk to the justices was under a statutory duty to keep a register giving particulars of justices' licences granted in the district, the question whether a licence had been granted to him was not one peculiarly within his knowledge. Hence the onus was on the prosecution to prove no licence had been granted to him. This argument about 'knowledge' rested on authorities some of them of great age. Lawton L.J. dismissed it. Following a review of the leading cases, he concluded:

> 'in offences arising *under enactments* which prohibit the doing of an act save in specified circumstances or by persons of a specified class or with specified qualifications or with the licence or permission of specified authorities . . .' (emphasis supplied)

Provided that it was a 'true construction of the statute', the burden of proving that he comes within the qualification rests on the defendant. Describing this as, in effect, an exception to *Woolmington*, Lawton L.J. said:

> 'if the true construction is that the enactment prohibits the doing of acts, subject to provisos, exemptions and the like, then the prosecution can rely on the exception.
>
> In our judgment its application does not depend on either the fact, or the presumption, that the defendant has peculiar knowledge enabling him to prove the positive of any negative averment.'

If this judgment was intended to rid the law of 'peculiar knowledge' as the basis for deciding to impose a reverse burden it has proved not to be the case. Not only does the Court of Appeal continue to regard knowledge as a key issue in express reverse burden cases, the Divisional Court did the same in the first reported post-*Lambert* decision on implied reverse burdens: *R on the application of Grundy & Co and Parry v Halton Divisional Magistrates' Court, The Forestry Commission* [2003] EWHC 272. Clarke L.J. held both that the offence/defence distinction was alive and well and that 'facts within the defendant's knowledge' justified the imposition of a proof burden on the accused. Gullible jury syndrome apparently extends to magistrates' courts. The imposition of only an evidential burden was described by Clarke L.J. [70] as 'unworkable'.

Although *Edwards* was tried on indictment the case focuses on s.101 of the Magistrates' Courts Act 1980. It provides:

> 'Where the defendant to an information or complaint relies for his defence on any exception, exemption, proviso, excuse or qualification, whether or not it accompanies the description of the offence or matter of complaint in the enactment creating the offence or on which the complaint is founded, the burden of proving the exception, exemption, proviso, excuse or qualification shall be on him; and this notwithstanding that the information or complaint contains an allegation negativing the exception, exemption, proviso, excuse or qualification.'

In *Hunt* [1987] 1 All E.R. 1, the House of Lords held that s.101 reflects the common law. In practice, therefore the mode of trial (summary or on indictment) makes no difference to the process of deciding whether the provision should be construed to impose a reverse burden of proof by implication.

What does 'construction' mean?

Under s.101(1) if the defendant relies on some wording in a statutory provision which operates as an exception, exemption, proviso, excuse or qualification, then he bears the burden of proving it. 'Construction' means demonstrating that the words in question operate in that way. The prosecution does this by looking at how the prohibited act and any exception, exemption etc. are related to each other in the wording of the offence. In the hypothetical at the start of this section of work, we said that the construction of the provisions differed. If you look back you should see that while the construction of Statute one does not give rise to any proviso at all, Statute two might be regarded as 'conditional' in the sense that the defendant will be guilty unless he brings himself within the ambit of the proviso i.e. lawful authority or excuse. This is reinforced if you imagine taking the phrase 'without lawful authority or excuse' and placing it more or less anywhere in the provision as follows.

Figure 9—Illustration of the meaning of 'construction'

It is an offence for a person to be in possession of an offensive weapon in a public place *without lawful authority* or excuse.
It is an offence, *without lawful authority* or excuse, for a person to be in possession of an offensive weapon in a public place.
It is an offence for a person, *without lawful authority* or excuse, to be in possession of an offensive weapon in a public place.
It is an offence for a person to be in possession of an offensive weapon *without lawful authority* or excuse in a public place.
Without lawful authority or excuse it is an offence for a person to be in possession of an offensive weapon in a public place.

We might conclude that the italicised words do indeed operate as a proviso within s.101. Professor Smith, (1987) 38 N.I.L.Q. 223 explained the correct approach by asking whether the conduct in question:

(a) tends towards criminality (e.g. being in possession of drugs); or

(b) is basically lawful (e.g. driving) but can become unlawful in particular circumstances (without a licence). Here the offence is in the exception.

The rule represented by s.101 implies that it is always possible to isolate the words constituting the 'offence' from the words which amount to an exception, exemption etc. However, if we take the offence of driving a vehicle without a licence, 'construction' would require us to think of 'driving' as the 'description of the offence', and possession of a licence as the exception, etc. This is plainly absurd. In *Hunt* (above) the House approved *Edwards* 'as an excellent guide to construction' though stressing that every case turned on its facts. The House was clear that *Edwards* is not a decision about an exception to a rule. Each time the prosecution claims s.101 is applicable, the court must decide afresh whether what has been created is an offence subject to an exception, exemption etc. which operates as a defence once the prosecution adduces credible evidence of a prohibited act. This has meant that the courts have been far from consistent in their approach to s.101 as can be seen by comparing the following decisions.

Figure 10—Judicial inconsistency in relation to section 101 of the MCA 1980

Case	Provision	Burden reversed?
Gatland v Metropolitan Police Commissioner [1968] 1 All E.R. 100	Highways Act 1961 s.161(1): offence for any person without lawful authority or excuse to deposit anything on a highway whereby any highway user is injured.	Yes
Cousins [1982] Q.B. 526	Offences Against the Person Act 1861 s.16: a person who without lawful excuse makes to another a threat, intending that the other would fear it would be carried out, to kill that other or a third party.	No
Hirst and Agu v Chief Constable of West Yorkshire [1986] 85 Cr. App. R. 143	Highways Act 1961 s.137(1): without lawful authority or excuse wilfully obstructing the free passage along a highway.	No
Polychronakis v Richards and Jerrom Ltd [1998] Env. L.R. 346	Environmental Protection Act 1990: failure to abate a nuisance contrary to s.80(4): If a person on whom an abatement notice is served, without reasonable excuse, contravenes or fails to comply with any requirement or prohibition imposed by the notice, he shall be guilty of an offence.	No

Some commentators reconcile *Gatland* and *Cousins* by a less than convincing argument that the latter is a direct offence against the person while the former is indirect. The decision in *Hirst* might be justified because of the word 'wilfully' which clearly imports mens rea. In *Polychronakis*, the court looked at other subsections of s.80 which provided expressly for reverse proof burdens. The absence of such wording in s.80(4) was regarded as deliberate choice by Parliament and was pivotal in the decision. Such assertion beggars belief. You will recall a similar approach to construction taken by Lord Phillips C.J. in *Keogh* (above para.1.9.2).

The case of Hunt [1987] 1 All E.R. 1 and wider issues

As we have seen, *Hunt* involves strong endorsement of the *Edwards* approach though the decision actually goes the other way. The defendant was charged with possession of a morphine compound. Prosecution evidence did not show that the amount of morphine in the compound was less than 0.2 per cent which made it an exempt preparation. The House held the provision about 0.2 per cent was a definitional element of the case and did not come within the Lawton L.J. guide. There were no exceptions, exemptions etc. nor any specified persons, classes, licences etc. provided for in the regulations in question.

However, the House said that a reverse proof burden might be implied where the 'construction' approach does not resolve the issue. Though Parliament must not be taken lightly to have placed (impliedly) the proof burden on a defendant, policy considerations, including both the seriousness of the offence, the mischief at which the provision was aimed, and ease or otherwise of proof, are legitimate issues for the court to consider. Although decided before *Hunt, Nimmo v Alexander Cowan & Sons Ltd* [1968] A.C. 107, a decision under the Factories Act 1961 s.29(1), is an example of just such a case. The section provides:

> 'There shall, so far as is reasonably practicable, be provided and maintained safe means of access to every place at which any person has at any time to work and every such place shall, so far as is reasonably practicable, be made and kept safe for any person working there.'

By a bare majority the House of Lords held that if the prosecution proved the working place was not safe, even though s.29(1) was not couched in terms of an exception, it was for the employer to prove that it was not reasonably practicable to make it so. *Nimmo* was cited with approval in *Bilton v Fastnet Highlands Ltd* [1998] S.L.T. 1323.

The judgment in *Hunt* has been poorly received by commentators not least by Healey ('Proof and Policy: No Golden Threads' [1987] Crim. L.R. 361) who says 'the majority's analysis defies formulation in prescriptive terms for the guidance trial judges, prosecutors and defending counsel' and characterises 'implied legislative intent as a conceit or fiction for judicial policy-making and judicial legislation.'

1.11.2 **Implied reverse burdens and the presumption of innocence**

In *Lambert* [35] Lord Steyn said:

> 'It is necessary to concentrate not on technicalities and niceties of language but rather on matters of substance. I do not have in mind cases within the narrow exception "limited to offences arising under enactments which prohibit the doing of an act save in specified circumstances or by persons of specified classes or with specified qualifications or with the licence or permission of specified authorities"; *R v Edwards* [1975] QB 27, 40; *R v Hunt (Richard)* [1987] AC 352; section 101 of the Magistrates Courts Act 1980.'

Although this statement might be interpreted to exclude implied reverse proof burdens from the scope of art.6(2) in *R. on the application of Grundy & Co Parry v Halton Divisional Magistrates' Court, The Forestry Commission* [2003] EWHC 272 [61] by Clarke L.J. held that the implied burdens in question did derogate from the presumption of innocence. His Lordship then considered justification and proportionality in the same process we have seen above in relation to express reverse burdens. He held that imposing a proof burden was justified.

We should conclude that both express and implied reverse proof burdens must be kept within the bounds of proportionality discussed in the authorities above.

1.12 The standard of proof in criminal proceedings

In criminal proceedings the prosecution must prove its case beyond reasonable doubt. Where a specific proof burden is on the defendant, he must discharge it on a balance of probability which is usually defined as 'more likely than not'. Failure to direct the jury on the requisite standard of proof may not lead to a conviction being quashed, whereas failure to direct a jury on the incidence of the burden of proof will always lead to that result: *Z* [1983] Crim. L.R. 484

The JSB suggests (Specimen Direction 2) that in directing the jury it is not normally necessary to use the phrase 'beyond reasonable doubt' at all. The traditional phrase is, however, deeply embedded, is supported by high authority (*Woolmington*) and continues to be used. An alternative would be to direct that the prosecution must have made the jury sure from the evidence it adduced that the defendant is guilty: *Summers* (1952) 36 Cr. App. R. 14. Whether one of these phrases is used or not, it is the overall effect of the direction which is crucial: *Ferguson v R* [1979] 1 All E.R. 877.

The expression 'beyond reasonable doubt' has caused problems in some cases where judges have attempted a gloss or explanation of its meaning. Where that has been done, 'satisfied' is insufficient explanation (*Gourley* [1981] Crim. L.R. 334) though 'completely satisfied' is sufficient and in *Ching* [1976] Crim. L.R. 687, the Court of Appeal did not disturb the verdict where the direction was:

> 'it is a doubt for which you can give a reason . . . it is sometimes said to be the sort of matter which might influence you were you to consider some business matter, for example a mortgage concerning your house.'

One of the best known explanations is that of Denning J. in *Miller v Minister of Pensions* [1947] 2 All E.R. 372, where he said:

> 'It need not reach certainty but it must carry a high degree of probability. Proof beyond a reasonable doubt does not mean proof beyond the shadow of a doubt. The law would fail to protect the community if it admitted fanciful possibilities to deflect the course of justice. If the evidence is so strong against a man as to leave only a remote possibility in his favour, which can be dismissed with the sentence "of course it is possible but not in the least probable" the case is proved beyond reasonable doubt, but nothing short of that will suffice.' (Reproduced by permission of Reed Elsevier (UK) Ltd, trading as LexisNexis Butterworths.)

In *Stephens* [2002] EWCA Crim 1529 a jury retired and then sent a note asking the judge: (i) what constituted reasonable doubt; (ii) how certain it was necessary for them to be. The Court of Appeal held the Judicial Studies Board guideline was well established as follows:

> 'How does the prosecution succeed in proving the defendant's guilt? The answer is—by making you sure of it. Nothing less than that will do. If after considering all the evidence you are sure that the defendant is guilty, you must return a verdict of "Guilty". If you are not sure, your verdict must be "Not Guilty".'

It is not helpful for the judge to try to distinguish between being sure and being certain.

1.13 Summary

(a) There are two senses in which the phrase 'burden of proof' is used—the overall and specific burdens.

(b) An evidential burden is not itself a proof burden.
(c) A party with a specific proof burden must also have an evidential burden.
(d) The overall burden of proof is on the prosecution as are most of the specific proof burdens.
(e) The content of the specific proof burdens is a matter of substantive law not evidence.
(f) A defendant in criminal proceedings may have an express or an implied burden reverse proof burden.
(g) Reverse proof burdens may violate the presumption of innocence in art.6(2) of the ECHR.

1.14 Exercise

In the table below try to answer the questions in the first column either without looking at the second and third column at all or by covering them.

Figure 11—Exercise

Proposition	True/false	Reason
The overall burden of proof on the case can move from prosecution to defence.	False	If true, then the accused would have to prove his innocence contrary to *Woolmington*.
The legal burden of proof of dishonesty in Theft Act 1968 s.1 moves from prosecution to defence and back again depending on the amount of evidence adduced by either side.	False	Legal (proof) burdens *never* shift. (If you said 'true' you have confused legal (proof) and evidential burdens.
The evidential burden of proof of recklessness in the Criminal Damage Act 1971 s.1 is on the defendant.	False	The expression 'evidential burden proof' is a contradiction.
Whenever a party has an evidential burden they must also have a legal burden.	False	Most defendants most of the time at worst have only an evidential burden.
The burden of proof decides who opens the case.	True	But only if we are referring to the overall burden.

1.15 Further Reading

Ashworth & Blake: The presumption of innocence in English Criminal Law [1996] Crim. L.R. 306

Birch, Hunting the Snark: The Elusive Statutory Exception [1988] Crim. L.R. 221
Dennis, 'Reverse Onuses and the Presumption of Innocence: In Search of Principle' [2005] Crim. L.R. 901
Doran, 'Alternative Defences: The Invisible Burden on the Trial Judge' [1992] Crim. L.R. 878
Hamer, 'The Presumption of Innocence and Reverse Burdens of Proof' [2007] C.L.J. 142
Healey, 'Proof and Policy: No Golden Threads' [1987] Crim. L.R. 361
Smith, 'Satisfying the Jury' [1988] Crim. L.R. 335

2 The Examination of Witnesses

2.1 Introduction

English criminal proceedings have traditionally been based on oral evidence from witnesses though there have been some recent statutory inroads into the orality principle. This principle means that although virtually every witness will have made a written statement relating to the facts in issue (e.g. a witness statement) they will give their evidence in person without reference to their written statement. The jury will not usually be aware from the proceedings in court that such statements exist and it is only in very exceptional circumstances that the jury would be allowed to see such statements. Putting it shortly and acknowledging exceptions, a witness's evidence consists of what they say in court today.

The current chapter envisages criminal proceedings against a defendant with witnesses called by the prosecution, the defence and possibly the judge. We investigate issues relating to the examination of witnesses. In particular we shall consider the questions which can and cannot properly be put to a witness. In the Introduction to this book we saw that the defendant is a competent witness in his own behalf and though reference will be made to him as a witness, this chapter is principally concerned with witnesses other than the defendant. Nevertheless, in both this and subsequent chapters we shall encounter special rules governing questioning of the defendant (both by the prosecution and any co-defendant) where he gives evidence.

2.2 The privilege against self-incrimination

> 'No one is bound to answer any question if the answer thereto would, in the opinion of the judge, have a tendency to expose the deponent to any criminal charge, penalty or forfeiture which the judge regards as reasonably likely to be preferred.' (per Lord Goddard in *Blunt v Park Lane Hotel* [1942] 2 All E.R. 187, 189).

The privilege does not apply to the defendant in respect of the offence at hand, only in respect of other possible offences. It is personal in the sense that it applies to the witness (and so can be waived by him) rather than to the evidence. It follows that even if a witness successfully claims the privilege, it may be possible to prove the facts in question by other means. The judge decides whether the claim is bona fide or whether the witness is 'trifling with the court' and is undesirous of giving the information: *Re Reynolds* [1881–85] All E.R. 997. It seems there is no rule that a judge must warn a witness that he is not bound to answer questions.

Problems have arisen in relation to statutory provisions which expressly or, as a matter of construction, violate the privilege but do not limit the use which can be made of answers in subsequent proceedings. In *Saunders v United Kingdom* (1997) 23 E.H.R.R. 313 the defendant had made statements under legal compulsion to inspectors of the Department of Trade and Industry. His answers were subsequently used in criminal proceedings against him. The ECtHR held that their use violated art.6 of the Convention. The court said the privilege not to incriminate oneself, like the right to silence:

> 'is a generally recognised international standard which lies at the heart of the notion of a fair trial under Article 6.'

It is closely linked to the presumption of innocence in art.6(2). The real issue was the use made by the prosecution of statements obtained in such circumstances. It was irrelevant whether their content was incriminatory because even neutral statements could be used by the prosecution to support its case. The public interest in combating fraud could not be invoked to justify the use of answers compulsorily obtained in a non-judicial investigation to incriminate at trial. (The law in question (Companies Act 1985 s.434) has been amended by s.59 and the third Schedule to the YJCEA.)

The principle in *Saunders* does not apply if the questioning is no more than a request for factual information. There is no right to refuse to provide such information on the basis of breach of the privilege. In *R. v Hertfordshire CC Ex p. Green Environmental Industries Ltd* [2000] 2 W.L.R. 373 a local authority made statutory inquiries of a company to determine factual issues concerned with the dumping of clinical waste. The company refused to answer the inquiries on the ground that the answers could be used against it in a subsequent prosecution. The House of Lords, dismissing the appeal, distinguished *Saunders* holding there was no illegality in the process whereby answers could be demanded compulsorily and, accordingly, no violation of art.6. The decision in *Orkem SA v Commission of the European Communities* (C374/87) [1989] E.C.R. 3283 drew the line at the point where the questioning compelled answers which might involve admission of a violation of the law. A mere request for factual information did not do that.

The same conclusion was reached by the ECtHR in *O'Halloran v UK* (App. No. 15809/02) and *Francis v UK* (App. No. 25624/02). The privilege was not breached by legislation which required the keeper of a motor vehicle to name the driver of the vehicle at a given time. Although the requirement to supply information was compulsion of a direct nature, car owners were aware of the regulatory scheme which was imposed because of the recognition that cars have potential to cause serious injury. It was not an offence of strict liability since it was not committed if the registered keeper neither knew nor, with reasonable diligence, could have known who was driving the vehicle. In the earlier case of *Stott v Brown* [2001] 1 W.L.R. 817 Lord Bingham C.J. held the same statutory provision could hardly be termed a disproportionate legislative response to the problem of road safety. (This begs the question of proportionality in relation to the privilege against self-incrimination.) While the keeper's reply to the police created new evidence, so do the results of a breathalyser and no one argues that that violates the privilege. Finally the only penalty for non-compliance was a fine (an incomplete statement as to which see below). His approach was approved in *O'Halloran* and *Francis*.

Penalty for non-compliance

It seems clear that the privilege will be breached where the penalty for non-compliance is imprisonment: *Heaney & McGuiness v Ireland* [2001] 22 E.H.R.R. 12. Section 52 of the

Offences Against the State 1939 (an Irish statute) made it an offence subject to imprisonment of six months to fail to account to a police officer for one's movements in respect of a specified terrorist offence. The ECtHR relied on its own decision in *Funke v France* (1993) 16 E.H.R.R. 297 where the penalty for failure to yield documents to customs authorities was an accumulation of fines. In *JB v Switzerland* [2001] Crim. L.R. 748 the penalty of approximately £800 was held to amount to improper compulsion. Given that the penalty for non-compliance in *O'Halloran*, *Francis* and *Stott* was a fine of up to £1,000, mandatory endorsement of the driver's licence and possible disqualification from driving it seems difficult to state clearly just how the question of penalty fits into the issue of violation of the privilege.

Evidence having an independent existence

In this section we consider a distinction first made by the ECtHR in *Saunders*. On the one hand there is evidence having 'an existence independent of the will of the subject' such as blood, hair or other physical or objective specimens such as a tacograph or betting slips: *Attorney General's Reference (No. 7 of 2000)* [2001] EWCA Crim 888. In *PG & JH v UK* (App. no. 44787/98), *The Times*, October 19, 2001 the ECtHR held non-incriminating tape recordings to be in this category. Secret bugging of premises had produced a tape indicating that a robbery was being planned. Following their arrest, in order to match the voices on the tape to the defendant, the police subsequently recorded conversations in the cells. Although some of the taping was not lawful and, therefore, represented a breach of art.8.2 the Court held there was no breach of art.6 because the privilege does not apply to this type of evidence.

On the other hand there is evidence obtained from the defendant by oral questioning under some form of compulsion as in *Saunders*. Whether the distinction between these types of evidence is tenable remains to be seen. It seems to depend on the reliability of real evidence but if it does, then the answers in *O'Halloran*, *Francis* and *Stott* should surely be excluded. In any event, it is a distinction which has blurred edges and it is by no means clear that it can carry the weight which the Court placed upon it.

This view is reinforced by the decision of the ECtHR in *Jalloh v Germany* (2007) 44 E.H.R.R. 32. The defendant had been observed removing plastic bags ('bubbles') from his mouth and selling them. On arrest he swallowed the bubble he had in his mouth. He refused a request to take medication to induce vomiting whereupon he was held down by four police officers while a doctor inserted a naso-gastric tube into his nose through which emetics were forcibly fed into his stomach. He was also injected with an emetic. He regurgitated a bubble of cocaine and was arrested. Convicted of dealing, he was sentenced to 12 months imprisonment suspended—reduced to six months on appeal.

The Court held a violation of arts 3 and 6. The cocaine was evidence of a substance having an existence independent of the will of the suspect (hence admissible under *Saunders*) but the force used to obtain the evidence, the breach of art.6 and violation of Jalloh's rights lead to exclusion. So far so good but the Court then muddied the waters by adding that admissibility should also take account of: (i) the weight of the public interest in the investigation; and (ii) the punishment of the offence at issue. Neither of these elements are referred to in *Saunders* and in fact run directly contrary to the judgment in that case.

2.3 The power of the court to call witnesses and ask questions

In criminal proceedings witnesses are normally excluded from the court until called to give evidence. Once called into court, the witness is examined in chief by the party calling him. He is cross-examined by the other side and may thereafter be re-examined by the party calling him. We shall explore these matters in detail shortly.

In such proceedings the judge can call a witness if he considers it necessary in the interests of justice (*Grafton* (1993) 96 Cr. App. R. 156) but according to Lord Taylor C.J. it is a power that should be exercised 'most sparingly and rarely.' While it is the prosecutor's duty to call (or offer to call) any witness who is both worthy of belief and can give evidence of the primary facts, the judge is entitled to inquire why such a witness is not being called and may, as above, call that witness himself.

It is common practice (and courtesy) for the re-examiner to ask the judge if he has any questions of a witness. Where the judge does so, the questions should 'clear up any uncertainties, fill gaps or answer any queries which might be lurking in the jury's mind' (per Auld L.J. in *Wiggan*, *The Times*, March 22, 1999). He must not cross-examine the witness nor must he 'descend into the forum' (per Cumming-Bruce L.J. in *Gunning* (1980) 98 Cr. App. R. 303) by making unwarranted interventions. In *Wiggan* the judge had asked 64 questions which was unwarranted and created a clear risk of prejudice to the party who called the witness.

2.4 Court procedures

Figure 12—Crown Court standard procedure—indictable and either-way offences

Counsel for the prosecution opens his case
First witness for the prosecution—examination in chief
Cross-examination of first witness for prosecution
Prosecution re-examination of its first witness
(Next witness for prosecution)
Submission of no case to answer
Counsel for the defence may open his case
First witness for the defence—examination in chief
Cross-examination of first witness for defence
Defence re-examination of its first witness
(Next witness for defence)
Counsel for the prosecution sums up his case
Counsel for the defence sums up his case
Summing up by judge to jury
Jury retires and returns with its verdict

Figure 13—Magistrates' Court standard procedure—summary and either way offences

Prosecution opens its case
First witness for the prosecution—examination in chief
Cross-examination of first witness for prosecution
Prosecution re-examination of its first witness
(Next witness for prosecution)
Submission of no case to answer
First witness for the defence—examination in chief
Cross-examination of first witness for defence
Defence re-examination of its first witness
(Next witness for defence)
Defence closing speech
The decision
Mitigation

Under the CEA s.2, if:

> 'The only witness to the facts of the case called by the defence is the person charged, he shall be called as a witness immediately after the close of the evidence for the prosecution.'

At common law and under the PACE s.79 if the defendant and another witness are to be called for the defence, the defendant must, unless the court directs otherwise, be called first. However, both the Act and the common law preserve discretion to vary the order in particular circumstances—e.g. where there is a purely formal or non-contentious witness for the defence who is likely to provide conclusive evidence of the defendant's innocence.

2.5 Submission of 'no case to answer'

At 'half time' (the close of the prosecution case) the defence may submit there is no case to answer. To avoid prejudice to the defendant and allow the judge to ask any relevant questions without inhibition, the submission should be made in the absence of the jury: *Crosdale v R.* [1995] 1 W.L.R. 864.

In *Galbraith* [1981] 1 W.L.R. 1039 the Court of Appeal held that when deciding whether there is a case to answer, the judge should consider whether the evidence adduced by the prosecution, if believed in itself together with any inferences to which it might give rise, would be sufficient to convict. The submission should succeed if there is no evidence that the defendant committed the offence or if the evidence was so tenuous that a properly directed jury could not convict. Where a decision as to whether there is a case to answer depends upon the view taken of the prosecution witness's credibility the case should go to the jury.

The *Galbraith* test has been criticised as too weak (Pattenden [1982] Crim. L.R. 558) and in at least one area of the law of evidence—disputed identification evidence—the courts have raised the bar with regard to both the quantity and quality of evidence required before a case can reach the jury: *Turnbull* (1976) 63 Cr. App. R. 132. (See Ch.10, para.10.3.2).

2.6 Direction to acquit or convict

We considered this in the Introduction to this book at para.0.4.

2.7 Examination in chief

This is the opening stage of examination and consists of questioning of the witness by the party calling him. It is designed to produce evidence favourable to the party calling the witness. As we noted above, a witness will usually have made some type of written statement such as a witness statement, proof of evidence or deposition, and the questioning will be based on it. A number of fairly strict rules govern what may be asked. In particular, the examiner must not ask leading questions (known as 'leading' the witness) that is must not ask questions in a way which tend to suggest the answer to the witness or 'put words into the witness's mouth' or which assume the existence of facts which have yet to be the subject of evidence. An example of the latter (Cross & Tapper, p.262) would be 'what did you do after Smith hit you?' before the witness had deposed to being hit by Smith.

Leading is permissible through the formal or introductory parts of testimony (name, address, occupation etc.); through undisputed issues such as 'did you work for Jones from 2003 to 2007?', where the witness is ruled hostile (see para.2.12.2.1) and any other areas by agreement between the parties.

The common law does not permit 'oath-helping' so the jury must assess witness testimony without assistance. It is not permissible to call an expert to say that a witness should be believed on his oath: *Robinson* [1994] 3 All E.R. 346. Such expert testimony might be allowed where the witness's credibility had been the subject of specific challenge by the other side, or where such challenge was anticipated and where the issue was outside the jury's experience. In *Tobin* [2003] Crim. L.R. 408 the defence to a charge of indecent assault was that the sexual activity had been instigated by the girl in question. Her mother was allowed to depose that her daughter got on well at school and with her siblings was polite and quiet, and had been brought up to respect others. That the mother was not an expert may account for the decision but more likely is the fact that the defendant had given evidence that he was married, had no previous convictions for sexual offences and had called a number of character witnesses.

2.7.1 Refreshing the memory

We noted in the Introduction to this chapter that criminal proceedings in England are based on the 'orality' principle—witnesses give oral evidence to the court of what they saw, heard etc. The common law tended to regard giving evidence as a memory test and frowned on the idea that a witness should be able to refresh his memory from his earlier statement. Given that it may be many months between the incident and trial such an approach made no sense and the common law retreated from it during the later part of the last century. In *G (Joel) (a Juvenile) (No. 1)* [2002] EWCA Crim 01 Henry L.J. said there were no 'fixed or immutable rules which must be followed before a witness may refresh his memory' from an earlier document.

2.7.1.1 Refreshment prior to giving evidence

It is common practice for a witness to be shown his statement before giving evidence. It is courtesy to inform the other side that it has happened. It must not represent an opportunity for witnesses to compare their statements or to get their heads together to decide what to say (*Richardson* [1971] 55 Cr. App. R. 244) or to discuss the evidence they may give even if this takes place under the guise of a case conference by the police: *Skinner* (1994) 99 Cr. App. R. 212. Neither should statements or proofs of evidence be read to witnesses in each other's presence.

2.7.1.2 Refreshment in court

The law is now a combination of common law and statute. By virtue of the CJA 2003 s.139(1):

'A person giving oral evidence in criminal proceedings about any matter may, at any stage in the course of doing so, refresh his memory of it from a document made or verified by him at an earlier time if—

(a) he states in his oral evidence that the document records his recollection of the matter at that earlier time, and
(b) his recollection of the matter is likely to have been significantly better at that time than it is at the time of his oral evidence.'

Under s.139(2) where the witness made an oral statement of which a sound recording was made the witness may refresh his memory from a transcript of the recording.

For the purposes of ss.137–139 (only) a document is defined by s.140 as 'anything in which information of any description is recorded but not including any recording of sounds or moving images.'

Provided the twin conditions in s.139(1) are met the witness is entitled to refresh and the judge has no role to play. Refreshment may occur either when the witness has departed from his previous statement or has omitted relevant matters. Refreshment may also occur in re-examination as where the witness deviates under cross-examination from his evidence in chief. Where a party is minded to seek permission to treat his own witness as hostile (see para.2.12.2.1), it is standard practice to ask, first, whether the witness would like to refresh his memory.

As a result of the statute, the witness no longer needs to have supervised or composed the previous statement in person, nor to have acknowledged its accuracy if compiled by someone else. However, the common law rules still apply in part. Once used in court to refresh memory, the other side can inspect the document without being bound to put it in evidence. At common law the document did not become evidence if used (narrowly) by the cross-examiner *only* to question on the issues involved in refreshment—but the document did become evidence if the cross-examiner used it more widely. The position seems to be the same under the statute (s.120(3)) though the position is not entirely free from doubt. Section 120(3)(b) refers to 'on which he is cross-examined' without distinguishing the narrower and wider aspects involved.

2.7.1.3 **Past recollection recorded**

Where a witness has made a previous statement but it does not refresh his memory of events, the document may be admissible provided the conditions in s.120(4) and (6) are met. They are: (4) that the witness could have given oral evidence of the matters; and (6) the statement was made when the matters were fresh in his memory but he neither remembers them nor can reasonably be expected to do so. The witness must be called (s.120(1)) but need not have complete lack of recall of the matters involved. This would be so where the issues were complex, highly technical or, for example, involved detailed measurements or calculations. We shall cover these matters below at para.2.12.1.

2.7.1.4 **Can the jury see the document?**

While the answer is generally 'no', if the form of the document(s) is relevant the jury may be allow to view it (them). In *Bass* [1953] 37 Cr. App. R. 51 it was suggested in cross-examination of two police officers that they had collaborated on their notebooks, a suggestion which they denied. The jury was allowed to see the books which were made up in identical words so tended to show the officers were lying. Similarly in *Sekhon* (1987) 85 Cr. App. R. 19 it was held that if the cross-examiner suggests the witness has concocted a document used for memory refreshment, then, if the form of the document might be taken by the jury to indicate that the allegation is false, it is admissible in evidence at the instance of the party calling the witness. The problem here is that the document is not evidence of its contents and the jury must be carefully instructed to this effect.

The jury cannot retire with the document unless the court considers it appropriate or all parties agree: CJA 2003 s.122.

2.7.1.5 **Courts' discretion to exclude evidence in out-of-court statements**

The powers below are without prejudice to that in PACE s.78(1) to exclude evidence on which the prosecution proposes to rely. This is fully explained in Ch.7.

Under the Criminal Justice Act 2003 s.125

Section 125 relates to half time at jury trials. If the court is satisfied that the prosecution case is based wholly or partly on an out-of-court statement which is important to the case and is so unconvincing that a conviction would be unsafe, the court can direct either an acquittal or a retrial. The 'out-of-court statement' refers to a statement made by a person not called as a witness in the proceedings. The contents of such a statement are hearsay (see Ch.4 below). The section is recognition of the possible unreliability of hearsay evidence and the risks posed by it where it constitutes an important element of the prosecution case.

Under the Criminal Justice Act 2003 s.126

Section 126(1) provides discretion applicable to all courts to exclude evidence in an out-of-court statement if:

> 'the court is satisfied that the case for excluding the statement, taking account of the danger that to admit it would result in undue waste of time, substantially outweighs the case for admitting it, taking account of the value of the evidence.'

Section 126(2) contains an express saving for s.78(1) of PACE.

2.7.1.6 **Coaching**

Part of the ratio of *Richardson* (above) is that coaching of witnesses is improper. The courts draw a distinction between witness training or coaching on the one hand and familiarisation on the other. The latter provides 'sensible preparation for the experience of giving evidence which assists the witness to give of his or her best' (per Judge L.J. in *Momodou* [2005] EWCA Crim 177 [62]). The judge should be made aware that witnesses have had familiarisation and records of it must be kept and available. You can find more information about it by reading *Salisbury* (unreported but see *http://www.inpracticetraining.com* accessed March 31, 2008).

2.8 Cross-examination

This is the second stage of questioning and is undertaken by the opposing party or parties. All witnesses, unless called merely to produce a piece of evidence (document) are liable to cross-examination by any party to the proceedings whether the witness has actually given evidence against that party or not. The cross-examiner has a wide scope for questions. Control of cross-examination is ultimately in the hands of the judge who may need to restrain the cross-examiner if the questions are considered unnecessary, improper or intrusive.

The court has power to allow witness anonymity and to order voice modulation. In *Davis, Ellis* [2006] EWCA Crim 1155 it was held that concealment of identity of witnesses is not inconsistent with the right to a fair trial even if the evidence of the anonymous witness is pivotal. A careful direction about the issues is obviously required [Davis over ruled by House of Lords [2008] EWHL 36]. We shall look again at these matters in Ch.4 (see para.4.7.8)

There are three possible areas of questioning in cross-examination

- facts in issue;
- the character of the witness (also referred to as 'credibility'); and
- the witness's capacity to give accurate evidence.

We shall look at each of these matters in detail below (para.2.8.2–2.8.4) after considering restrictions on questioning.

2.8.1 Restrictions on questions in cross-examination

A party to legal proceedings is normally represented by a lawyer but according to Lord Bingham C.J. in *Brown (Milton)* [1998] 2 Cr. App. R. 364 British tradition has always permitted individuals to represent themselves in both civil and criminal proceedings. The case is reported on the common law power of the judge to regulate cross-examination of a witness by a defendant in person by protecting the witness, controlling the questioning, and preventing a party in person from abusing the rules relating to repetition of questions and relevance which would apply to a lawyer. Much of what his Lordship referred to has been overtaken by statutory provisions in the form of Special Measures Directions for Vulnerable and Intimidated Witnesses (see para.2.10) but the report contains valuable guidance in relation to any issues outside the statutory scheme.

Under the YJCEA s.34 no person charged with a sexual offence may in any criminal proceedings cross-examine in person a witness who is the complainant either about the sexual or any other offence with which he is charged in those proceedings.

Under the same statute, there are restrictions on the type of questions (as well as the evidence that can be adduced on the defendant's behalf) that can be put in cross-examination of such a complainant (s.41) and also in respect of children who have given evidence through a video recording (s.35). These are covered later in this chapter at para.2.11, and Ch.3 respectively.

Section 36 of the YJCEA gives the court discretion in all criminal proceedings to prevent the defendant cross-examining a witness in person. A direction to this effect can be triggered by an application from the prosecutor or the court can do so of its own motion: s.36(1). The court may give such a direction if it appears both that without it the quality of the evidence will be diminished, *and*, that with it, the quality will be improved. The direction must also not be contrary to the interests of justice. The court must have regard to the criteria in s.36(3). 'Quality' is defined in s.16(5) as 'completeness, coherence and accuracy'; coherence refers to answers which 'address the questions put to the witness and which can be understood both individually and collectively'.

Section 38 engages if the court makes an order under s.36. The court must invite the defendant to arrange legal representation for the cross-examination (s.38(2)) and if he does not do so the court may appoint a qualified legal representative to do it in his interests: s.38(4). The representative is not responsible to the defendant: s.38(5). The judge 'must give the jury such warning (if any)' that no prejudice attaches to the defendant either from the fact that he was prevented from cross-examining in person or that the cross-examination was carried out by a court-appointed representative rather than his own lawyer (if any): s.39(1).

Figure 14—Summary of restrictions on cross-examination by defendant in person in Chapter 11 of the Criminal Justice Act 2003

Section 34

(i) Sexual offence
(ii) Witness is complainant
(iii) Not about sexual or any other offence also charged

Section 35

(i) Offences against children
(ii) W is child complainant or witnessed commission of offence

Section 36

(i) Neither ss.34 nor 35 applicable
(ii) Quality of evidence diminished without direction
(iii) Quality of evidence improved with direction
(iv) Not contrary to interests of justice
(v) Criteria in s.36(3)

Section 38

(i) D to arrange own legal representative
(ii) If does not do so, court can (ss.3) or must (ss.4) appoint

Section 39

Warning to jury not to draw adverse inferences

2.8.2 Facts in issue

The object of cross-examination is to undermine the witness's evidence in favour of the party who called him and obtain testimony in favour of the cross-examiner. The scope of cross-examination is wider than examination in chief. Leading questions are permissible.

There is a rule of practice of examination in chief that all a party's evidence must be 'in' by the time he finishes presenting (closes) his case. One consequence of this rule is that material to be put by the prosecution to the defendant or his witnesses in cross-examination should normally have been led by the prosecution as part of it evidence in chief: *Dartey* (1986) 84 Cr. App. R. 352. The defendant is entitled to know the whole of the case against him before he opens his defence. By way of example suppose on a charge of murder the prosecution conducts its case solely on the basis that the deceased was killed by a karate kick to the head by the defendant. All prosecution witnesses are examined-in-chief on that basis. The prosecution seeks to cross-examine either the defendant or defence witnesses to the effect that the defendant was seen to throw a punch at the deceased, knocking him to the ground. Such questioning should not be permitted because no foundation for it has been laid by the prosecution as part its case in chief. (Based on *Carr* [2000] 2 Cr. App. R. 149).

A cross-examiner's failure to question a witness amounts to tacit acceptance of the witness's evidence in chief. Consequently, the cross-examiner will not be permitted to invite the jury not to believe the witness. If the cross-examiner proposes to contradict a witness by calling contrary evidence, the witness must be informed of this during cross-examination so that he can explain any discrepancy. Failure to observe this rule may well lead the judge not to permit contradiction. In *Fenlon* (1980) 71 Cr. App. R. 307 it was held the rule applies not only to the prosecution but also to co-defendants numbers 2 to 6 when the first defendant has given evidence in conflict with that which numbers 2 to 6 would give. Citing Lord Herschell in *Browne v Dunn* (1894) 6 R. 67 the Court of Appeal held it was counsel's duty to draw the attention of *any witness* to evidence which it was intended to impeach and, accordingly, the trial judge had not erred.

The rule as to challenge is not 'inflexible and it has been held to be unsuitable to proceedings before lay justices, and less applicable to parties, including the complainant in a sexual case'. (Cross & Tapper, p.292). What amounts to 'informing' the witness of a challenge to their evidence depends on the facts of the case. In *Lovelock* [1997] Crim. L.R. 821 the Court of Appeal indicated that a 'raised eyebrow' approach might be sufficient. It is clear that there does not need to be a detailed challenge to every aspect of the testimony. The whole tenor of the cross-examination may indicate challenge.

2.8.3 Matters of credit (credibility)

Cross-examination on the facts in issue may well elicit answers favourable to the cross-examiner but cross-examination as to the witness's credit may undermine the value of his evidence in chief by showing him to be unworthy of belief. This is also known as 'impeachment of the witness'. When judges and commentators refer to 'credit' they mean matters which would affect whether a witness should be believed on issues material to the case and which affect the likelihood generally of a person telling the truth—whether he is trustworthy. Such matters include character, convictions, reputation, chastity and any previous statements the witness may have made.

Questions to a witness other than the defendant as to his bad character are governed by s.100 of the CJA 2003. This is explained at para.2.8.6 and in Ch.9, para.9.5. For the moment we assume the evidence passes the statutory test of admissibility.

The witness's answers to questions about his credibility are:

(i) collateral to the facts in issue; and

(ii) generally final.

This does not mean the party asking the questions or the court must accept the answers as true, merely that the party asking them cannot call contrary evidence. We shall postpone detailed discussion of both of the above matters until we consider them as exceptions to the rule as to finality (see para.2.8.6). However, we should note here that it is the finality rule which distinguishes cross-examination as to credit from cross-examination both: (i) on facts in issue; and (ii) as to the witness's capacity to give accurate evidence. It is to the latter issue that we now turn.

2.8.4 The witness's capacity to give accurate evidence

Questions may be designed primarily to show that the witness is *mistaken* rather than *untrustworthy*. In other words the jury should not believe a witness on the particular evidence which they have given because there are physical matters (hearing, eyesight, memory etc.) or he has mental attributes or features which affect his capacity to tell the truth. As we noted a moment ago, the answers here are not final—they can be rebutted by affirmative evidence.

In *Toohey v MPC* [1965] 1 All E.R. 506 the House of Lords held the evidence in chief of a doctor that drinking alcohol could exacerbate hysteria and that a witness in the case was more prone to hysteria than was a normal person had been wrongly excluded. Prior to *Toohey* the law excluded the evidence of a medical expert who, while having reservations about a witness could not go so far as to say that he would not believe the witness on his oath. Such an expert had not been allowed:

> 'to testify, as is desired in the present case, to the abnormality and unreliability of the witness or, as may happen in some other case, to the fact that the witness, by reason of some delusion would, on some matters, not be credible whereas on others he might be quite reliable.' (Per Lord Pearce).

His Lordship emphasised the importance of the distinction between, on the one hand, 'mental disturbance' and, on the other, bad reputation and character. In general terms the principle which his Lordship articulated is that medical evidence is admissible to show a witness suffers from some disease, or physical or mental defect or abnormality which renders him not capable of giving a true or reliable account to the jury. Amnesia would be an example of this. It is allowable for 'medical science' to reveal this 'hidden fact' to the jury. The evidence must be outside the normal competence of the jury. The rule applies to both prosecution and defence.

2.8.5 Finality of answers

We have seen that answers to questions about the witness's credit are generally final and cannot be challenged by contrary evidence even if it is available. The reason is to prevent a multiplicity of collateral issues the exploration of which would often be of marginal relevance and at a not insignificant cost. The test of a 'collateral' issue is whether the cross-examiner would have been allowed to introduce the evidence in question as part of his case in chief. If not, the issue is collateral.

By way of example, in *Harris v Tippett* (1811) 2 Camp 637, a defence witness denied under cross-examination that he had attempted to dissuade one of the victim's witnesses from attending the trial. It was held that his answer was final. Again in *Piddington v Bennett* (1940) 63 C.L.R. 533 a witness to an accident in a supermarket car park was cross-examined about his presence at the scene. He said he had delivered goods to the supermarket. It was held that the manager of the supermarket should not have been called to prove that no goods were delivered by the witness that day—the issue was collateral. The cross-examiner would not have been allowed to call the manager as part of his case in chief evidence because it would not be relevant to the facts in issue.

Though easy to state, the test may be difficult to apply. In *Att-Gen v Hitchcock* (1847) 1 Exch 91 the issue was whether a bribe had been *offered* to a witness. The court held the denial was final though if the issue had been whether the witness had accepted it, the denial would not have been since it would have gone to issue of bias—as to which see para.2.8.6.3.

2.8.6 Exceptions to finality

As noted above the CJA 2003 governs the admission of evidence of bad character. Bad character under the Act consists of evidence of 'misconduct' which itself consists of offences or other reprehensible behaviour but excluding 'evidence which has to do with the alleged facts of the offence': s.98. The Act distinguishes the admissibility of evidence of bad character of defendants from that of non-defendants. The latter is governed by s.100(1) which permits such evidence either where it is admitted by agreement, or is important explanatory evidence, or has substantial probative value in relation to a matter of substantial importance in the proceedings.

The current section of work assumes the court has permitted questioning of a non-defendant witness under s.100 of the CJA 2003 (Questions to both defendants and non-defendants are considered in detail in Ch.9). The Act applies only where the questions relate to the witness's (mis)conduct or behaviour. To repeat, we are concerned with whether answers given by the witness must be accepted as final by the cross-examiner.

2.8.6.1 **Previous inconsistent statements**

Where the witness denies having made a previous statement inconsistent with his evidence in court today; this is covered at para.2.12.2.

2.8.6.2 **Previous convictions**

The CPA s.6 (as amended) provides:

> 'If upon a witness being lawfully questioned as to whether he has been convicted of any crime, he either denies or does not admit the fact, or refuses to answer, it shall be lawful for the cross-examining party to prove such conviction.'

To be 'lawful' within the section, the questions would need to comply with s.100 of the CJA 2003. Given that the witness is being cross-examined as to his credibility, it might be thought that questioning would be limited to convictions for offences involving dishonesty or untruthfulness. This is not the case. In principle (and subject to the next paragraph) there is no restriction on which offences may be proved.

While the Rehabilitation of Offenders Act 1974 does not apply (s.7(2)(a)) to criminal proceedings it was said in *Nye* (1982) 75 Cr. App. R. 247 that Parliament's intention must be respected and judicial discretion to permit evidence of spent convictions 'should be exercised, so far as can be, favourably towards the' defendant (per Talbot J. at 251). On the facts, in respect of minor convictions spent more than five years previously, the Court of Appeal was inclined to allow the defendant to be represented of good character but expressly refused to interfere with the decision of the trial judge who fully understood and dealt with material before him. There is a practice direction on this issue (Direction No. 1.6) on the website of the Ministry of Justice as follows: *http://www.justice.gov.uk/criminal/procrules—fin/contents/practice—direction/pd—consolidated.htm* (accessed March 31, 2008).

2.8.6.3 **Bias**

A denial by the witness of bias towards one of the parties may be proved by contrary evidence. Relationships between witnesses can give rise to obvious possible bias (e.g. within a family/friends) but this may not always be clear and it is then permissible to rebut any denial. In *Phillips* (1938) 26 Cr. App. R. 17, the Court of Criminal Appeal held the defendant should have been allowed to call evidence to rebut his daughter's (B) denial that she had been schooled by her mother to give evidence against him. He was charged with incest of B and his other daughter, I gave evidence against him. He had previously been convicted of indecent assault on B and, again, I had given evidence against him.

In *Mendy* (1977) 64 Cr. App. Rep. 4, while a police officer was giving evidence against the defendant, a man (T) was seen writing notes which he then took outside and showed to the defendant's husband, H. When H gave evidence, he denied receiving a note. The Court of Appeal held that he was rightly contradicted by the evidence of T even though it was a collateral issue. The jury was entitled to know that H was prepared to cheat and lie to deceive them. Is this very different from *Harris*?

The provisions of s.100 of the CJA 2003 might well apply to cases such as *Mendy* which are based on the alleged conduct of the witness. Relationship cases would seem to be outside the reach of the Act.

2.8.6.4 **Police misconduct**

As we have seen, under s.98 of the CJA 2003 evidence of 'bad character' is defined as misconduct 'other than evidence which has to do with the alleged facts of the offence'. (The precise meaning of the phrase is considered in Ch.9, para.9.4.2.1.) It follows the section does not bite where the defendant wishes to cross-examine police officers about their alleged misconduct in relation to the current proceedings e.g. questions about whether they planted evidence or falsified admissions ('verballing') or incriminating silences ('non-verballing'). Once it is clear s.98 does not bite the question of cross-examination will be decided under the common law where the only issue is relevance.

In *Busby* (1982) 75 Cr. App. R. 79 two officers were cross-examined to show they had 'verballed' the defendant and to show they had visited one of his potential witnesses, W, to persuade W not to give evidence. W was called by the defendant but the trial judge held W's evidence would be collateral to the main trial and the defendant's guilt (burglary and handling). On appeal it was held not to be collateral but relevant to a fact in issue—namely what lengths police were prepared to go in order to secure convictions. *Busby* may be a specific example of the bias exception covered above (para.2.8.6.3) but not everyone is convinced of this or that *Busby* is correctly decided. The decision was nevertheless treated as correct in *Funderburk* [1990] 90 Cr. App. R. 466, which is mentioned at para.2.8.6.5 and covered in detail at para.2.12.2.2. The questions would be outside the CJA 2003 since they are 'to do with the facts of the alleged offence.'

Where the defence wishes to cross-examine police officers to show they gave false evidence in previous cases where there had been verdicts of not guilty or appeals allowed (*Edwards* [1991] 93 Cr. App. R. 48) s.98 and therefore s.100 of the CJA 2003 does bite. To repeat what we saw in para.2.8.6, under s.100 such evidence can be admitted either by agreement, or if it is important explanatory evidence, or has substantial probative value in relation to a matter of substantial importance in the proceedings.

In *Edwards* the Court of Appeal held that because verdicts of not guilty or appeals being allowed did not necessarily impugn the credibility of the officers, questioning was admissible only where there was independent evidence which cast doubt on officers' credibility. In any event as an attack on the officers' credibility their answers would be final. Murphy (p.556) distinguishes the outcomes in *Busby* and *Edwards* arguing that the former 'involved a direct interference by the officers with potential evidence in the instant case, rather than an attack on their credibility by reference to their conduct in other cases'.

The principle in *Edwards* has been applied where there had been a positive disciplinary finding (not a mere allegation) of professional misconduct against police officers: *Guney* [1998] 2 Cr. App. R. 242. However, in *Edwards (Maxine)* [1996] Cr. App. R. 345 Beldam L.J. referred to cases where there was a 'suspicion of perjury' by police officers which clearly extends the limit imposed in *Edwards*. In *Fraser* [2003] EWCA Crim 3180 'a suspicion of perjury that infects the evidence in this case' was the basis on which convictions for possession of drugs were quashed. (per Auld L.J. [19])

Edwards also holds the defence is entitled to be informed of any convictions or disciplinary findings recorded against police officers involved in the present case, or any decisions by trial judges where a trial was stopped, or Court of Appeal judgments where a conviction was quashed because of misconduct or lack of veracity of identified police officers who are also involved in the present case. The court regarded its findings as applicable to all professional people.

2.8.6.5 **The rule in *Funderburk***

In the area of sexual offences, the courts have been unwilling to draw a distinction between questions or evidence relating to facts in issue and those relating to the credibility of the complainant: *Funderburk*; *Nagrecha* [1997] 2 Cr. App. R. 401. In the latter case Rose L.J. quoted Watkins L.J. in *R. v Knightsbridge Crown Court Ex p. Goonatilleke* (1985) 81 Cr. App. R. 31 that:

> 'a matter going to the credit of a witness in a criminal case cannot be said to be collateral to the vital issue; that is to say guilt or otherwise, especially where, as here, the witness in question provides the only evidence upon that issue.'

If the matter is not collateral the cross-examiner can rebut any denial by the witness and evidence received in this context *would* be evidence of its contents. (See further para.2.12.2.2 below.)

Figure 15—Finality of answers to questions in cross-examination

	Final	**Exceptions**	
Facts in issue	No	No	
Credit	Yes	Yes	Previous inconsistent statements; Convictions; Bias; Police misconduct; Rule in *Funderburk*.
Accurate/reliable evidence	No	Yes	Rebuttal evidence inadmissible if issue within jury competence.

2.9 Re-examination

Re-examination is the third and final possible stage of questioning (apart from questions from the judge). It is limited to questions to clarify issues raised in cross-examination and to explain any inconsistencies between the witness's evidence in chief and cross-examination. Questions about issues raised only in examination in chief should therefore not be asked. Where the cross-examiner has accused the witness of fabricating his evidence in chief, the party calling the witness may be allowed to prove that the witness made a previous out of court statement which is consistent with his evidence today. (See para.2.12.1.)

It appears the judge has residual discretion about questions so as to ensure that the jury is not misled as to the existence of some fact or the terms of any previous statement by the witness: *Ali (Hawar Hussein)* [2003] EWCA Crim 3214. The discretion does not permit the re-examiner to reinstate the evidence of a witness merely where inconsistencies are shown up by cross-examination. This would affect the finality rule and falls some way short of the test of whether the jury would otherwise be misled.

The following table summarises the previous section of work and represents in tabular form what we saw above at 2.4 in relation to proceedings in the Crown Court.

Figure 16—Summary table

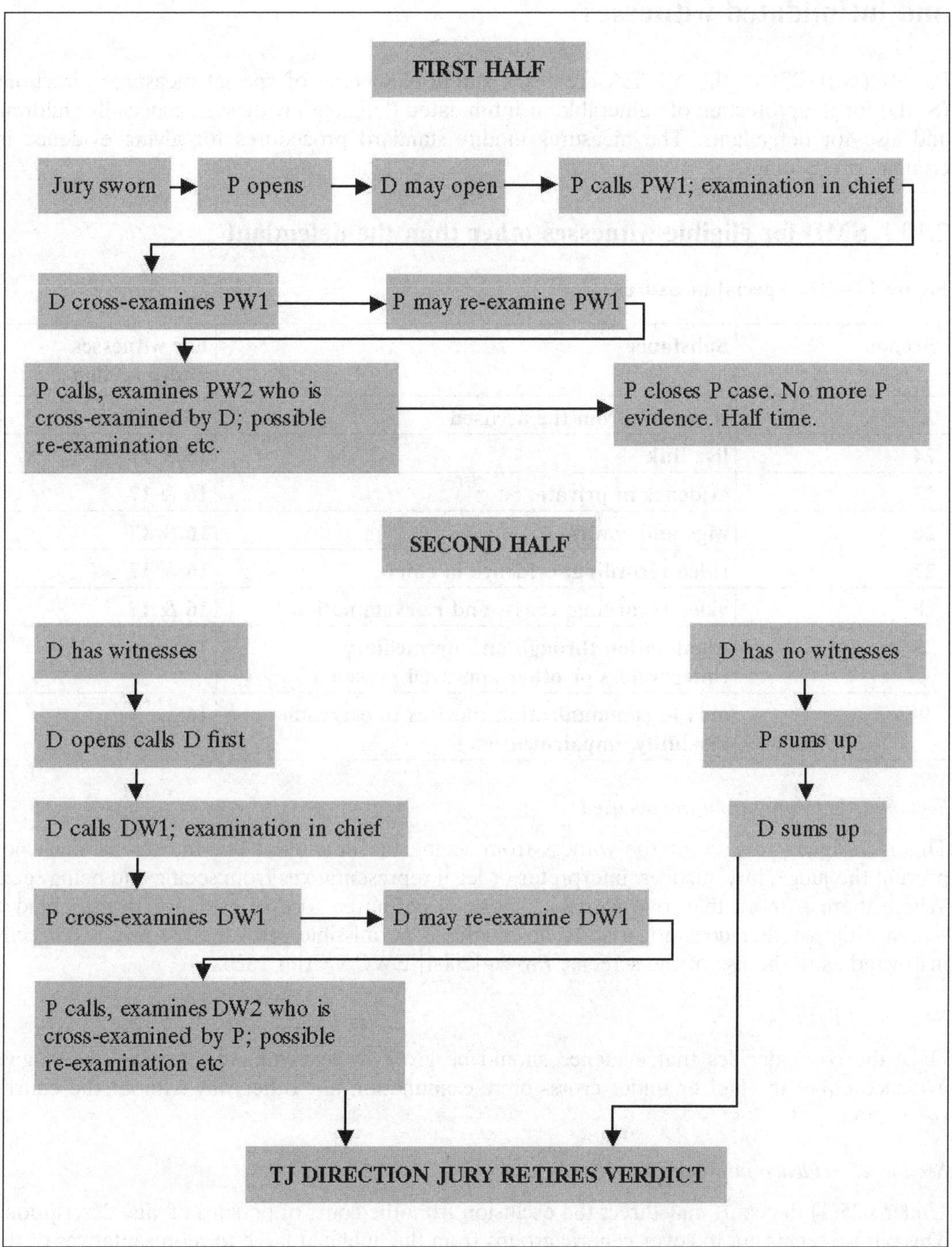

2.10 Special Measures Directions for defendants and vulnerable and intimidated witnesses

Part II (ss.16–33) of the YJCEA creates a statutory scheme of special measures directions (SMD) for the protection of vulnerable or intimidated ('eligible') witnesses, especially children, and also for defendants. The measures modify standard procedures for giving evidence in criminal proceedings.

2.10.1 SMD for eligible witnesses other than the defendant

Figure 17—The special measures

Section	Substance	For witnesses under section
23	screening from the accused	16 & 17
24	live link	16 & 17
25	evidence in private	16 & 17
26	wigs and gowns	16 & 17
27	video recording; evidence in chief	16 & 17
28	video recording; cross- and re-examination	16 & 17
29	examination through an intermediary (interpreters or other approved persons)	16
30	aids to communication (devices to overcome disability, impairment etc)	16

Section 23 screening from the accused

This is designed to prevent the witness from seeing the defendant but the screen must not prevent the judge, jury, justices, interpreter or legal representatives from seeing and being seen. Where there is more than one witness, or one is permitted to give evidence from behind a screen while another does not wish to do so, this is permissible provided the jury is correctly instructed as to the use of the screens: *Brown* [2004] EWCA Crim 1620.

Section 24 live link

Once the court decides that evidence should be given by live link, the witness cannot give evidence either in chief or under cross- or re-examination any other way without the court's permission.

Section 25 evidence in private

Under s.25(1) the court may direct the exclusion from the court of persons of 'any description'. This phrase seems apt to cover generic groups from the public at large to representatives of the media but it does not seem apt to cover particular named individuals. The SMD may not exclude the defendant, or legal representatives acting in the proceedings or interpreters: s.25(2). Under s.25(3) an SMD excluding the media shall be expressed so as not to apply to one named individual nominated by the media for that purpose.

An SMD under s.25 applies only to sexual offences (subs.(4)(a)) or where the court has reasonable grounds to believe that someone other than the defendant has sought or will seek to intimidate the witness in connection with giving evidence (subs.(4)(b)). Given that the latter is likely to be a named person, it seems even more odd that s.25(1) refers to excluding by 'description'.

Sections 27 & 28 video recordings of evidence in chief, cross- and re-examination

These measures can apply to any eligible witness whatever their age. Their full meaning is dealt with in Ch.3, para.3.3.3.

Section 32 provides that in trials on indictment where an SMD has been given the judge 'must give the jury such warning (if any) as he considers necessary to ensure that the fact that' an SMD was given does not prejudice the accused. This badly drafted section appears to be both mandatory ('must') and discretionary ('if any').

2.10.2 Categories of eligible witness

This Part of the Act is structured as follows. Sections 16 and 17 define an 'eligible witness'. Such a witness can be the beneficiary of an SMD. In general terms, a witness will benefit from an SMD where, without it, there would be a diminution in the quality of his evidence. The special measures themselves are to be found between ss.23 and 30. The power of the court to order an SMD is contained in s.19(2). As the following table indicates, there are four categories of eligible witness.

Figure 18—Categories of eligible witness other than the defendant

'Eligible witness'	Gateway—if W	Criteria
Section 16(1)(a)	is under 17 years at hearing.	
Section 16(2)	suffers from mental disorder, significant impairment of intelligence and social functioning, or physical disability or disorder.	(i) If quality of evidence likely to be diminished because of such circumstances. (ii) Court must consider W's view.
Section 17(1)	suffers fear or distress in connection with testifying.	(i) If quality of evidence likely to be diminished because of circumstances opposite (subs.(1)). (ii) Nature & circumstances of offence. W's age. Social/cultural/ethnic origins of W; domestic & employment circumstances; religious beliefs or political opinions. Behaviour of D, his family, associates or likely witness towards W (subs.(2)). (iii) W's views (subs.(3)).
Section 17(4)	is complainant in sexual proceedings.	Unless W has told court does not wish to be eligible.

2.10.3 SMD for the defendant

By virtue of s.33A of the Act a defendant is eligible for assistance as the following table indicates. Although the defendant will usually be present in court there are circumstances—such as where he misbehaves himself badly—when the trial can continue without his physical presence.

Figure 19—Defendant eligibility for SMD

D as witness	**Evidence by live link**	**Specific condition**	**General conditions**
	On D's application.		
D is under 18 years.	Yes.	Ability to participate effectively as a witness is compromised by level of intelligence or social functioning, and ability to participate effectively would be improved by giving evidence over a live link: s.33A(4).	Interests of justice.
D is 18 or above.	Yes.	Unable to participate in the proceedings effectively because has a mental disorder or a significant impairment of intelligence or social function, and ability to participate effectively would be improved by giving evidence over a live link: s.33A(5).	Once direction made, D must give all evidence (in chief, re- & cross-examination) by live link.

While the assistance is limited to giving evidence via a live television link, s.19(6) preserves the powers of the court to make orders or give leave of any description in exercise of its inherent or other powers and this could apply to a defendant. In *R. (D) v Camberwell Green Youth Court* [2005] UKHL 4 Baroness Hale said the court had inherent power to assist the defendant to give the best evidence he could. She instanced a detailed statement being read to the jury so it was clear what he wished to say.

2.10.4 **Section 19**

An SMD is triggered either if a party makes an application in respect of a witness or the court raises the issue of its own motion: s.19(1). The court must then decide (s.19(2)) whether an SMD would improve the quality of the evidence and which measures, either singly or in combination, to employ. From the table above, it should be clear that the diminution/ improvement issue does not apply to witnesses under s.16(1)(a) or s.17(4). However, the view of a s.17(4) witness as to whether he wants an SMD is paramount. This is because one witness might be too frightened to face the defendant while another might have no qualms. Otherwise in considering diminution/improvement in quality the witness's view is a factor of which account must be taken as is whether the SMD might inhibit effective testing of the evidence in question.

2.10.5 **The meaning of 'quality'**

Section 16(5) defines quality of a witness's evidence in terms of 'completeness, coherence and accuracy'. 'Coherence' is further defined as 'a witness's ability in giving evidence to give answers which address the questions put to the witness and can be understood both individually and collectively'.

2.11 The complainant's sexual behaviour—Youth Justice and Criminal Evidence Act 1999 s.41

Until 1976 it was common in rape trials for the defence to ask questions of the victim with a view to exploring her sexual history. Detailed questioning to the point of causing distress and humiliation was permitted under the guise of relevance. A law designed to restrict such questioning was introduced in 1976 with limited success. Section 41 is the latest attempt to provide what is sometimes known as a 'rape shield', though it should be stressed that the section is not limited to the offence of rape and protects both male and female complainants.

By virtue of s.41(1) when a person is charged with a sexual offence (as defined in s.62) then except with leave of the court 'no evidence may be adduced and no question may be asked in cross-examination by or on behalf of any accused at the trial about the sexual behaviour of the complainant'. The embargo applies to questions to any witness and is not limited to questions to the complainant.

2.11.1 **The meaning of 'sexual behaviour'**

Section 42(1)(c) unhelpfully tells us that '"sexual behaviour" means any sexual behaviour or other sexual experience whether or not involving any accused or other person.' In *Mukadi* [2004] Crim. L.R. 373 the Court of Appeal entertained doubts whether getting into a large, expensive car driven by a man much older than the complainant and exchanging telephone numbers with him amounted to sexual behaviour.

One problem the courts have encountered is whether questions/evidence that the complainant has made previous false complaints, or no complaint when it might have been expected, are within s.41. In *T (Complainant's Sexual History)* [2001] EWCA Crim 1877 the Court of Appeal held they were not. Each case will, however, depend on its facts. Counsel must have evidence to support the contention that the questions/evidence will not violate the embargo and the court will not allow such questions to be a cloak for doing so. What constitutes an 'evidential basis' is contentious. A typical argument that such a basis exists would be that the victim withdrew the complaint or refused to cooperate with the police following initial complaint: *Garaxo* [2005]

EWCA Crim 1170; *V* [2006] EWCA Crim 1901. If the court finds there is an evidential basis for the questions, the matter is outside s.41 but the questions might well be caught by s.100 of the CJA 2003 which governs the admissibility of evidence of bad character of persons other than the defendant. This is covered in Ch.9, para.9.5.

2.11.2 **The initial procedure**

Lifting the embargo is possible but there are a number of conditions which must be satisfied before the court will allow questions/evidence. In *F* [2005] EWCA Crim 493 Judge L.J said that if the conditions are satisfied there is no discretion to refuse the questions/evidence; the section establishes a judgment—it is not based on discretion.

Once an application is made, the first step is that court must be satisfied the questions/evidence relate to specific instances of alleged sexual behaviour on the part of the complainant: s.41(6). Next the court must be satisfied that it is neither the purpose nor main purpose of the questions/evidence to impugn the credibility of the complainant as a witness (s.41(4)) even if it has that effect: *Martin* [2004] EWCA Crim 916. The defendant wished to show that two days prior to the incident in question the complainant had 'pestered' him for sex as well as performing an act of oral sex on him but that he had rejected her suggestion of further sexual relations. The current complaint was, allegedly, the revenge of a woman scorned. The judge had refused leave but was reversed on appeal. The Court of Appeal held that even if one of the purposes of the questioning was to impugn the complainant's credibility it was neither 'the' nor 'the main' purpose. The decision is defensible on the ground that the questioning was not a *direct* attack on the complainant's credibility but sought only to undermine her credibility with regard to the offence in question.

Section 41(4) applies to s.41(3) not to s.41(5) (see para.2.11.3).

The following chart indicates the situation explained so far.

Figure 20—Flow chart of initial procedure for section 41 applications

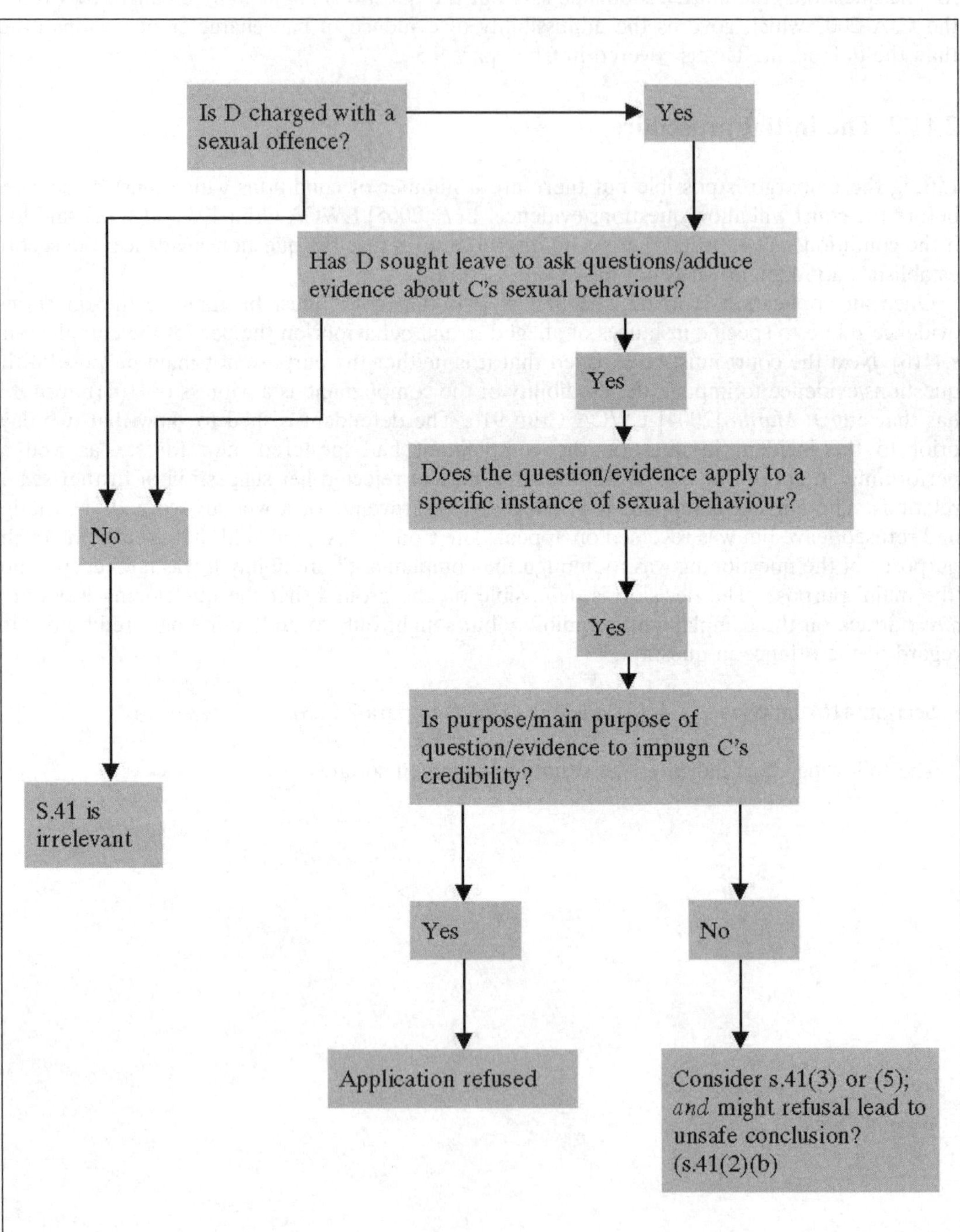

The prohibition may be lifted (subs.(2)) only if either subss.(3) or (5) applies *and* the court is satisfied that refusal might result in an unsafe conclusion in relation to any trial issue.

2.11.3 Questions/evidence under s.41(5)

Subsection (5) allows the defence to rebut or explain any evidence about the complainant's sexual behaviour adduced by the prosecution provided the defence goes no further than rebuttal or explanation. In *F* (above) the defendant was charged with a number of counts of sexual offences against C while she was under 16 years. It was accepted the parties had had a consensual adult sexual relationship from the time C was 18 until she was 24. C's contention was that the adult relationship was a continuation of the childhood abuse and that she had been too scared of the defendant to finish it. The defendant said he brought the adult relationship to an end and C was motivated by revenge in making the complaints of under-age abuse. The judge held the adult relationship was relevant and admissible, and the prosecution had lead evidence of it. The Court of Appeal held the defendant had been entitled to cross-examine C under subs.(5) in relation to her evidence in chief. He should, however, also have been allowed to cross-examine her on videos and photographs compiled during the adult relationship which showed C in a number of sexually suggestive poses in which she appeared happy and at ease.

2.11.4 Questions/evidence under s.41(3)

2.11.4.1 Is consent in issue?

If the questions/evidence do not relate to consent and provided they relate to a specific instance(s) of sexual behaviour (s.41(6)), the only issue is whether, without the question or evidence, any conclusion of the jury might be unsafe: s.41(2)(b). Provided the questions/evidence are relevant and comply with subs.6 it is difficult to imagine when refusal of leave would not lead to an unsafe verdict.

2.11.4.2 When would the questions/evidence not relate to consent?

One example would be if the accused denied the offence completely—as where he suggested that it was a case of mistaken identity. Another would be if he raised the issue of belief in consent rather than consent itself: *A (No.2) (Complainant's sexual history)* [2001] UKHL 25.

2.11.4.3 What about when consent is in issue?

Where the questions/evidence relate to consent, they will be admissible only if either subs.(b) or either part of subs.(c) of s.41(3) is satisfied.

2.11.4.4 What is the meaning of s.41(3)(b)?

> '. . . it is an issue of consent and the sexual behaviour of the complainant to which the evidence or question relates is alleged to have taken place at or about the same time as the event which is the subject matter of the charge against the accused;'

The behaviour covered by the subsection might take the form of acts of familiarity between complainant and defendant at about the same time as the alleged incident. In *A* Lord Steyn said an 'example . . . would be where it is alleged that the complainant invited the accused to have sexual intercourse with her earlier in the evening'. It is not immediately obvious how an invitation amounts to 'behaviour'.

His Lordship further held that what he termed 'the temporal restriction' ('at or about the same time') in subs.(b) could not extend to acts done in days, weeks or months before the acts in question—it seems that 24 hours is about the limit. This would seem to apply also s.41(3)(c)(ii) (see below) though in *T* [2004] EWCA Crim 1220 Waller L.J. referred to a possible different construction for this phrase in s.41(3)(c)(ii). He did not explain why.

Murphy (p.215) says the phrase 'the event which is the subject matter of the charge' is unclear 'but seems designed to embrace more than the conduct constituting the offence'.

2.11.4.5 **The meaning of s.41(3)(c)**

Section 41(3)(c) permits leave to be given where the question/evidence relates to consent and the sexual behaviour of the complainant is so similar to any of his/her sexual behavior which took place:

- as part of the event in question (s.41(3)(c)(i)); or
- at or about the same time as the event (s.41(3)(c)(ii)

that the similarity cannot be explained as coincidence.

The questions/evidence governed by subs.(3)(c) must show what amounts to a similarity between the complainant's behaviour and that alleged to have occurred as part of, or at or about the same as the events in question. According to Lord Clyde in *A* [133] the similarity need be neither 'rare' nor 'bizarre'.

The subsection covers (though is not limited to) questions/evidence of 'situational similarities' such as the *Romeo and Juliet* balcony scenario. The defendant is alleged to have met C at a party, followed her home, climbed up a balcony, entered C's bedroom and raped her. He says that C invited him to come to her home and re-enact the balcony scene in *Romeo and Juliet*, which he did, after which they had consensual sex. The defendant wishes to prove that a few days before and also a few days after the night in question, precisely the same thing happened with other young men—picked up at a party, invited to come to C's home and re-enact the scene, invitation accepted, followed by consensual sex. (Baroness Malalieu; House of Lords February 8, 1999 Hansard Column 45.)

In *T* [2004] EWCA Crim 1220 it was held that evidence of previous consensual sexual intercourse between the same parties inside the climbing frame in a children's play-area in a park was admissible where the instant charges related to identical behaviour but alleged rape.

In *A* Lord Steyn said it would apply where the defendant alleges that after an act of consensual intercourse the complainant tried to blackmail him by alleging rape. The defendant now wishes to ask the complainant whether she ever tried to blackmail other men after intercourse. We may accept this both as 'behaviour' and as 'part of the event' in question but it is difficult to see how such a demand constitutes *sexual* behaviour.

The question in *A* was whether the defendant could cross-examine the complainant as to whether before the alleged rape they had had a three-week consensual sexual relationship and that their last act of intercourse had occurred about one week prior to the events in issue. The court was between a rock and a hard place. The non-coincidental 'similarity' requirement can hardly be satisfied either by showing sexual behaviour with the defendant or by what might be termed 'standard' acts of prior intercourse. On the other hand, to refuse to permit such questions would seem to invite an allegation of an unfair trial under art.6 of the ECHR.

The ratio of the case appears to be that the questions *might* be admissible under s.41(3)(c)(i). Whether they were was a question for the judge at the resumed trial. Although not addressed expressly by Lord Steyn, the implication is that the questions could be brought only (if at all) within subs.(3)(c)(i) because of the temporal restrictions in subs.(3)(c)(ii). It is anyone's guess as to how the evidence could possibly comply with the phrase 'as part of the event' in subs.(3)(c)(i).

The House rejected the invitation to make a declaration of incompatibility between s.41 and art.6 choosing instead to operate under the interpretative obligation within s.3(1) of the HRA. Lord Steyn held that the 'blanket exclusion of prior sexual history' in s.41(1), subject to only narrow exceptions in the remainder of the section, raised questions of proportionality and the extent to which the embargo was excessive.

Practice and procedure

Under s.43(1) an application for leave must be heard in private in the absence of the complainant. The judge must (s.43(2)) specify in open court in the absence of the jury the reasons for his decision and the extent of any leave granted.

Counsel does not need to have evidence to prove the correctness of his assertion that the complainant witness should be cross-examined about his or her previous sexual behaviour. There must, however, be some basis for the proposed questions supported by reasonable grounds—counsel must have instructions giving reasonable grounds for making the assertion for which leave is sought. The trial judge can ask counsel what the questions are and what support there is for them: *Howes* [1996] 2 Cr. App. R. 490. There is provision under s.43(3) for rules of the court to be made under which a party seeking leave to adduce such evidence or questions must specify their grounds as well as enabling the court to request information to assist the court in reaching a decision on the application.

2.12 Previous statements: Criminal Justice Act 2003 & Criminal Procedure Act 1865 ss.3–5

A witness in criminal proceedings will usually have made a statement about the events in question. The earlier statement may be oral or written, sworn or unsworn, and it may be either consistent or inconsistent with the evidence which the witness has given in court today.

This section of work explains changes in the common law brought about by Ch.2 of Pt II of the CJA 2003. For the purposes of Ch.2, a statement is defined in s.115(2) as 'any representation of fact or opinion made by a person by whatever means; and it includes a representation made in a sketch, photofit or other pictorial form.'

2.12.1 Previous statements consistent with present testimony: the rule against narrative

Under the common law rule against narrative (or self-serving statements) a party is not allowed to ask a witness they have called whether he made a previous statement consistent with his evidence today. In so far as there were common law exceptions to this rule, the statements were evidence only of consistency, not of their contents.

However, the effect of s.120(2)–(8) of the CJA 2003 is that such statements are admissible as evidence of their contents in the circumstances of each subsection. In summary, such statements are evidence both of consistency *and* of their contents provided the witness could have given oral evidence thereof.

Section 120(2)—rebutting allegation of recent invention

If a cross-examiner puts it to a witness that his evidence has been fabricated or invented, the party calling the witness may be allowed to reinstate his evidence by proving his previous consistent statement during re-examination. This not automatic and the judge would need to be convinced that the matters had progressed beyond pointing out inconsistencies or severe cross-examination. The jury is not entitled to see the statement: *Beattie* (1989) 89 Cr. App. R. 302.

Section 120(3) memory refreshment

See para.2 7.1.2

Section 120(4)

The subsection provides:

> 'A previous statement by the witness is admissible as evidence of any matter stated of which oral evidence by him would be admissible, if—
>
> (a) any of the following three conditions is satisfied, and
> (b) while giving evidence the witness indicates that to the best of his belief he made the statement, and that to the best of his belief it states the truth.'

The three alternative conditions referred to in (a) above are contained in s.120(5)–(7).

Section 120(5)

Under a long-standing common law rule a witness's evidence of a previous out-of-court identification (such as at a formal identification process) of the defendant is admissible: *Osborne and Virtue* (1973) 57 Cr. App. R. 297. The justification for the rule is that it showed the witness's consistency over a period of time and lessened the likelihood of error in identification. The statutory rule extends to descriptions of objects and places.

Section 120(6)

> 'the statement was made by the witness when the matters stated were fresh in his memory but he does not remember them, and cannot reasonably be expected to remember them, well enough to give oral evidence of them in the proceedings.'

We mentioned this subsection at para.2.7.1.3 ('Past recollection recorded') to which reference should be made.

Section 120(7) and (8)

These subsections reform the common law doctrine of 'recent complaint' in sexual cases and extend it to all offences. With the extension of the law in this way, the common law rules outlined below will provide guidance on admissibility. Subsection (7) provides as follows:

> (a) the witness claims to be a person against whom an offence has been committed,
> (b) the offence is one to which the proceedings relate,
> (c) the statement consists of a complaint made by the witness (whether to a person in authority or not) about conduct which would, if proved, constitute the offence or part of the offence,
> (d) the complaint was made as soon as could reasonably be expected after the alleged conduct,
> (e) the complaint was not made as a result of a threat or a promise, and
> (f) before the statement is adduced the witness gives oral evidence in connection with its subject matter.
>
> (8) For the purposes of subsection (7) the fact that the complaint was elicited (for example, by a leading question) is irrelevant unless a threat or a promise was involved.'

Evidence from a third party that a complaint was made to him by the victim of an offence is admissible provided the statutory conditions are fulfilled. The terms of the complaint must be narrated by the third party (*White v R.* [1999] 1 Cr. App. R. 153) but (para.(f)) the victim must give evidence first. In *White* Lord Hoffman said the court did not go so far as to say that the victim could not mention that he had spoken to a third party but it was crucial to ensure that if the complaint were to be admissible its terms must be proved by the person to whom it was made.

While admissibility of the complaint depends on whether its terms overall support the evidence of the victim, there is no requirement that the evidence and the complaint must be in identical terms: *Spooner* [2004] EWCA Crim 1320. The case also holds that the content of the complaint must disclose evidence of material and unlawful (sexual) contact which could support the victim's credibility. There is no rule that the whole of the detail must be in the complaint before it is admissible.

Subsection (7)(d) is based on the decision in *Valentine* [1996] 2 Cr. App. R. 213. This moved away from the common law decisions which required more immediacy. Given that a victim may be seriously traumatised by the experience, there is no reason to insist on immediacy.

Subsection (8) reverses the common law rule that the complaint is inadmissible if made in response to a leading question.

2.12.2 Previous statements inconsistent with present testimony

2.12.2.1 Hostile witnesses: Criminal Procedure Act 1865 section 3

Imagine that in examination in chief the witness has given all the answers expected of him by the party by whom he was called. We say he has 'come up to proof'. Suppose, however, the witness gave some expected answers but also some unexpected ones—he says he cannot remember something. Where a witness's evidence does not correspond (in part) with his pre-trial statement—whether oral or written—he is said to be 'unfavourable' to the party calling him as where he 'suffers a singular lack of recognition' and we say he has 'not come up to proof'.

If a witness called by party A to prove a fact in issue or relevant to the issue, fails to prove such fact or proves an opposite fact then A may contradict him by calling other evidence, and is not thereby precluded from relying on those parts of the witness's evidence as A does not contradict: *Ewer v Ambrose* (1825) 3 B&C 746. Holroyd J. said: 'I take the rule of law to be that, if a witness proves a case against the party calling him, the latter may show the truth by other witnesses'.

Suppose, however, A's witness either refuses to speak at all ('stands mute') or gives answers which indicate either that he is lying or that he will not give the required information. Such a witness is 'hostile' defined as 'one who is not desirous of telling the truth at the instance of the party calling him.' A witness may exhibit hostility in chief or (unusually) at re-examination: *Norton and Driver (No. 2)* [1987] Crim. L.R. 699. Party A may then apply for leave to treat his witness as hostile. It is standard practice to offer the witness the chance to refresh his memory before applying to treat him as hostile, though there are occasions when the witness is so hostile that this is inappropriate. The judge has unfettered discretion on the application. All this should be done in the presence of the jury who can assess the witness's demeanour and answers: *Darby* [1989] Crim. L.R. 817.

It is a common law principle that a party cannot 'impeach' or cross-examine (i.e. attempt to discredit) his own witness. However, if leave to treat the witness as hostile is given, party A can question his witness 'in the manner of a cross-examination' to the extent to which the judge considers necessary for the purpose of doing justice. Questioning will be governed by the CPA 1865 s.3 which, while referring only to a witness 'proving adverse', has been interpreted to mean 'hostile': *Greenough v Eccles* (1859) 5 C.B.N.S. 786. Under s.3 (and see *Conway* (1980) 70 Cr. App. R. 4) the circumstances of the alleged statement 'sufficient to designate the particular occasion, must be mentioned to the witness and he must be asked whether or not he has made such statement.'

If leave is given party A can ask leading questions, questions as to the facts in issue, matters relating to the accuracy, veracity and credibility of the witness and previous statements. This is the limit of impeachment. He may not, therefore, question his witness to show he is of bad character by questions as to convictions and or misconduct nor to show that he should not to be believed on oath. We shall see (see Ch.9) that the bad character of a non-defendant can be proved by virtue of ss.98–100 of the CJA 2003. However, by virtue of s.112(3)(a), s.100 does not apply to the CPA s.3. Accordingly, the embargo on a party impeaching *his own* hostile witness by evidence of bad character remains. Such a witness may, of course, be subject to cross-examination on his character by the other side.

Although at common law a statement proved under s.3 is evidence only of inconsistency, by virtue of the CJA 2003 s.119(1) it is also evidence of its contents. The jury might choose to rely on the out of court statement (which they will have heard at least in part though not seen) rather than on the witness's evidence (if any). Where the witness has been called by the prosecution, a conviction may, therefore, be based in part on a statement the truth of which the maker of which is no longer prepared to acknowledge.

There is common law authority that a party cannot call a witness whom they know to be hostile: *Blastland* [1985] 2 All E.R. 1095. Where a witness has made inconsistent out of court statements a party may nevertheless be entitled to call him to see if he will resort to his original statement. However, if he does not, he may be cross-examined on the original statement with a view both to illuminating the differences between the two accounts and inviting the court to accept the previous statement as evidence of its contents: CJA 2003 s.119(1). This may prejudice the defendant but is inherent in the process. In *Dat* [1998] Crim. L.R. 488 the Court of Appeal said the questioning of a prosecution witness in these circumstances should be undertaken with care to limit the damage to the defendant.

If the hostile witness adopts or confirms part of the contents of his earlier statement it becomes to that extent part of his evidence. The judge must remind the jury of any inconsistency and say the first matter for them is to decide whether the witness is worthy of any belief at all. If he is, the jury should then be invited to consider which parts of the evidence might be accepted and which rejected: *Maw* [1994] Crim. L.R. 841.

2.12.2.2 **Criminal Procedure Act 1865 section 4**

Section 4 permits cross-examination of the witness by the other side on a previous inconsistent statement (oral or written and whether or not on oath). Thus, for example, the defence would wish to ask a prosecution witness who said in his out of court statement that he could not tell who had started a fight why, in his evidence today, he was quite sure it was the defendant. While questioning is not leave-dependent, s.4 creates two threshold conditions.

First, the previous statement must be 'relative to the subject matter of the indictment or proceedings'. This is a question for the judge, and it is arguable it is limited to facts in issue in the trial. If so, it would not apply if the previous statement were relevant only to the witness's credit. However, as we shall see shortly, the distinction between facts in issue and issues of credit may be more apparent than real.

Secondly, the statement can be put to the witness only if he does not 'distinctly admit' having made it. So if the witness admits, or does not deny making the previous statement, the cross-examiner should not be permitted to put the statement to him.

Where a previous statement is put to the witness, the effect may well be to damage him in the eyes of the jury, albeit any inconsistency between the evidence and statement is quite limited. As we have seen, once the statement is proved against the witness, it is evidence of its contents: CJA 2003 s.119(1). Again as we have seen, unless the cross-examiner accuses the witness of fabrication of today's evidence, the examiner in chief is not entitled to reinstate his witness's evidence by proof of any prior consistent statement. In this way, ss.3 and 4 of the CPA do not operate symmetrically.

The distinction between facts in issue and issues of credit

In *Funderburk* (above) the defendant was charged with three counts of unlawful sexual intercourse with a girl under the age of 13 years. The complainant said in chief that she was a virgin prior to the events in question. The defence was that she was lying and in order to show how a girl of her age, if lying, could give such a detailed account of sexual intercourse, wanted to question her to ascertain the extent of her prior sexual experience, and, in particular, to show that she had told a defence witness that she had had prior sexual intercourse with other men. The Court of Appeal held the questions were proper as relevant to an issue in the case. The Court further held that her answers would not be final, and that the defence would be allowed to call witnesses to show her answers were untrue. While on the face of it questions as to her sexual experience might appear relevant principally if not exclusively to the complainant's credibility and therefore be collateral, the Court took the view that the circumstances in which she lost her virginity were directly relevant to the defendant's guilt.

Funderburk was approved in *Nagrecha*. The complainant said the defendant had indecently assaulted her at a restaurant. There were no witnesses. She was cross-examined as to (allegedly false) allegations of sexual impropriety she had made against other men. In the Court of Appeal Rose L.J. held that where, as here, there were no witnesses to the events, the question of whether the complainant had made similar prior allegations might, technically, go only to her credit. However, the matter of prior allegations went to the heart of the case, and it was not possible to draw a hard and fast distinction between facts in issue and credit. In such circumstances the distinction between matters going to the issue and those going to credit is reduced to vanishing point. Evidence to contradict her answers should have been permitted.

Murphy (p.553) says it is difficult to see how the previous complaints shed any light on what happened at the restaurant, whereas the previous (alleged) statements in *Funderburk* did bear on the facts in issue. It has also been observed (Commentary to *Nagrecha* [1998] Crim. L.R. 65) that allowing rebuttal evidence on such facts opens 'the sort of debate which the rule of finality exists to prevent, for, whatever the answer, the cost of discovering it is likely to be out of all proportion to the benefit to the jury in deciding what went on behind closed doors between' the parties.

It should be remembered that at least some of the questioning in this type of case would be subject to the restrictions in s.41 of the Youth Justice and Criminal Evidence Act 1999 (see above para.2.11.).

2.12.2.3 **Previous statements in writing: Criminal Procedure Act 1865 section 5**

A witness can be *cross-examined* on such a statement without showing him the writing but it must be shown if the writing is to be used to contradict him. Under the section the judge can call for the writing, inspect it and make such use of it as he considers proper. It is not necessary for the judge to permit the whole of the previous statement to be read or shown to the jury. Although at common law a document admitted under s.5 was not evidence of contents, as a result of the changes brought about by the CJA 2003 the document would be admissible as evidence of its contents in accordance with the law as stated above (paras 2.12.1 and 2.12.2).

Figure 21—Summary regarding previous statements

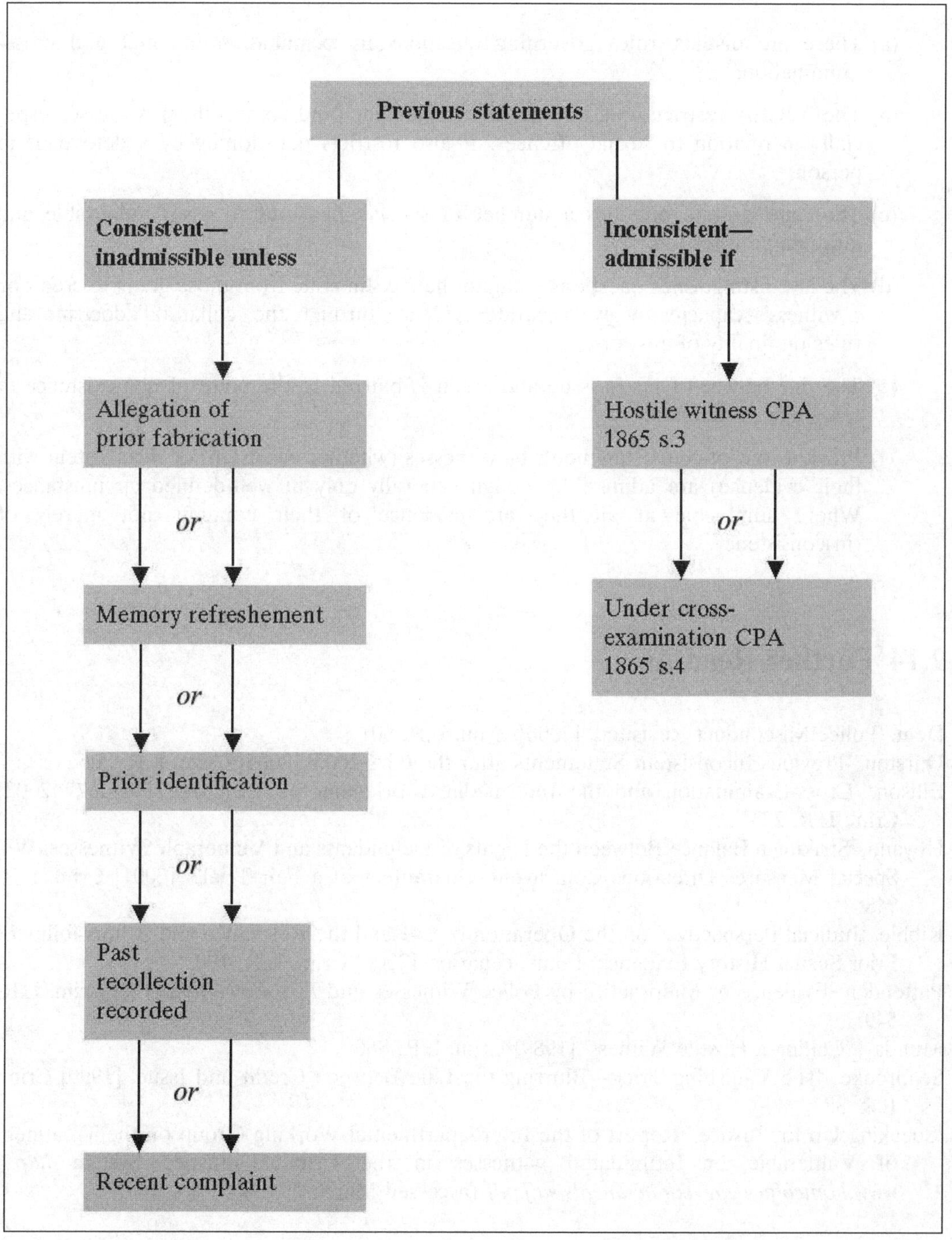

2.13 Summary

(a) There are distinct rules governing questions in examination in chief and cross-examination.

(b) The YJCEA restricts questioning of complainant (and some other) witnesses especially in relation to sexual offences. It also restricts questioning by a defendant in person.

(c) The same statute provides a number of special measures to assist vulnerable and intimidated witnesses.

(d) The law distinguishes questions going to the facts in issue from those going to credit or a witness's capacity to give accurate evidence through the 'collateral' doctrine and rules on finality of answers.

(e) The line between facts in issue and credit is blurred to the point of non-existence in cases like *Funderburk*.

(f) Previous out-of-court statements by witnesses (whether consistent or inconsistent with their evidence) are admissible though generally only in well-defined circumstances. Where admissible at all they are evidence of their contents not merely of (in)consistency.

2.14 Further Reading

Dein, 'Police Misconduct Revisited' [2000] Crim. L.R. 801

Durston, 'Previous Inconsistent Statements after the CJA 2003' [2005] Crim. L.R. 206

Ellison, 'Cross-Examination and the Intermediary: Bridging the Language Divide?' [2002] Crim. L.R. 223

Hoyano, 'Striking a Balance Between the Rights of Defendants and Vulnerable Witnesses: Will Special Measures Directions Contravene Guarantees of a Fair Trial?' [2001] Crim. L.R. 948

Kibble, 'Judicial Perspectives on the Operation of s.41 and the Relevance and Admissibility of Prior Sexual History Evidence: Four Scenarios' [2005] Crim. L.R. 190

Pattenden: Evidence of Malpractice by Police Witnesses and *R. v Edwards* [1992] Crim. L.R. 549.

Munday, 'Calling a Hostile Witness' [1989] Crim. L.R. 866

Seabrooke, 'The Vanishing Trick—Blurring the Line Between Credit and Issue' [1999] Crim. L.R. 387

'Speaking Up for Justice.' Report of the Interdepartmental Working Group on the Treatment of Vulnerable or Intimidated witnesses in the Criminal Justice System *http://www.homeoffice.gov.uk/documents/sufj.pdf* (accessed March 29, 2008)

3 Competence and compellability

All statutory references in this chapter are to the Youth Justice and Criminal Evidence Act 1999 (YJCEA) unless otherwise indicated.

3.1 Introduction

A witness is competent if he can lawfully be called on to give evidence and is compellable if he can lawfully be required to give evidence. At common law competence implies compellability though there have always been some exceptions to this principle.

3.2 Basic issues

The statutory rule of competence

By virtue of s.53(1) all persons are competent to give evidence in criminal proceedings whatever their age. 'Proceedings' covers every aspect of a trial from committal to evidence in mitigation of sentence.

The statutory test of competence

Under s.53(3) a person is not competent to give evidence in criminal proceedings if it appears to the court that he is not a person who is able to:

(a) understand questions put to him as a witness; and

(b) give answers to them which can be understood.

While the test of competence is the ability to understand questions, and to communicate evidence in an intelligible and coherent way, the courts have adopted a purposive rather than formal approach. The courts have seen it as important both to protect vulnerable witnesses and to give them a voice in court. In *D* [2002] EWCA Crim 990 (a case on children's evidence (see also para.3.3.3)) Swinton Thomas L.J. said that the ability to distinguish between truth and fiction or between fact and fantasy was built into the statutory test of competence. If a child witness gave a coherent account of events, it was a question of fact for a jury whether they believed the evidence. If, subsequent to such an account, the child witness purported to retract it, the judge must warn the jury strongly about relying on it. The jury was entitled to consider such evidence against the case as a whole and act on it if it considered it was sound, the retraction notwithstanding.

In a similar vein in a case concerning an adult witness (*Sed* [2004] EWCA Crim 1294) Auld L.J. held the competence test in s.53 was satisfied in the context of a complaint of rape by an 81 year old woman suffering from Alzheimer's disease. His Lordship said of the complainant:

> 'the video-film of her interview shows that she did have some appreciation of why she was being questioned, namely about a man who had recently done something to her, namely sticking his penis into her in an unpleasant way, a matter to which she referred a number of times during the interview. Whilst she did not always answer the question put to her and sometimes rambled off into other occurrences and places involving other people, her reference to such sexual assault by a man was a strong theme in her discourse with the officers. Sometimes her answers were hard to understand or bore little relation to the question asked, but at the end of the interview, the abiding picture was of a woman whose account and responses to questions were somewhat patchy, but who was nevertheless complaining repeatedly of a particular recent sexual assault by a man in which he had stuck, or had tried to, stick his penis into her more than once and that she had not liked it.'

His Lordship made it clear that the judge must not approach competence in a formulaic or mechanistic manner and he emphasised the difference between *competence* (which is a question for the judge) on the one hand and *reliability* or *cogency* of the evidence (a question for the jury) on the other.

Procedure for establishing competence

The issue of witness competence can be raised by any party to the proceedings or by the court. Once raised it is a matter for the judge alone (s.54(1)) and it is for the party calling the witness to prove competence on a balance of probability: s.54(2). Competence of witnesses should be determined in the absence of the jury (s.54(4)), in the presence of the parties (s.54(6)) and expert evidence is admissible: (s.54(5)).

Figure 22—Interim summary chart

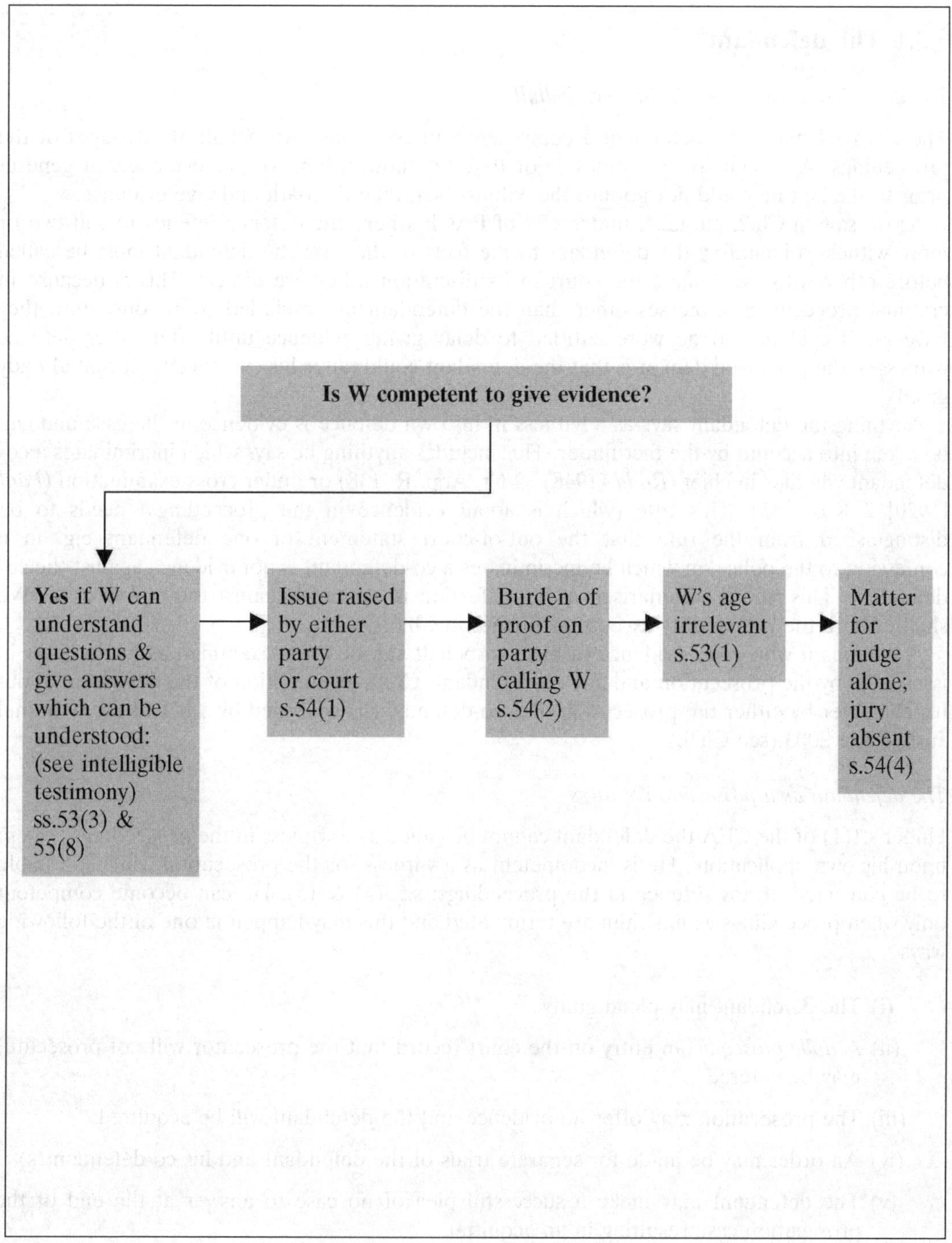

3.3 Special classes of witness

3.3.1 The defendant

The defendant as a witness in his own behalf

The CEA s.1 made the defendant a competent witness in his own behalf at all stages of the proceedings. Although some statutes prior to 1898 allowed him to give evidence, in general prior to the Act he could not go into the witness box, take the oath and give evidence.

As we saw in Ch.2, para.2.4, under s.79 of PACE where the defence intends to call two or more witnesses including the defendant to the facts of the case the defendant must be called before other witnesses unless the court in its discretion otherwise directs. This is because in criminal proceedings witnesses other than the defendant are excluded from court until they have given evidence. If he were entitled to delay giving evidence until after other defence witnesses, the perceived danger is that the defendant could tailor his evidence to fit that already given.

Anything the defendant says as a witness in his own defence is evidence in the case and can be taken into account by the fact-finder. This includes anything he says which incriminates a co-defendant whether in chief (*Rudd* (1948) 32 Cr. App. R. 138) or under cross-examination (*Paul* [1920] 2 K.B. 183). This rule (which is about evidence in the proceedings) needs to be distinguished from the rule that the out-of-court statement of one defendant e.g. in a confession to the police, in which he incriminates a co-defendant is not evidence against the co-defendant. This rule is summarised as 'a confession is evidence against the maker only'. We shall explore the rule and its exceptions further in Ch.6.

A defendant who gives evidence in his own behalf can be cross-examined as to the facts in issue both by the prosecution and any co-defendant. Cross-examination of the defendant about his character by either the prosecution or a co-defendant is governed by s.101 of the Criminal Justice Act 2003 (see Ch.9.)

The defendant as a prosecution witness

Under s.1(1) of the CEA the defendant cannot be called as a witness in the proceedings 'except upon his own application'. He is incompetent as a witness for the prosecution while still liable to be convicted of any offence in the proceedings: s.53(4) & (5). He can become competent only when proceedings against him are terminated and this may happen in one of the following ways

(i) The defendant may plead guilty.

(ii) A *nolle prosequi* (an entry on the court record that the prosecutor will not prosecute) may be entered.

(iii) The prosecution may offer no evidence and the defendant will be acquitted.

(iv) An order may be made for separate trials of the defendant and his co-defendant(s).

(v) The defendant may make a successful plea of no case to answer at the end of the prosecution case resulting in an acquittal.

Where the question of sentence arises, practice varies as to whether it should occur before or after the (former) defendant gives evidence as a prosecution witness. There are arguments both ways. If un-sentenced, there is an obvious motive (which the defence will not be slow to exploit) for axe grinding against the current defendants. But if sentenced, there is always the risk that the witness will decide there is now nothing to gain (and the possibility of reprisal) from giving evidence and will refuse to answer questions when called.

In *Pipe* (1966) 51 Cr. App. R. 17 it was held that an accomplice against whom proceedings are pending (as in (iv) above) but who is not being tried in the proceedings in question should not be called as a witness for the prosecution unless he has been given an undertaking that proceedings against him will be discontinued. This seems to a matter of discretion for the judge rather than a rule of law. In *Turner* (1975) 61 Cr. App. R. 67 Lawton L.J. said that a judge has discretion to prevent the prosecution calling a witness against whom proceedings are pending and who might be required to incriminate himself.

The defendant (D1) as a witness for a co-defendant (D2)

Until proceedings against D1 are terminated, he is competent (s.53(1)) but not compellable as a witness for D2: CEA s.1(1). Once terminated, he becomes compellable.

3.3.2 Spouses and civil partners

Section 80 of PACE as amended by the Civil Partnership Act 2004 provides (so far as relevant):

> '(2) In any proceedings the spouse or civil partner of a person charged in the proceedings shall, subject to subsection (4) below, be compellable to give evidence on behalf of that person.
>
> (2A) In any proceedings the spouse or civil partner of a person charged in the proceedings shall, subject to subsection (4) below, be compellable—
>
> (a) to give evidence on behalf of any other person charged in the proceedings but only in respect of any specified offence with which that other person is charged; or
>
> (b) to give evidence for the prosecution but only in respect of any specified offence with which any person is charged in the proceedings.
>
> (3) In relation to the spouse or civil partner of a person charged in any proceedings, an offence is a specified offence for the purposes of subsection (2A) above if—
>
> (a) it involves an assault on, or injury or a threat of injury to, the spouse or civil partner or a person who was at the material time under the age of 16;
>
> (b) it is a sexual offence alleged to have been committed in respect of a person who was at the material time under that age; or
>
> (c) it consists of attempting or conspiring to commit, or of aiding, abetting, counselling, procuring or inciting the commission of, an offence falling within paragraph (a) or (b) above.'

Figure 23—The effect of section 80 of PACE

SPOUSE OR CIVIL PARTNER	COMPETENT YJCEA	COMPELLABLE PACE
As prosecution witness	All cases (s.53(1)) unless the spouses/partners are charged in the same proceedings	No except for 'specified' offences: (i) assault or injury to spouse/civil partner of defendant or person under 16 years: s.80(3)(a); or (ii) sexual offence against person under 16 years s.80(3)(b); or (iii) inchoate offences etc. under above: s.80(3)(c)
As witness for spouse's or partner's co-defendant	All cases s.53(1)	No except for 'specified' offences as above
As witness for own spouse/partner	All cases s.53(1)	Yes (s.80(2)) unless charged in same proceedings: s.80(4)
As witness for each other	All cases s.53(1)	No

Sections 80(5) provides that a person who *has been* but is no longer married to (or in a civil partnership with) the defendant shall be competent and compellable to give evidence as if that person and the defendant had never been married (or in a civil partnership). By virtue of s.80A the prosecution shall not comment on the failure of the spouse/civil partner of any person charged in any proceedings to give evidence.

The common law principle of non-compellability of one spouse—now including a civil partner—as a witness against the other (which is largely enshrined in s.80) applies only to lawfully wedded persons and to those who have contracted civil partnerships under the Civil Partnership Act 2004. It does not apply to bigamous marriages or marriages otherwise unlawful under English law.

3.3.3 Children

We have considered (see para.3.2) both the statutory rule and test of competence. In this context, provided the child passes the test of competence in s.53(3) his evidence is admissible. The statutory process for determining competence applies to all witnesses irrespective of age.

The provisions of s.55 determine whether a witness gives sworn evidence. The issue can be raised by any party or the court: s.55(1). By virtue of subs.(2) there are two conditions which must be met before the witness can give sworn evidence. First, he has attained the age of 14. If he is under 14 years, his evidence must be unsworn. This is reinforced by s.56(2) which provides that the evidence of a competent witness who is not permitted to be sworn 'shall be given unsworn'.

Secondly, the witness must (s.55(2)(b)) have sufficient appreciation of the solemnity of the occasion and of the particular responsibility to tell the truth which is involved in taking an oath. This test in s.55(2)(b) replicates the common law test in *Hayes* [1977] 64 Cr. App. R. 194 which was used for the same purpose. The test was, and under the statute remains, secular in nature. A witness is presumed (s.55(3)) to have sufficient appreciation of the solemnity of the occasion and of the particular responsibility to tell the truth if he is able to give 'intelligible testimony'. The test of intelligible testimony is found in s.55(8) as where the witness both (a) understands questions put to him and (b) can give answers which can be understood.

The following chart builds on Fig.23 with particular reference to children's evidence.

Figure 24—Competence and sworn testimony of children

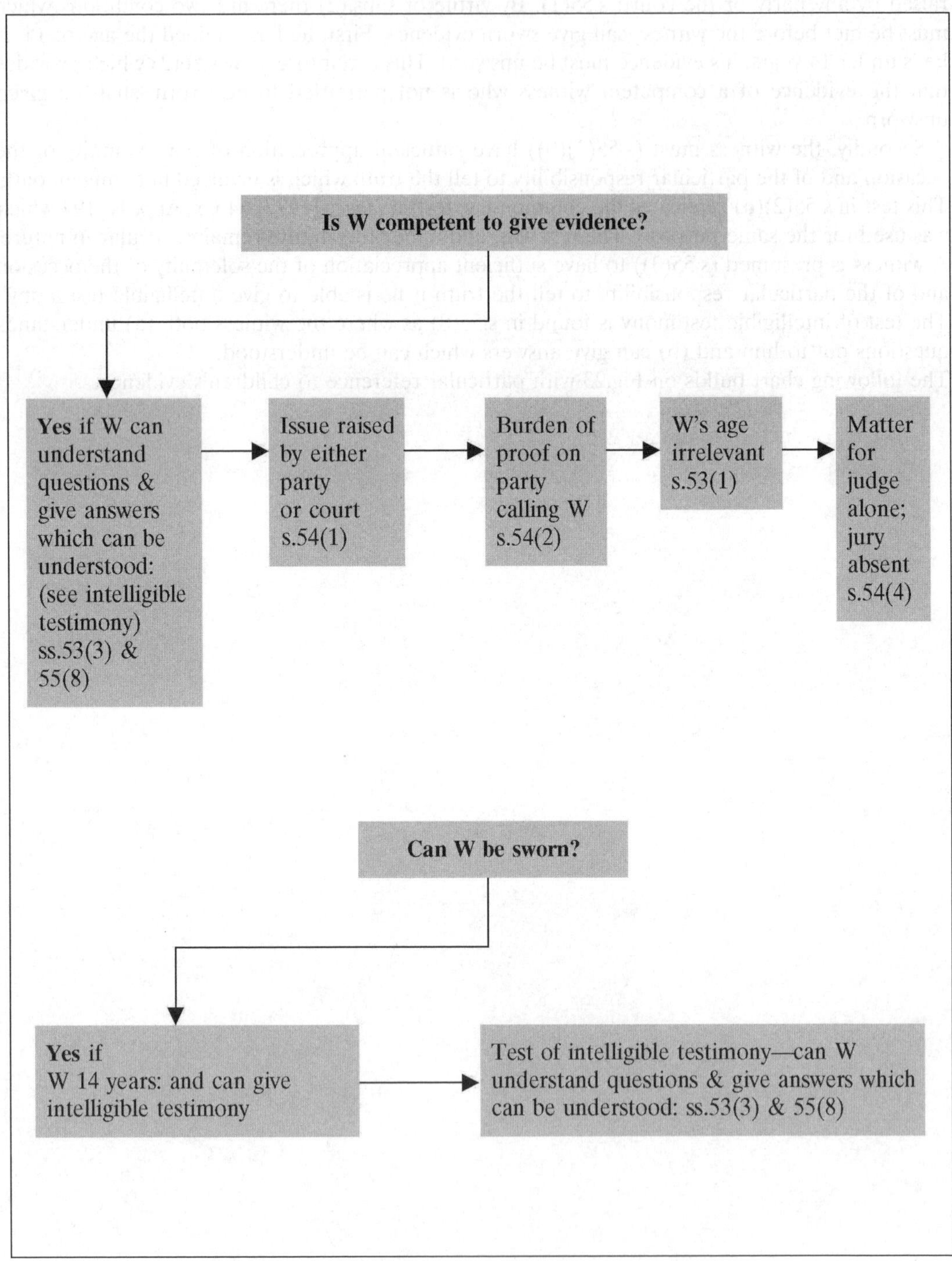

The outcome of s.55 is that a witness who is competent and has reached 14 years will always give his evidence sworn. The only reason why a competent witness will give evidence unsworn is because he has not reached 14 years. In all other respects the witness will be treated as though he were an adult.

There are occasions when a witness's evidence is given in a video recording. Where the witness was under 14 years when he made the recording but is over that age at the trial he should be sworn, at the latest, before any questions are put to him by counsel: *Sharman* [1998] 1 Cr. App. R. 406. The witness had made a video while 13 years but was 14 years at trial. Because the video contained admissible and inadmissible evidence which was inextricably mixed, the bulk of the witness' evidence was by live link but she was neither sworn nor did she make a solemn affirmation. The Court of Appeal held that this was no 'mere technicality' but amounted to a material irregularity. A retrial was ordered.

Where a witness who should have been sworn is, inadvertently, permitted to give their evidence unsworn, this omission cannot be cured by asking him at the close of cross-examination if his evidence was truthful: *Simmonds* [1996] Crim. L.R. 816.

No minimum age

In *Z* [1990] 2 All E.R. 971 Lord Lane held that statutory reforms had superceded the common law and that there was no minimum age for giving evidence. His Lordship doubted whether a five-year-old could ever satisfy the statutory requirements of competence but held the issue was one of discretion for the judge according 'to the circumstances of the case, the nature of the case, and the nature of the evidence which the child is called on to give'. *Z* was considered and approved in *DPP v M* [1997] 2 All E.R. 749 where the child was four years of age. The Divisional Court said there would come an age at which a child was so young that he could not understand questions and answer them in a coherent manner. But where, as here, there was video evidence, a court must permit that evidence to be given and the judge had no discretion to refuse to admit it only on the ground of the child's age.

As we have seen, expert evidence is receivable on the question of whether the witness may be sworn for the purpose of giving evidence on oath: s.55(6). Such evidence should not be called as a matter of course but only where the emotional or mental condition of the witness gives rise to concern.

3.3.4 **Competence and compellability of a judge**

Can a judge be called to give evidence of matters arising in his court? In *Warren v Warren* [1996] 4 All E.R. 664 Lord Woolf M.R. held that judges are competent to give evidence as to issues relating to and arising out of their judicial function. While a judge would not be compellable, the Court of Appeal said that if the situation arose where the evidence was vital, a judge must be relied on not to assert his non-compellability as a reason for refusing to give evidence. This decision does not apply to magistrates who are not judges for this purpose.

3.4 Evidence via deposition

3.4.1 **Deposition**

By virtue of s.56(3) a deposition of evidence from a person whose evidence would be unsworn may be taken as if the evidence had been given on oath. Section 56(4) in effect provides that the court 'shall' receive in evidence any deposition made under subs.(3). (A deposition is an out of court statement taken on oath under questioning from both sides to a legal dispute.)

3.5 Evidence via television live link and video recording

3.5.1 Criminal Justice Act 1988

Under s.32(1) a person other than the defendant can give evidence by live link if he is outside the United Kingdom. In *Forsyth* [1997] 2 Cr. App. R. 299 it was held it was not a ground for refusing this facility that the witness was speaking from a country from which they could not be extradited if they gave perjured evidence.

> 'In general, once it is shown that there is difficulty in obtaining the evidence of witnesses abroad whose evidence is relevant to the defence, we consider the court should lean in favour of permitting evidence to be given in this way, even though in particular cases there may be reasons to refuse it.' (per Beldam L.J. at p.311).

3.5.2 Criminal Justice Act 2003

Under Pt 8 (ss.51–56) there is general provision for the use of live link in criminal proceedings for witnesses other than the defendant. (The defendant is now covered by s.33A of the YJCEA as we saw in Ch.2, para.2.10.3). Section 51(4) provides that evidence shall not be given in this way unless the court is satisfied it is in the interests of efficient or effective administration of justice. Subsection (7) contains seven further conditions of which the court must take account. The court must give its reasons for refusing an application in open court: subs.(8).

3.5.3 Youth Justice & Criminal Evidence Act 1999

As we saw in Ch.2, para.2.10, the Act provides a scheme whereby witnesses may be eligible for a special measures direction (SMD). A witness who is under 17 years at the time of the hearing is eligible within s.16(1) and is known as a child witness within s.21. This section permits or requires (according to circumstances) that the evidence of a child in chief shall be given by a video. Dennis (p.628) describes the drafting of s.21 as 'fearsomely complex' and asks whether it was necessary to create such a 'labyrinthine procedure'.

The key to understanding the section is that all child witnesses, irrespective of the offence charged, are governed by what is known as the 'primary rule' and that a limited class of child witnesses within the main group is, because of the nature of the offence, 'in need of special protection'. We shall look at the primary rule first then consider those witnesses in need of special protection and the measures which apply to them.

Section 21, special measures and the 'primary rule'

To repeat, the primary rule governs all child witnesses irrespective of the offence. The court is bound (s.21(3)) by the 'primary rule' before it considers any other special measures. The rule is in two parts namely that

(a) evidence in chief shall be in the form of a video recording (s.27); and

(b) any evidence given in the proceedings otherwise than by video must (whether in chief or under cross-examination) be given by live television link (s.24).

Since the underlying purpose of a special measure is to enhance the quality of the evidence, the court is not bound by the primary rule if compliance would not maximise its quality: s.21(4)(c). Where the primary rule applies any cross-and re-examination of the child may (and sometimes must) be by video under s.28. A video under s.28 would then displace a live television link under s.21(3)(b).

Admission & exclusion of the video under s.27

The section is inclusionary in nature—the video should be admitted unless excluded in the interests of justice (subs.(2)) and this extends to admitting parts of it (subs.(3)). In *R. (on the application of the DPP) v Redbridge Youth Court* [2001] Crim. L.R. 473 the Divisional Court considered the 'interests of justice' formula under former legislation (CJA 1988 ss.32 and 32A). It held that video evidence should be permitted only if the witness could be upset, intimidated or traumatised by giving evidence in court. This does not, apparently, extend to mere 'embarrassment' about giving evidence. Given that the whole scheme of the 1999 Act is the protection of witnesses, the court's interpretation of 'the interests of justice' is not purposive and would render the scheme much less effective than expected.

Under s.27(4) the court can exclude the video where

(i) the child will not be available for cross-examination; or

(ii) the parties have not agreed that the child need not be available; or

(iii) rules governing disclosure of the circumstances in which the recording was made have not been complied with.

Unless the court has instructed that cross- and any re-examination should be given otherwise than by in-court testimony, the child must be called by the party tendering the video (subs.(5)). The child may not be examined in chief on any matter which is dealt with adequately in the video. If an issue is raised in the recording, the witness may give evidence about it only with the permission of the court: s.27(5)(b)(ii).

Subject to s.27(2), it is not necessarily a ground for excluding the video that it contains hearsay statements or that it tends to show that the speaker has been 'coached'. The video should be made in accordance with 'Achieving Best Evidence on Criminal Proceedings: Guidance for Vulnerable or Intimidated Witnesses, including children'. It can be viewed at *http://www.cps.gov.uk* (accessed March 31, 2008).

Under previous legislation, it was held that failure to adhere to the terms of the predecessor of the Guide may be a ground for excluding video evidence: *G v DPP* (1997) 2 Cr. App. R. 78. In *K* [2006] EWCA Crim 472 it was held that the key issue is, not withstanding breaches of the Guide, whether the evidence is reliable as being credible, accurate and complete. Additional evidence might assist in deciding whether breaches of the Guide affected credibility or accuracy but reliability remains the key: *Hanton* [2005] EWCA Crim 2009. The court will consider the age of the child ('not an insurmountable problem for the prosecution') and whether there was substantial delay between the incident and the video recording: *Powell* [2006] EWCA Crim 3, per Scott Baker L.J. This is because a young child's memory is much less stable than an adult's. Social workers should appreciate that the contents of a therapeutic interview with a child are generally not acceptable to a court as evidence where e.g. there is an allegation of abuse.

Child witnesses in need of special protection

The table below indicates when a child witness will be in need of special protection. As you will see, it is determined by the offence charged against the defendant.

Figure 25—Child witnesses in need of special protection

(a)	Sexual offences under PCA 1978 or SOA 2003 Pt 1
(b)	Kidnapping/false imprisonment or abduction under CAA 1984 ss.1 and 2
(c)	Cruelty to persons under 16 years under C&YPA 1933 s.1
(d)	Offence involving 'assault on, or injury to or a threat of injury to any person'

In *Lee* [1996] 2 Cr. App. R. 266 (a case under previous similar legislative provision) it was held that s.35(3)(d) above is satisfied if injury to a person is a real possibility. The threat of injury to a person need not have been made directly by the defendant nor is the subsection limited to the situation where the child witness is the person threatened. *Lee* was approved in *McAndrew-Bingham* [1999] 2 Cr. App. R. 293. The appellant had been convicted of child abduction contrary to s.2 of the CAA an offence which does not depend on whether the child consented or whether force was used. It was held that child abduction involves at least a risk of injury to the mental health of the child or its carer. The Court emphasised that the law required 'injury' so mere emotions such as fear, distress or panic were insufficient.

Requirements where the child is in need of special protection

As we have seen the court may exclude the whole or part of a video if its admission would be contrary to the interests of justice: ss.21(4)(c) and 27(2). However, s.21(5) provides that the court cannot disapply the primary rule where the child witness is in need of special protection. The effect of subs.(5) is that where the child is in need of special protection his evidence in chief *must* be given by video.

In *R on the application of (D) v Camberwell Green Youth Court* [2005] UKHL 4, it was held that subs.(5) is compliant with art.6 of the ECHR in so far as (because it is mandatory) the subsection prevents individualized consideration of the necessity for a special measure at this stage of the proceedings. The House of Lords held there was no violation of the requirements of the ECtHR in *Kostovski v Netherlands* (1990) 12 E.H.R.R. 434 in that all of the relevant evidence is adduced at trial and can be seen and challenged by the defendant.

Cross- or re-examination of a child in need of special protection

Under s.21(6) where the offence falls within s.35(3)(a) (sexual offences under the Protection of Children Act 1978 or the SOA Pt 1) the court *must* direct that any cross- or re-examination shall also be by video in accordance with s.28 unless the child informs the court he does not wish this to apply to him. This measure does not apply to the offences contained in s.35(3)(b)–(d).

Figure 26—Summary of Primary and Special Protection Rules

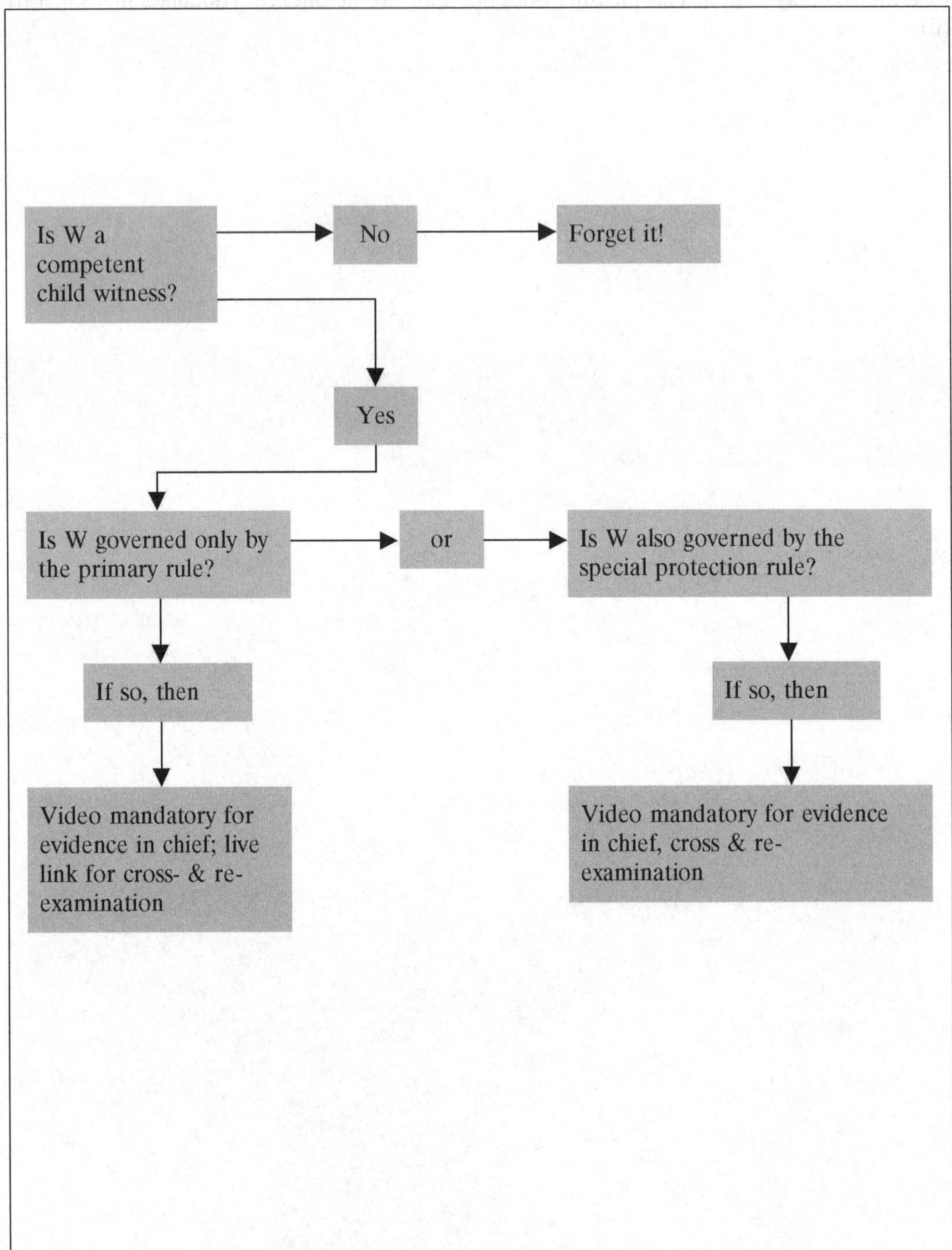

Figure 27—Section 28—video for cross-and re-examination

Section 28 with subsections	
	Contents
2	Judge and the parties must be able to communicate with those present at the recording; defendant must not but must be able to see and hear the examination and communicate with his lawyer.
5	Evidence from video and any live link cross-examination cannot be subject of further oral questioning. Court may at discretion order further recording.
6	Strict conditions on a further recording under subs.(5) especially in 6(a)—new issue since recording which could not have been ascertained with due diligence.

Replaying the video

The jury should not normally be allowed a second viewing of a video: *M* (evidence: replaying video) [1996] 2 Cr. App. R. 56. Repetition of evidence is a departure from the standard way of giving evidence and any exception should be kept to a minimum. The judge might permit it where it was needed to enable the jury to understand a particular point that was being made but it should not be the norm.

If it is a matter of the jury being reminded of the words the judge can do this from his notes but if it is a question of how the words were spoken he can permit a replay of the video:

(a) in open court; and

(b) with the parties present; and

(c) with a warning not to attach too much weight to the video only because they were rehearing it well after all the other evidence; and

(d) reminding them from his notes of the cross- and any re-examination of the witness.

In *Atkinson* [1995] Crim. L.R. 490 it was held that the jury must be warned against treating the replayed video as more important than any other item of evidence. The same warning applies where the judge reminds the jury of video evidence from his notes instead of permitting the video to be replayed: *McQuiston* [1998] 1 Cr. App. R. 139.

Can the jury see the transcript of the video?

In *Welstead* [1996] 1 Cr. App. R. 59 the Court of Appeal held that it is proper to allow the jury a transcript if it assists them to understand what they are hearing on the tape—as where the sound is of poor quality or witnesses' answers are partly inaudible. The jury should be told that the transcript is not evidence, and to concentrate on the oral evidence. They cannot normally take the transcript with them when they retire. The jury should also be warned not to give disproportionate weight to the transcript. The court stressed that while the tape is admissible, it is not the tape per se which is evidence but the oral statements on it.

3.6 Summary

(a) Competence and compellability of witnesses are matters of law for the judge. The test of competence is secular and is based on being able to respond to questions by giving intelligible answers.

(b) The burden of proving competence is on the party calling the witness on a balance of probability.

(c) A defendant cannot be called by the prosecution to give evidence while proceedings are pending against him.

(d) Children are treated as competent to give evidence unless and until they indicate some fallibility.

(e) A person cannot give sworn evidence until they have reached 14 years.

(f) Special Measures for vulnerable and intimidated witnesses under the YJCEA include provision for video evidence and live television link for evidence in chief, cross- and re-examination. Section 21 and succeeding sections contain provisions in respect of the evidence of children generally under the 'primary rule' and the sub-group of children in need of special protection because of the nature of the offence charged.

3.7 Further reading

Birch, 'A Better Deal for Vulnerable Witnesses?' [2000] Crim. L.R. 223

Cooper, 'Pigot Unfulfilled: Video Recorded Evidence under section 28 of the YJCEA 1999' [2005] Crim. L.R. 456

Hoyano, 'Striking a Balance Between the Rights of Defendants and Vulnerable Witnesses: Will Special Measures Directions Contravene Guarantees of a Fair Trial?' [2001] Crim. L.R. 948

Hoyano, 'Variations on a Theme by Pigot: Special Measures Directions for Child Witnesses' [2000] Crim. L.R. 250

'Speaking Up for Justice: Report of the Interdepartmental Working Group on the Treatment of Vulnerable or Intimidated witnesses in the Criminal Justice System' *http://www.homeoffice.gov.uk/documents/sufj.pdf* (accessed March 28, 2008)

4 Hearsay

All statutory references in this chapter are to the Criminal Justice Act 2003 unless otherwise indicated.

The hearsay provisions in the Act are contained in Pt 11 Ch.2, which embraces ss.114–136 inclusive.

4.1 Introduction

The law relating to hearsay is reputedly the most difficult part of the law of evidence. It is perhaps, therefore, surprising, that it is not only a commonly used word but also that in its basic meaning is well understood. This is easily demonstrated. When we gossip we often preface our latest piece of scandal with the phrase 'well I know it's only hearsay but . . .' In doing this we not only draw attention to the fact that we do not *know* what we are talking about in the sense that we cannot vouch for the facts in question. At the same time we illustrate why the common law is traditionally hostile to hearsay as a means of proving anything—it is notoriously fallible.

The 'say' element of the word hearsay is apt to give an incomplete picture. While it is true that much hearsay is spoken, it is also found in documentary form. If I write out my gossip and hand it to you the writing is as much hearsay as if I had spoken it if it is proved in court by anyone other than me. The same applies in principle to any medium in or on which information is recorded such as an audio or video tape, emails and text messages—the information is capable of being hearsay. Hearsay can also be found in conduct as in a gesture, a nod or shake of the head.

At common law, hearsay evidence is governed by an exclusionary rule: hearsay evidence is inadmissible unless rendered admissible by virtue of an express exception. The first major reform of the law of hearsay occurred with the Civil Evidence Act 1968. Reform was completed by the Civil Evidence Act 1995 which abolished the hearsay rule in civil proceedings.

Reform in criminal proceedings was slower but under the CJA 2003:

- the common law rules governing the admissibility of hearsay in criminal proceedings are abolished by s.114(1);
- eight common law exceptions to the rule excluding hearsay are preserved: s.118(1); and
- both oral and documentary hearsay are admissible subject to conditions: ss.114–117.

Hearsay was, and to some extent, remains an inadmissible *means* of proving facts rather than a rule which prevents proving the facts at all. A party may always to choose to adduce the evidence in question by some non-hearsay means.

When you are dealing with possible hearsay evidence, it is vital to separate definition from admissibility. If the evidence is not hearsay its admissibility is likely to be subject only to the principle of relevance. If it is hearsay the party seeking to rely on it will need to satisfy some admissibility conditions before being allowed to do so. The definition of hearsay and the admissibility conditions are each governed by the Act of 2003. We look first at definition starting from its common law base.

4.2 Initial definition

Building from the threshold of gossip we could define hearsay as 'the things you told me.' This does not constitute and will not suffice as a legal definition but from this relatively simple idea we can move on to an initial definition of hearsay in more legal terms. It is said that at common law oral or written statements made by persons, other than the witness who is testifying, are not receivable *to prove truth of matter stated*. The reason why part of this statement is in italics is explained at para.4.4.1.4 below. While helpful this is as much a statement about exclusion as definition.

Illustration

Imagine a student (S) rushes into his tutor's (M) room hand covered in blood and asks for help saying, 'I've just cut myself on a broken window in the corridor'. Suppose later that morning over coffee M tells his colleague (T) what happened. As a virtuous employee M also makes an entry in the accident book. Improbably all this ends up in court.

Some of the evidence would be direct and some hearsay. The hearsay evidence is of two types—first hand and multiple as explained in the following table.

Figure 28—Explanatory table

The evidence	Direct yes or no?	Hearsay yes or no?	If hearsay then first hand or multiple?
S's evidence is:	Yes—S is 'relevant person'—has knowledge of facts		
If M gave evidence in court that			
(i) S entered the room	Yes—as above for S		
(ii) S's hand was covered in blood	Yes—as above for S		
(iii) S had spoken	Yes—as above for S		
(iv) S told me how his injury had occurred	No	Yes—M does not know whether S's statements are true	First hand; M heard it from relevant person
T tells the court everything M told T	No	Yes—neither does T	Multiple—T heard it from M who heard it from S (etc.)
Entry in the accident book	No	Yes. M did not know the truth of what he wrote	First hand if vouched for by M; otherwise multiple

We give the student the letter S because he is the supplier of the information—S has actual knowledge of how the injury occurred and his evidence would be direct. In the CJA 2003 the person with actual knowledge is called the maker of the statement or 'the relevant person': s.116(1)(b).

As the table above illustrates, M's evidence of the events would be a mix of direct evidence and hearsay. Without any hearsay, M could say that S entered his room, his hand was covered in blood, and that S spoke to M. There would be no hearsay because M would be testifying as to what M saw and heard. This is sometimes expressed as what M 'saw and heard with his own unaided senses.' This part of M's testimony would constitute direct evidence.

The move from direct to hearsay evidence would come if M were asked: 'What did S say to you?' If M replied 'S told me he had cut his hand on a broken window in the corridor' the answer would be hearsay because M does not know the truth of his answer except in the sense that S told him.

It follows that T's testimony as to what he was told by M would also be hearsay. The difference between M and T is that whereas M heard the story directly from the person who knew what happened (S), T is one step further down the line. While M's evidence would be first hand hearsay T's evidence would be multiple. This difference can be significant (see para.4.6.3 below).

The entry in the accident book would be hearsay since it purports to be evidence of a workplace accident made by a person (M) who does not know whether it is true (S might have cut his hand in a fight in the street). The book would be multiple hearsay if produced to the court by anyone other than M or unless M vouched for its contents. The book is, in this way, just like T's testimony.

4.3 Common law hostility

This was noted in the introduction to this chapter. A number of reasons have been advanced.

- If S is not called as a witness he cannot be cross-examined.
- The risk of concoction or fabrication of evidence.
- S was not on oath when he made the statement.
- The court cannot consider S and his demeanour.
- The effect of art.6(3)(d) of the ECHR (right of the defendant to examine or have examined witnesses against him).
- It is not the best evidence—it is secondary and hence inferior.

These factors were never sufficient to justify a total ban on the admission of hearsay evidence at common law. While the CJA 2003 provides for an inclusionary approach to hearsay, they may be relevant to deciding, in the circumstances of the individual case, whether to admit hearsay evidence which in principle satisfies the scheme of the Act or any preserved common law exceptions under s.118.

4.4 Hearsay, assertions and original evidence

In *Illustration* (above), we found that what S said to M would be hearsay if repeated by M 'to prove the truth of the matter stated'—how S's injury had occurred. There are at least two reasons why the words 'to prove the truth of the matter stated' are important and they relate to the crucial question of the *purpose* of admitting the evidence in question.

The first reason is concerned with what are known as assertions which are of two types—express and implied. The second is concerned with 'original' evidence.

4.4.1 Assertions

4.4.1.1 Express assertions

There is an express assertion if (as in *Jones v Metcalfe* [1967] 3 All E.R. 205) a witness tells a police officer 'The number of the car was ABC 123.' If in court the officer relied exclusively on what he was told by the supplier of information the officer's evidence would be hearsay though not necessarily inadmissible. In *Gibson* (1887) 18 QBD 537 the defendant was charged with unlawful wounding. A witness was allowed to narrate words, spoken by unknown person, 'the man who threw the stone went in there' while pointing at the defendant's house. It was held the words were hearsay (and inadmissible).

Assertion-free statements?

Logically, if a statement does not contain any assertion it cannot be hearsay. Since such a simple greeting as 'good morning' contains an assertion (albeit at a very low level), you may be wondering when a statement would not. The case of *Sean Lydon* (1987) 85 Cr. App. R. 221 provides an illustration. A gun bearing ink was found on the ground, and paper with the words 'Sean rules' and 'Sean rules 85' in the same ink was found nearby. Since the writing did not contain any assertion in respect of guilt in respect of an alleged robbery, it was held to be admissible. The paper was regarded as a (weak) item of circumstantial evidence that 'Sean' was connected to the gun.

While the decision in *Lydon* seems clear, other cases present greater difficulty. How should we treat the name on a baggage tag or a ticket? Does the tag or ticket contain an assertion and if so of what? In *Rice* (1963) 47 Cr. App. R. 79 the prosecution wished to establish that Rice and another person (M) had flown London to Manchester on a particular day and wished to put in evidence a used ticket for the flight in Rice's name. Rice contended the ticket was hearsay evidence of its contents and was wrongly admitted at trial. In a judgment of extraordinary subtlety Winn J. held that while the ticket could not be used to speak to its contents ('I was issued to Rice and M') it was evidence that two persons boarded that particular flight leaving the jury to infer one of them was Rice.

The ticket cannot be regarded merely as a travel warrant permitting a person access to the aircraft irrespective of their identity. Murphy (p.219) says the decision treats the ticket as an item of real evidence 'from which the court can draw conclusions using its senses.'

Although never expressly overruled, *Rice* is considered incompatible with the decision of the House of Lords in *Myers v DPP* [1964] 2 All E.R. 881—a case which raised similar issues. By a majority the House held that records of car manufacture created from data recorded by different persons working on the vehicles at various stages of the manufacturing process, and of which no person had overall personal knowledge, were hearsay and inadmissible.

'Performative utterances'

There are many occasions when words are regarded as having particular legal effect. Examples from civil law are offer and acceptance, and defamation. Where making a statement has legal effect the words used are not caught by the hearsay rule. In *Woodhouse v Hall* (1981) 72 Cr. App. R. 39 the defendant was charged with management of a brothel. Police officers observed the premises (a sauna) and subsequently entered as genuine customers. They were offered 'hand relief' or 'topless hand relief' by women working there. The legal issue was whether there had been an offer of a sexual service.

Reversing the magistrates, the Divisional Court held that the officers' testimony was evidence of such offer. In the words of Professor Smith, since an offer cannot be true or false, if the fact that it was made is relevant, evidence of it cannot be hearsay. We need to distinguish (i) whether anything was said at all from (ii) if it was what was it? Clearly evidence of (i) is admissible but it involves evidence of (ii) which the prosecution wishes to rely on, though not to prove its truth. The prosecution is not relying on any assertion in the words spoken by the women. On such facts the evidence cannot be hearsay.

Woodhouse was considered in two drugs cases (*Harry* (1986) 86 Cr. App. R. 105 and *Kearley* [1992] 2 All E.R. 345) involving implied assertions and this is our next area of study.

4.4.1.2 **Implied assertions**

Imagine you were picking up a rental car. The dispatch clerk tells you to look around the car to check for damage before you drive away. The clerk watches you walk around the car, get in and drive away. Can we imply from your conduct that the car was damage-free? Are you (effectively) saying the car is damage-free and, if you are, could the clerk's testimony be regarded in any way as hearsay evidence of the lack of damage? Situations like this involve what are sometimes referred to as 'speech acts' which means drawing inferences from words or actions by persons not called as a witness. Might we say that driving the car away gives rise to an implied assertion that it was undamaged?

Prior to the Criminal Justice Act 2003 it was held in *Kearley* [1992] 95 Cr. App. R. 88 that implied assertions were subject to the exclusionary hearsay rule. The defendant was charged with possession of drugs with intent to supply. The police remained at his premises following his arrest receiving both telephone calls and personal callers asking for drugs. The prosecution did not call the callers as witnesses relying instead on the evidence of police officers who had received the calls or spoken to the callers. The defence objected to the admission of the officers' evidence the purpose of which was, of course, not to prove the truth of the words spoken by the callers but to invite the jury to infer the defendant was dealing. (The parallel is between the police officers and the dispatch clerk at the car rental desk.) By a majority, the House of Lords held the evidence was inadmissible because it merely illustrated the state of mind of the callers who believed they could obtain drugs from the premises. (On this basis the evidence was simply irrelevant, and whether or not it is hearsay is not relevant either). Lord Ackner said that while the callers could have been called to give direct evidence that they had previously been supplied by the defendant and had called or visited on the day in question for their regular supply, the hearsay rule (at that time) prevented the police giving this evidence. The majority also rejected the argument that the words used by the callers could be seen as a kind of 'act' and that, from this combination of words and acts, it was permissible to infer that the defendant dealt in drugs.

Section 115 is designed to carry implied assertions (such as those in *Kearley* or in greetings or questions) outside the reach of the hearsay rule. Whether it achieves its aim is debateable. Under the heading 'Statements and matters stated' it provides:

(1) In this chapter references to a statement or to a matter stated are to be read as follows.

(2) A statement is any representation of fact or opinion made by a person by whatever means; and it includes a representation made in a sketch, photofit or other pictorial form.

(3) A matter stated is one to which this chapter applies if (and only if) the purpose, or one of the purposes, of the person making the statement appears to the court to have been—

(a) to cause another person to believe the matter; or

(b) to cause another person to act or a machine to operate on the basis that the matter is as stated.

The combined effect of ss.114(1) and 115(2) & (3) was intended to be that when a person makes a statement but it is neither his purpose nor one of them to communicate the contents of the statement to another but those contents may be implied or inferred, the statement would be outside the hearsay rule. If a caller asks Kearley 'Can I have my usual stuff' he does not intend someone to believe (i.e. in the language of the statute it is neither his purpose not one of his purposes to make another person believe) that Kearley is a dealer—it is simply a request for drugs and not hearsay under the Act. Similarly if a caller said to Kearley 'The stuff you sold me last week was bad' it would not have been one of the purposes of the statement to make someone believe Kearley was a dealer. Dealing may be an implication but it was not the purpose of the speaker to make another believe it.

With the rental car, although driving the vehicle away may well be a representation (subs.(2)) of satisfaction that the vehicle is undamaged, was it your purpose (or one of them) in driving away to cause the clerk to believe you were satisfied about lack of damage? In other words is subs.(3)(a) satisfied? In so far as the pivotal distinction seems to be between inducing another to believe a matter and such matter merely being an underlying assumption it is arguable that the line is unclearly drawn. Suppose the dispatch clerk's parting words to you were: 'The documents do not show any damage to the car but look around and get back to me before you leave the depot if you see damage.' You look around and wave to him as you leave. Such conduct may well be not be covered by s.115(3), and would be treated as hearsay. Your conduct in waving and driving away might well be seen as a representation of fact (s.115(2)) one purpose being to cause the clerk to believe the car was undamaged. On these facts evidence of your conduct would amount to hearsay. It might of course be admissible but that is not the point here.

Keane (p.292) cites *Teper v R.* [1952] A.C. 480 to support his view that s.115 does not achieve its aim of carrying implied admissions outside the reach of the hearsay rule. The defendant was charged with arson of his wife's shop. His defence was alibi. In order to place him at the scene evidence was admitted that an unknown woman had been heard to say to a motorist resembling the defendant: 'your place burning and you going away from the fire'. The Privy Council held the words were inadmissible hearsay:

> 'It is not clear that s.115(3) operates to reverse this decision. It would turn upon whether it appears to the court that one of the purposes of the unidentified woman, in making her statement, was to cause one or more of the bystanders to believe that Teper was present but departing.' (Keane p.292.)

As the section is drafted, it might be sufficient that it was the purpose of the unidentified woman to convince Teper himself that she had seen him, knew it was his place and that he was running away.

On the other hand the case of *Singh* [2006] EWCA Crim 660 seems clear. The issue was whether telephone records of calls to and from a cell phone were admissible. The record is a statement within s.115(2), but is outside subs.(3). Rose L.J. held that since the record did not fall within any of the rules preserved in s.118(1) by s.118(2) and was not caught by s.115(3) it was not hearsay so its admissibility depended only on its relevance.

In *Knight* [2007] EWCA Crim 2307 it was held that the contents of her niece's diary containing statements from when she was 14 years of a sexual relationship with the defendant starting with kissing and progressing to various sado-masochistic acts could be narrated to the court by her aunt. The aunt's evidence fell outside s.115, since the niece had not intended for other people to read the diary: *N (Kenneth)* (2006) EWCA Crim 3309.

Whatever reservations there may be about the effect of s.115(3) it does seem clear that when we consider 'purpose' it relates to the purpose of the person making the statement *at the time he made it*. The common law distinguished hearsay from original evidence by focusing on the purpose of admitting the evidence at trial. In other words, chronologically, 'purpose' has migrated from the time at which it was sought to admit the statement into evidence to the much earlier time of when the statement was made. In addition, while the common law focused only on the purpose of admitting the evidence, under the Act it is the maker's purpose in making the statement which distinguishes hearsay from non-hearsay. To reiterate, if it was neither the purpose nor one of the purposes of the maker of the statement to cause another believe the matter in question then the statement cannot be hearsay. Admissibility then turns on relevance. On this basis the outcome of the case of *Kearley* would be unchanged because the statements made by the callers were relevant only to their state of mind—they believed Kearley was dealing drugs but this was not relevant to whether he was in fact doing so.

4.4.1.3 **Negative hearsay**

It may be necessary for a party to prove that some event did not occur. In *Patel* [1981] 3 All E.R. 94 the prosecution sought to prove a person was an illegal immigrant by demonstrating the absence of his name from a register. The conviction was quashed primarily on the ground that the Criminal Evidence Act 1965 (the then applicable statute) did not apply to this type of record which was hearsay at common law. The problem can be solved now in one of the following ways. First, the register would be admissible under s.117 (see para.4.7.2) so the jury would be asked to make the necessary inference from the absence of the name in question. Alternatively, it is arguable that since it was not the purpose of the person compiling the record to cause anyone else believe it (s.115(3)(a)), the record is not hearsay under the Act. Finally it might be argued the register is hearsay under the Act but that it is admissible under the 'safety valve' condition in s.114(1)(d) (see para.4.7.1).

4.4.2 **Hearsay and original evidence distinguished**

When a witness (W) gives evidence of what someone else (S) said it will be hearsay if the *purpose* of the testimony is to prove the truth of S's information. It is said that the court is relying on W's evidence 'testimonially'. However, it will not be hearsay if the purpose of W's testimony is merely to prove that something was said or that a conversation occurred irrespective of its content. The evidence would then be tendered as a relevant fact rather than as a means of proving a fact. W's testimony is regarded as original evidence of the conversation. (see para.4.2 with regard to M's evidence of a conversation with S.) The key to the distinction lies in the *purpose* of adducing the evidence.

In *Subramaniam v Public Prosecutor* [1956] 1 W.L.R. 965 the defendant pleaded duress to a charge of unlawful possession of ammunition. It was argued that he could not tell the court what the terrorists had threatened, because such evidence would be hearsay. The Privy Council said that the words of the threat were admissible to prove that the threats were made, i.e. it was original evidence rather than evidence of its facts.

In *Mawaz Khan and Amanat Khan v R.* [1967] A.C. 454 the prosecution wished to prove the defendants' confessions not for the purpose of proving the statements were true, but to show that together, and apparently independently, they constituted an innocent account of a killing when, against all the evidence in the case, they could be seen as obviously fabricated. A properly instructed jury might therefore draw an inference of guilt from such facts. Since the prosecution was not relying on the statements testimonially (as evidence of their contents) the hearsay rule was not infringed.

4.5 Preserved common law exceptions

As we saw in the introduction to this chapter, the Act of 2003 abolishes the common law rules with regard to the admissibility of hearsay evidence in criminal proceedings save for the eight #exceptions in s.118(1). Of the preserved exceptions, we shall cover 'Reputation as to character' (para.2) in Ch.9 and 'Confessions etc.' (para.5) in Ch.6. We now consider only one more preserved exception—Res gestae under para.4.

4.5.1 **Res gestae**

At common law, statements which accompanied and explained facts in issue were admissible as res gestae—loosely translated as 'the transaction' or 'events occurring' or 'things happening'. The rationale for admitting such statements was their probable reliability given their close connection with the events in question. Sometimes such statements fell into the category of 'excited utterances'—when the very pressure of the events was, in effect, responsible for a person making the statement. On other occasions the statement would have been in less dramatic circumstances and accompany and explain events. The other major importance of res gestae statements was that they were admissible to explain the state of mind of the speaker. (In all cases, the statement was narrated to the court by someone other than the maker but was treated as evidence of its contents). No matter into which category they fell, such statements were not inadmissible notwithstanding that they were hearsay.

Res gestae is preserved by s.118(1) under three heads as follows.

4.5.1.1 **Persons emotionally overpowered**

A hearsay statement is admissible where its maker was so 'emotionally overpowered by an event that the possibility of concoction or fabrication can be disregarded.' This formulation owes much to the opinion of Lord Wilberforce in *Ratten v R.* (1971) 56 Cr. App. R. 18. The defendant was charged with the murder of his wife by shooting which he alleged was accidental. A telephone operator (T) was allowed to depose that she had, at relevant times, received a telephone call from a woman who was frightened and hysterical and who had asked for the police before she rang off. Ratten contended that he made the only outgoing phone call from the house at the relevant time. On this basis T's testimony was direct evidence to the contrary. It was relevant and admissible as such.

The hearsay dimension of the case lies in T's evidence that the wife asked to be connected to the police. There is an implied assertion that she was under threat from her husband. T did not know any of this directly. As the law stood, such evidence could be admitted only as an exception to the rule excluding hearsay in the category of 'excited utterance'. (As a request by the wife to T rather than a 'representation of fact,' the evidence would no longer be hearsay: s.115(3)). Lord Wilberforce stated the proper test of admissibility.

> 'The possibility of concoction or fabrication, where it exists, is . . . probably the real test which judges in fact apply. In their Lordships' opinion this should be recognised and applied directly as the relevant test: the test should not be the uncertain one whether the making of the statement was in some sense part of the event or transaction. This may often be difficult to establish: such external matters as the time which elapses between the events and the speaking of the words (or vice versa) and differences in location being relevant factors but not, taken by themselves, decisive criteria. As regards statements made after the event, it must be for the judge, by preliminary ruling, to satisfy himself that the statement was so clearly made in circumstances of spontaneity or involvement in the event that the possibility of concoction can be disregarded. Conversely, if he considers that the statement was made by way of narrative of a detached prior event so that the speaker was so disengaged from it as to be able to construct or adapt his account, he should exclude it. And the same must be true in principle of statements made before the event. The test should not be the uncertain one, whether the making of the statement should be regarded as part of the event or transaction. This may often be difficult to show. But if the drama, leading up to the climax has commenced and assumed such intensity and pressure that the utterance can safely be regarded as a true reflection of what was unrolling or actually happening, it ought to be received. The expression *res gestae* may conveniently sum up these criteria, but the reality of them must always be kept in mind; it is this that lies behind the best reasoned of the judges' rulings.'

It is clear that the possibility either of 'fabrication' (*Ratten*) or 'concoction or distortion' (s.118(1)) should lead to exclusion and in *Nye & Loan* (1977) 66 Cr. App. R. 252 the Court of Appeal added 'error'. The victim of an assault misidentified his assailant as the driver of a car when he had in fact been a passenger. Holding that it was difficult to imagine a more spontaneous identification which left no chance for concoction (itself dubious on the facts) Lawton L.J. said concoction should include error. Section 118(1) does not include error and the draftsman could have done so expressly. It remains to be seen whether the courts will subsume 'error' within 'distortion'. In the meantime the status of *Nye & Loan* as authoritative is subject to some doubt. You will have noticed that Lawton L.J. spoke of 'spontaneity' though Lord Wilberforce was clear that this no longer represented the law.

In *Tobi v Nicholas* (1988) 86 Cr. App. R. 323 a 20 minute gap between a collision and the identification of the defendant as one of the drivers was held, on its facts, to be outside the parameters approved in *Nye & Loan*. By way of contrast in *Carnall* [1995] Crim. L.R. 944 the victim of a vicious assault with a baseball bat and knives had taken an hour to crawl from the scene to houses where he was seen by witnesses to whom he named the defendant as his attacker. In answer to a leading question from a police officer as to who was responsible the victim again named the defendant. The Court of Appeal upheld the judge in admitting the evidence. The (now deceased) victim's mind had been dominated by survival.

> 'The judge had taken account of the appalling nature of the attack itself, the frightful injuries that were inflicted, the pain that P was undergoing, and the obsession he had at the time with trying to get help and to stay alive.'

The judge had acknowledged the victim's life-long reputation for dishonesty but held it was irrelevant to the particular issues at hand. Neither did it matter that one of the identifications was in response to a leading question.

Ratten was approved by the House of Lords in *Andrews* [1987] 84 Cr. App. R. 382. The (now deceased) victim recognised and told police officers the name of one of his assailants (though there was some confusion as to what exactly the deceased had said). Given there was additional evidence implicating the defendant it was held the judge had correctly admitted the police officers' evidence notwithstanding there was some evidence that the victim had a motive to incriminate the defendant. Lord Ackner's speech contains a guide to admissibility of res gestae at common law. He referred to error involving no more than 'the ordinary fallibility of human recollection' as generally going to weight rather than admissibility of the evidence. However, 'special features' going beyond ordinary fallibility (his Lordship instanced drunkenness) might cause a judge to exclude the evidence. In *Edwards & Osakwe v DPP* [1992] Crim. L.R. 576 the Divisional Court upheld justices who allowed police officers to narrate the statement of the victim who was not called as a witness ('they're the ones . . . those two mugged me of my wallet'; 'they just stole my wallet') though he was drunk. The court emphasised that res gestae is not to be used as a device to circumvent calling a witness, though there was no suggestion of that here.

Res gestae used to circumvent calling direct evidence

In both *Tobi v Nicholas* (1988) 86 Cr. App. R. 323 and *Edwards & Osakwe* the court said res gestae must not be used as a device to avoid calling direct evidence where it is available. The *Attorney General's Reference (No. 1 of 2003)* [2003] EWCA Crim 1286 does look like attempted avoidance. The victim of an assault, the defendant's mother, made it clear that she would not give evidence against her son. Accordingly, the prosecution sought, under the res gestae principle, to rely on her statements to witnesses at the time of the assault that her injuries were inflicted by him. The judge excluded the witnesses evidence under the principle that it was not the 'best' available—the mother was available to the prosecution. The Court of Appeal held the proper approach was to agree that the evidence of the witnesses was admissible but to exclude it under s.78(1) of PACE due its adverse impact on the fairness of the proceedings. It is difficult to agree with the court that the prosecution was not seeking to take advantage of res gestae as 'a device'. The sole reason for not calling the mother was that if she had given evidence and had been cross-examined by her son, the prosecution case would have been bound to fail.

Res gestae is limited to explaining facts in issue

In all the cases we have considered to date, the statements admitted under the res gestae principle explained or accompanied one of the facts in issue—especially identity. In *Gilfoyle* [1996] 1 Cr. App. R. 302 the defendant was charged with murder of his wife in circumstances apparently consistent with suicide by hanging. Initially he had produced a suicide note in his wife's handwriting. He had (falsely) told her that he was on a course concerned with suicide and had asked her to write some suicide notes which he dictated to her. He had then taken her into the garage to show her how to arrange a rope. The following day she told work colleagues about these events. The judge excluded their evidence as inadmissible hearsay.

The Court of Appeal permitted the colleague's evidence to be received under the well established res gestae principle relating to the state of mind of the speaker which is the next area of res gestae to be considered. The wife's statements to colleagues were about the notes, not about the fact in issue i.e. whether she committed suicide. The state of mind principle does not permit her statements to be used to prove either that the defendant told her to write the notes or that he told her what to write but the judgment of Beldam L.J. suggests that they could be admitted to prove just that. Employing the words of Lord Wilberforce in *Ratten*, Beldam L.J. in effect bridged the 'emotionally overpowered' and 'state of mind' principles.

> 'In this case the statements themselves suggested that the events which prompted them were still dominating [her] mind. The statements were made the morning after the letters had been written as soon as ordinarily have been expected. The possibility of invention or unreliability could be discounted and there was little room for inaccuracy in the reporting of the statements.'

Beldam L.J. said the evidence should be admissible if the conditions under which the statement was made were 'a circumstantial guarantee of trustworthiness'. This is a significant extension of the *Ratten* principle. Commenting on the case, Dennis (p.732) says it represents 'a hint that the courts might be prepared to rely on the *Andrews* rationale to justify extending the exception to statements about evidentiary facts as opposed to restricting it to statements about facts in issue.'

4.5.1.2 **Statements accompanying and explaining relevant acts**

Under s.118(1) para.4(b) a statement is admissible as evidence of any matter stated if the statement accompanied an act and the act can be properly evaluated only if considered in conjunction with the statement. Most of the cases in this area are old but *McCay* (1990) 91 Cr. App. R. 84 is more recent. A witness at an identification parade identified the suspect with the words 'it is number eight'. At trial the witness could not recall the relevant number and the parade officer gave evidence that the defendant had occupied position eight. The officer was then asked what the witness had said to him and objection was taken that if the officer now replied 'he said to me "it is number eight"' then that answer would be hearsay and inadmissible. The evidence was admitted. The appeal against conviction was dismissed. The witness's words were res gestae, i.e. they accompanied and explained a relevant act, that of identification.

Under this principle, words are admissible only to explain an otherwise equivocal act. But in *McCay* there was nothing equivocal about the witness's act—the words do not so much 'accompany and explain' the act of identification as constitute it. Other criticisms of the reasoning of the Court of Appeal's reasoning in *McCay* (which were accepted in *Lynch* [2007] EWCA Crim 3035) can be found at [1990] Crim. L.R. 340.

4.5.1.3 **Statements about physical sensations or mental state**

Under s.118(1) para.4(c) 'a statement is admissible as evidence of any matter stated if the statement relates to a physical sensation or mental state (such as intention or emotion).'

We encountered this in looking at *Gilfoyle* [1996] 1 Cr. App. R. 302 above para.4.5.1.1. (See also Ch.5). Admissibility is limited to the fact of physical sensation or mental condition and excludes evidence of the cause(s) thereof. In *Parker* (1960) 45 Cr. App. R. 1 it was held the words 'he shot me he said he would' spoken by the defendant's wife to a neighbour should have been excluded.

4.6 The Police and Criminal Evidence Act 1984 s.74

The section reads as follows:

'Conviction as evidence of commission of offence

(1) In any proceedings the fact that a person other than the accused has been convicted of an offence by or before any court in the United Kingdom . . . shall be admissible in evidence for the purpose of proving, where to do so is relevant to any issue in those proceedings, that that person committed that offence, whether or not any other evidence of his having committed that offence is given.

(2) In any proceedings in which by virtue of this section a person other than the accused is proved to have been convicted of an offence by or before any court in the United Kingdom . . . he shall be taken to have committed that offence unless the contrary is proved.

(3) In any proceedings where evidence is admissible of that fact that the accused has committed an offence, in so far as that evidence is relevant to any matter in issue in the proceedings for a reason other than a tendency to show in the accused a disposition to commit the kind of offence with which he is charged, if the accused is proved to have been convicted of the offence—

(a) by or before any court in the United Kingdom;

(b) . . . he shall be taken to have committed that offence unless the contrary is proved.

(4) Nothing in this section shall prejudice—

(a) the admissibility in evidence of any conviction which would be admissible apart from this section; or

(b) the operation of any enactment whereby a conviction or a finding of fact in any proceedings is for the purposes of any other proceedings made conclusive evidence of any fact.'

In summary the section allows the prosecution to prove the conviction of a person other than the defendant where to do so is 'relevant to any issue' in the proceedings against the defendant. Suppose that, at an earlier trial, D1 pleaded or was found guilty of conspiracy to an offence on an indictment which also referred to D2 who was at liberty at the time. Suppose further D2 is subsequently arrested and tried for the offence in question. Provided it is relevant—as it probably would be—s.74 permits the prosecution to prove D1's earlier conviction at D2's trial.

In *Lunnon* (1988) 88 Cr. App. R. 71 four defendants were jointly charged with conspiracy to steal. The judge distinguished whether there was a conspiracy from the parties to it. D1's plea of guilty to the conspiracy did not prevent the jury acquitting any of D1–D4. While D1's plea tends to prove the conspiracy it does not itself prove who the parties were. It is clearly different if the allegation is that there were only two parties to the conspiracy or act in question.

Evidence admitted under subs.(1) is not merely proof that D1 was convicted (whether or not on a plea of 'guilty') but is evidence that D1 'committed the offence'. This is reinforced by subs.(2) by virtue of which D1 'shall be taken to have committed that offence unless the contrary is proved.'

The courts have approached the section with caution for two reasons. First, it permits the reception of evidence which, if tendered by the prosecution in the form of statements by others (D1) involved in the offence alleged against D2, would be inadmissible under the rule that confessions are admissible only against their maker (see Ch.6, paras 6.1 and 6.9). Secondly the inherent prejudice to D2. The principal authorities are *Kempster* [1989] 1 W.L.R. 1125; *Robertson* (1987) 85 Cr. App. R. 304; and *Mattison* [1990] Crim. L.R. 117. They focus on the prejudicial effect on the subsequent trial of D2 if the prosecution is allowed to adduce evidence of D1's conviction.

Some of the problems for D2

(i) He is deprived of the right to cross-examine D1 (though cross-examination will not necessarily favour D2).

(ii) It deprives the jury of the opportunity to see D1 under cross-examination.

(iii) It makes it much less likely that the jury will find D2 did not conspire with D1.

(iv) He is in a difficult position when during the trial D1 changes his plea to guilty while D2 maintains his not guilty plea: *Fredrick* [1990] Crim. L.R. 403. Is a fair trial really possible in these circumstances?

(v) The problems often arise but are not confined to nominate charges of conspiracy. For example if D1 pleads guilty to having committed an act of gross indecency with D2, who denies it, the jury should not be told of D1's plea; the judge should exclude it under s.78(1) of PACE: *Mattison*.

Judicial direction of the jury

In *Boyson* [1991] Crim. L.R. 274 the Court of Appeal set out four propositions.

(i) The conviction must be clearly relevant to an issue in the case. In *Mahmood, Manzur* [1997] 1 Cr. App. R. 414 three men had sexual intercourse with a woman in about an hour. The second man to do so pleaded guilty to rape and his conviction was admitted under s.74(1). On appeal it was held that the conviction could not possibly be relevant to whether the woman consented to intercourse with the first man which, he asserted, was consensual.

(ii) Section 74(1) should be used sparingly. We noted above the reasons for this. There is authority (*Chapman* [1991] Crim. L.R. 44) it should not be used if there is ample other evidence that the defendant committed the offence.

(iii) The judge should consider s.78(1) and whether the evidence would have the specified adverse effect on fairness. This should now embrace art.6 though the issues of fairness are identical.

(iv) The judge must direct the jury clearly as to why the evidence is before them and to what issue it is directed as well as the issues to which the conviction is *not* relevant.

In *Dixon, The Times*, November 2, 2000, the defendant pleaded not guilty to attempted burglary. The judge admitted evidence of guilty pleas of her two co-defendants instructing the jury that they could 'take it that there was an attempted burglary'. This was a misdirection. It did not follow from the admission of the guilty pleas that the jury must accept the attempted burglary as a fact. The defendant had said she had been with one of her co-defendants on the relevant evening and no burglary had been attempted—a direct conflict with her co-defendant's evidence. Evidence of the guilty pleas was admissible but the direction to the jury was erroneous.

Similarly in *Mahmood, Manzur* [1997] 1 Cr. App. R. 414 (for the facts see above), the judge failed to direct the jury about the possible reasons for the second man's guilty plea. Until it is clear *why* a person has pleaded guilty, it is impossible to locate the relevance of the conviction.

The overall cautious approach in was approved in *Smith* [2007] EWCA Crim 2105. Hughes L.J. noted [17] that under the hearsay and bad character provisions of the CJA 2003 (see para.4.7 and Ch.9 respectively) 'in some respects the ambit of evidence with which a jury can be trusted is wider than the law formally allowed'. Nevertheless s.74(1) must be used sparingly particularly where it closes off possible avenues otherwise open to the defence. His Lordship said [16]:

> 'That is particularly so where the issue is such that the absent co-defendant who has pleaded guilty could not, or scarcely could, be guilty of the offence unless the present defendant were also. In both those situations the court needs to consider with considerable care whether the evidence of the conviction would have a disproportionate and unfair effect upon the trial. With those cases can be contrasted the kind of case in which there is little or no issue that the offence was committed, and the real live issue is whether the present defendant was party to it or not. In those circumstances, commonly, the pleas of guilty of other co-defendants can properly be admitted to reinforce the evidence that the offence did occur, leaving the jury independently to consider whether the guilt of the present defendant is additionally proved.'

The reference to fairness ('unfair') in the extract is to the fact that the judge did not undertake the kind of assessment of fairness required by s.78(1) in light of the 'considerable power' [23] of evidence admitted under s.74(1). It might also be observed that if 'there is little or no issue that the offence was committed' it is arguable that the prejudicial effect of admitting the evidence outweighs any probative value it may have.

His Lordship said the conviction was also admissible under s.114(1)(d) but balancing was still required under s.114(2) and s.78(1). (See para.4.7 and Ch.7.)

4.7 Criminal statutory hearsay

Subject to conditions, the CJA 1988 Pt II permitted the reception of documentary hearsay in criminal proceedings. While Pt II has been repealed by the CJA 2003 many of the conditions applicable to the admissibility of evidence under the later Act are either similar or identical to the conditions under the earlier Act. It follows that case law arising under the 1988 Act will often apply under the Act of 2003. Under the CJA 2003 documentary hearsay continues to be admissible. The major innovation is that first hand oral hearsay statements are now admissible in principle as evidence of their contents.

Unless otherwise decided by the court, a party seeking admission of hearsay evidence must comply with Rule 34 of the Criminal Procedure Rules by giving requisite notice.

'A statement' and 'a matter stated'—ss.114(1) and 115(2) & (3)

As we have seen (para.4.4.1.2 above), a statement not made in oral evidence in the proceedings is admissible as evidence of any matter stated if any of the conditions in s.114(1) are met. 'Statement' and a 'matter stated' are the building blocks of hearsay whether oral or documentary under the Act. They are defined by s.115(2) and (3) respectively and we considered their meaning in detail at the same reference. The effect of these provisions is that any statement not made in oral evidence in the proceedings in question whether written, spoken or implied from conduct where the maker's purpose was not to cause another to believe its contents is no longer hearsay.

4.7.1 **Oral hearsay**

The effect of ss.114—116 CJA 2003 is to make oral hearsay available in criminal proceedings. Section 114(1) is the 'gateway to admissibility'. It provides that a statement not made in oral evidence is admissible as evidence of any matter stated either:

(a) under this Chapter (ss.114–136) of the Act;

(b) under any rule of law preserved by s.118(1) of the Act;

(c) if the parties agree to it; or

(d) if the court is satisfied that to do so would be in the interests of justice (the 'safety valve').

Under s.114(2) in deciding whether a statement not made in oral evidence should be admitted under subs.(1)(d), the court must have regard to the following factors (and to any others it considers relevant).

(a) How much probative value the statement has (assuming it to be true) in relation to a matter in issue in the proceedings, or how valuable it is for the understanding of other evidence in the case;

(b) what other evidence has been, or can be, given on the matter or evidence mentioned in para.(a);

(c) how important the matter or evidence mentioned in para.(a) is in the context of the case as a whole;

(d) the circumstances in which the statement was made;

(e) how reliable the maker of the statement appears to be;

(f) how reliable the evidence of the making of the statement appears to be;

(g) whether oral evidence of the matter stated can be given and, if not, why it cannot;

(h) the amount of difficulty involved in challenging the statement;

(i) the extent to which that difficulty would be likely to prejudice the party facing it.

In *Taylor (S)* [2006] EWCA Crim 260 the Court of Appeal considered the phrase 'must have regard'. It held that the judge was under nothing more than a duty to consider the nine factors but 'there is nothing in the wording . . . to require him to reach a specific conclusion in relation to each or any one of them.' (per Rose L.J. [39]). This seems to be a very relaxed interpretation of the word 'must.' It seems that circumstances will dictate the relative importance of each of the factors. Given the courts' preference for direct oral evidence, it should be for the party seeking to rely on hearsay evidence to satisfy the court with regard to factors (b) and (g) in all cases. Factors (d) and (e) are particularly important where one defendant seeks to rely on an out-of-court statement by a co-defendant where they are running 'cut-throat' defences (see Ch.10, para.10.3): *McLean* [2007] EWCA Crim 219.

The scope of section 114(1)(d)

In *Prosecution Appeal (No.2 of 2008): R v Y* [2008] EWCA Crim 10 the defendant (Y) was charged with murder. Another person (X) had previously pleaded guilty to the same murder and had named Y as also involved in a conversation with his (X's) girlfriend (G). X would give neither a statement nor evidence and the prosecution sought leave to admit G's statement as part of its case. Court of Appeal considered the following issues in relation to the operation of the subsection.

(i) Although the background to the subsection is that it was designed to avoid miscarriages of justice (such as in *Sparks v R* [1964] A.C. 964) it permits reception of evidence even though it might well be admissible under some other section of this chapter of the Act or under one of the common law rules preserved by s.118.

(ii) It applies to all evidence irrespective of which party (including co-defendants) seeks to rely on it.

(iii) G's statement was admissible. The court accepted the common law rule that a statement by one co-defendant is not evidence against another co-defendant and that the jury must be warned to this effect: see Ch.6, paras 6.1 and 6.9. However once the judge decides to admit such a statement under subs.(1)(d) no such warning is necessary.

The table below summarises the position so far.

Figure 29—Summary chart

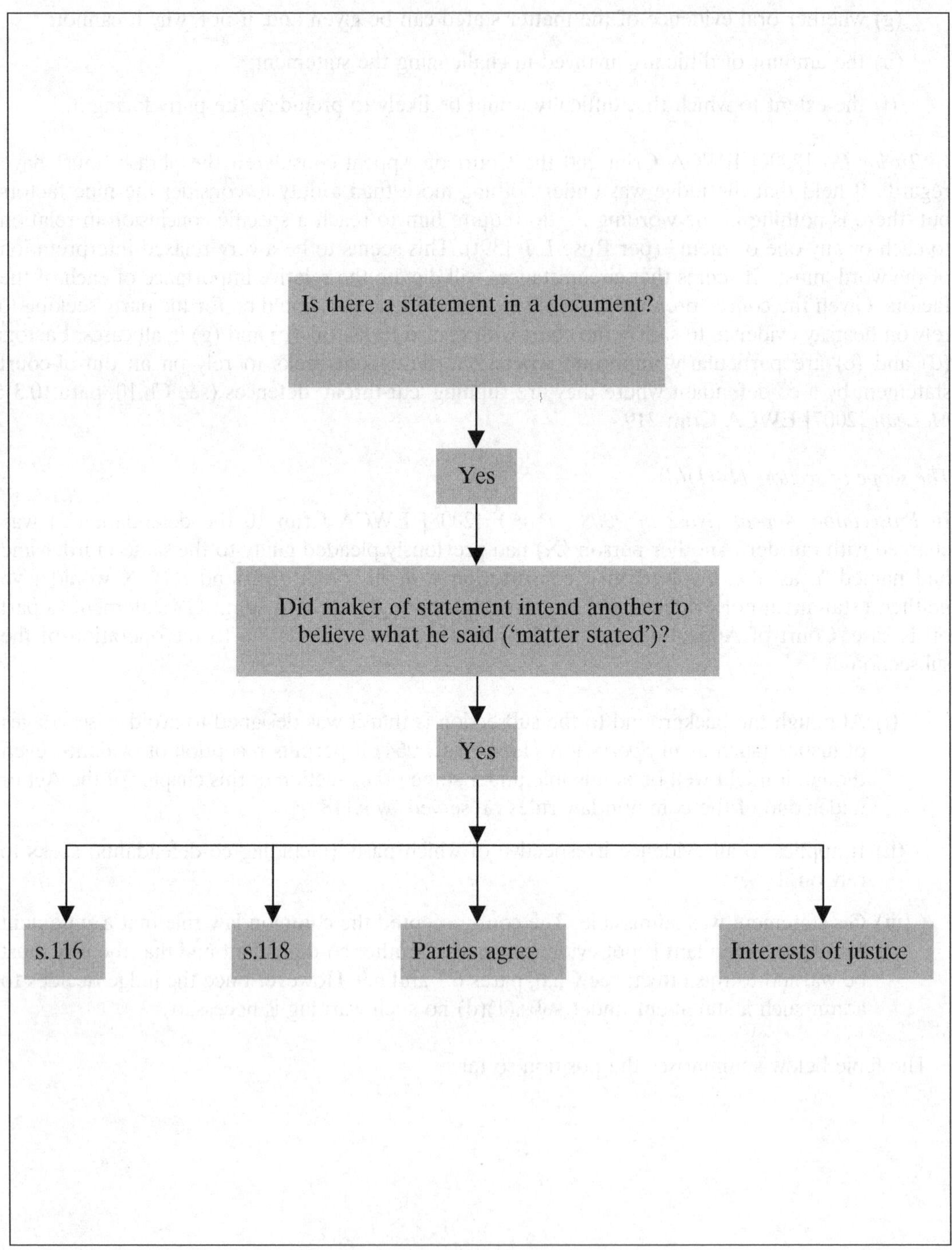

4.7.1.1 **Oral hearsay admitted under Chapter II of Part 11, s.116(1)**

By virtue of s.116(1) oral hearsay will be admissible under this Chapter where the maker of the statement is 'unavailable' provided three conditions are satisfied.

Figure 30—Admissibility of oral hearsay

S.116(1)	**Content**
(a)	oral evidence given in the proceedings by the person who made the statement (known as 'the relevant person') would be admissible as evidence of the matter(s) stated
(b)	the maker is adequately identified
(c)	any of the conditions listed in s.116(2) is satisfied

Limitation to first hand hearsay

Since a 'statement' is defined in s.115(1)(a) as a 'representation of fact' s.116(1)(a) prevents the admission of a statement which is itself hearsay. In other words, evidence cannot be given of any matter of which the maker of the statement did not have personal knowledge. If Minnie gives evidence that Elsie told her that Ken had been caught stealing subs.(1)(a) is satisfied provided Elsie had personal knowledge of the facts.

Whosay—s.116(1)(b)

As we saw (para.4.4.1.1 above) in *Gibson* an unknown man was heard to utter 'the man who threw the stone went in there' while pointing at the defendant's house. The evidence might fall into a preserved common law category (s.118 para.4) but if it did not, it would raise the identity issue in subs.(1)(b). If the maker of the statement remains unidentified how can the defence properly challenge his reliability?

Section 116(2)—the absence (unavailability) conditions

Section 116(2) stipulates the conditions one of which must be proved by the party seeking to rely on the oral hearsay as justification for the absence of the relevant person (maker of the statement). The conditions are virtually identical to those found in (now repealed) s.23(2) and (3) of the Criminal Justice Act 1988, which was limited to the admission of hearsay statements in documents. Much of the case law remains authoritative. Whenever an application is made to admit evidence under either s.116 (or s.117 for business and other documents) and irrespective of which party makes the application, cross-examination of any witnesses must be permitted. In *Wood & Fitzsimmons* [1998] Crim. L.R. 213 the Court of Appeal held that this was a fact-finding exercise to establish whether the criteria in the sections had been fulfilled. Both the examination and cross-examination might properly explore issues arising under the sections. The cases of *Feest* [1987] Crim. L.R. 766 and *Bermudez v Chief Constable of Avon and Somerset* [1988] Crim. L. R. 452 hold that before a party can adduce statutory hearsay evidence, they must lay down 'a proper foundation' for the evidence and show why a particular condition applies. A 'bold assertion' will not be sufficient (*Feest*).

The conditions in subs.(2) are—

Figure 31—Conditions applicable to section 116(2)

S.116(2)	Content—the relevant person
(a)	is dead
(b)	is unfit to be a witness because of his bodily or mental condition
(c)	is outside the United Kingdom and it is not reasonably practicable to secure his attendance
(d)	cannot be found although such steps as it is reasonably practicable to take to find him have been taken
(e)	through fear does not give (or does not continue to give) oral evidence in the proceedings, either at all or in connection with the subject matter of the statement, and the court gives leave for the statement to be given in evidence.

The conditions explained

(a) is dead

(b) unfit to be a witness because of his bodily or mental condition

This subsection applies equally to the mental and physical condition of a witness: *Setz-Dempsey, Richardson* (1994) 98 Cr. App. R. 23. The witness in that case was an amnesiac who was physically capable of attending court. The issue was whether the witness could testify capably once there. Reliance on a witness's mental condition is less problematic when the condition arises subsequent to the making of their statement. It is clearly more difficult when reliance is placed on mental condition subsisting both now and at the time when the statement was made while asserting its coherence as evidence. However, the courts have held that subs.(2)(b) is concerned only with the potential preservation of evidence: *D* [2002] EWCA Crim 990; *Sed* [2004] EWCA Crim 1294. At this stage, the only question for the judge is whether the bodily or mental condition of the relevant person makes him unfit to be a witness so enabling the reception of hearsay evidence. The issue of the quality of the evidence arises only later.

(c) outside the United Kingdom and it is not reasonably practicable to secure his attendance

There are two conditions in the subsection and it necessary to prove them both. In *Bray* (1989) 88 Cr. App. R. 354 the only person who could authenticate a computer record was in South Korea and had been for a considerable period before trial. The prosecutor asked the court to apply the 'absence abroad' provision because she had been informed only on the morning of the trial that the witness was outside the United Kingdom. It was held that since the prosecution could not prove (factually) that it was not reasonably practicable to secure his attendance, the condition was not met and the appeal was allowed. The Court of Appeal rejected the argument that it was not reasonably practicable at the time the prosecution found out—preparatory work must be done.

The amount of such work will vary from case to case but the party seeking admission of the document must be able to justify why it is not reasonably practicable to secure the attendance of the missing witness. The reasons should be based on up-to-date evidence. In the words of McCowan L.J. in *Gonzales* (1993) 96 Cr. App. R. 399 '. . . if (the section) is to be fairly applied . . . any investigating authority . . . must get its tackle in order before it seeks to rely on it.' The court considered it was inadequate to ask a witness whether they were prepared to come to the UK to give evidence without questioning the reason for any refusal. In *C* [2006] EWCA Crim 197 it was held that if the party wishing to tender the evidence cannot show what efforts have been made to get the witness to attend (or arrange a live link) the court might exclude the evidence. (See also *Radak* [1999] 1 Cr. App. 187 (see para.4.6.8)).

(d) cannot be found . . . such steps as it is reasonably practicable to take to find him have been taken

What has been said in relation to subs.(2)(c) is equally applicable here.

(e) through fear . . . does not give oral evidence either at all or in connection with the subject matter of the statement, and the court gives leave for the statement to be given in evidence.

The first question is whether the witness is in fear. Although case law under the CJA 1988 suggested 'fear' involves some form of violence s.116(3) requires the court to construe it widely to include inter alia fear of death or injury or of financial loss. Might it cover fear of a witness's homosexuality being exposed (*Valderrama-Vega* [1985] Crim. L.R. 220)? This was insufficient on its own to found the basis of the defence of duress by threat. As a matter of policy, failure to give evidence because of a fear of being prosecuted for perjury should be insufficient to trigger the operation of the section.

The best evidence of fear is that of the witness himself. In *Greer* [1998] Crim. L.R. 572 the Court of Appeal held it was 'helpful and sensible' where the recorder had heard unsworn evidence from persons who were, allegedly, too frightened to give evidence. If the witness in fear does not appear before the court his fear must be proved by admissible evidence. This might be done as res gestae under the preserved common law exception to the rule against hearsay (s.118(1)). In *Neill v Northern Antrim Magistrates' Court* [1992] 97 Cr. App. R. 121 a testifying police officer told the court that he had been told by the mother of two boys that they were too frightened to give evidence. Repetition by the officer of those fears was held to be inadmissible hearsay. Had the officer been told of their fear by the boys personally, rather than by their mother, he could have given direct evidence as to their contemporaneous state of mind. The officer's evidence might then be regarded as non-hearsay or (now) admitted as an exception to the hearsay rules under s.116 provided the admissibility conditions under the section are met.

The 'fear' in question must be of fear at the time of the proceedings so that stale evidence may well be inadmissible: *H* [2001] Crim. L.R. 815. In *H* the Court of Appeal indicated that a video or audio tape from the witness would be an alternative to direct oral testimony of fear.

In *R. v Ashford Magistrates' Court Ex p. Hilden* [1993] 2 All E.R. 154 that it was held the court could decide for itself whether the witness was in fear. It is unnecessary for the court to hear independent evidence to that effect. Additionally, the statutory requirements are fulfilled if the magistrate is 'apprised' of the contents of the statement; the magistrate need not read the statement in its entirety.

Once fear is demonstrated, the subsection is wide enough to cover a witness who either does not give evidence at all or gives some evidence while refusing to speak on other matters. This overcomes differences of judicial opinion on the interpretation of former legislation in *Ashford*.

Although there is no reference in s.116(2)(e) to the origin of the fear the effect of s.116(5) is that a party cannot rely on any of the conditions in subs.(2) if he is responsible for bringing that situation about. It would not prevent his opponent from seeking to admit the evidence.

Interests of Justice

Evidence should be admitted under subs.(2)(e) 'only if the court considers that the statement ought to be admitted in the interests of justice' (subs.(4)) taking account of the specific issues in (a)–(c) in subs.(4) and 'to any other relevant circumstances' (subs.(4)(d).

Once the judge decides to admit the hearsay evidence he should not explain to the jury—even if asked—the reason for doing so: *Churchill* [1993] Crim. L.R. 285 especially where the reason may prejudice the defendant in the jury's eyes.

Figure 32—Summary chart

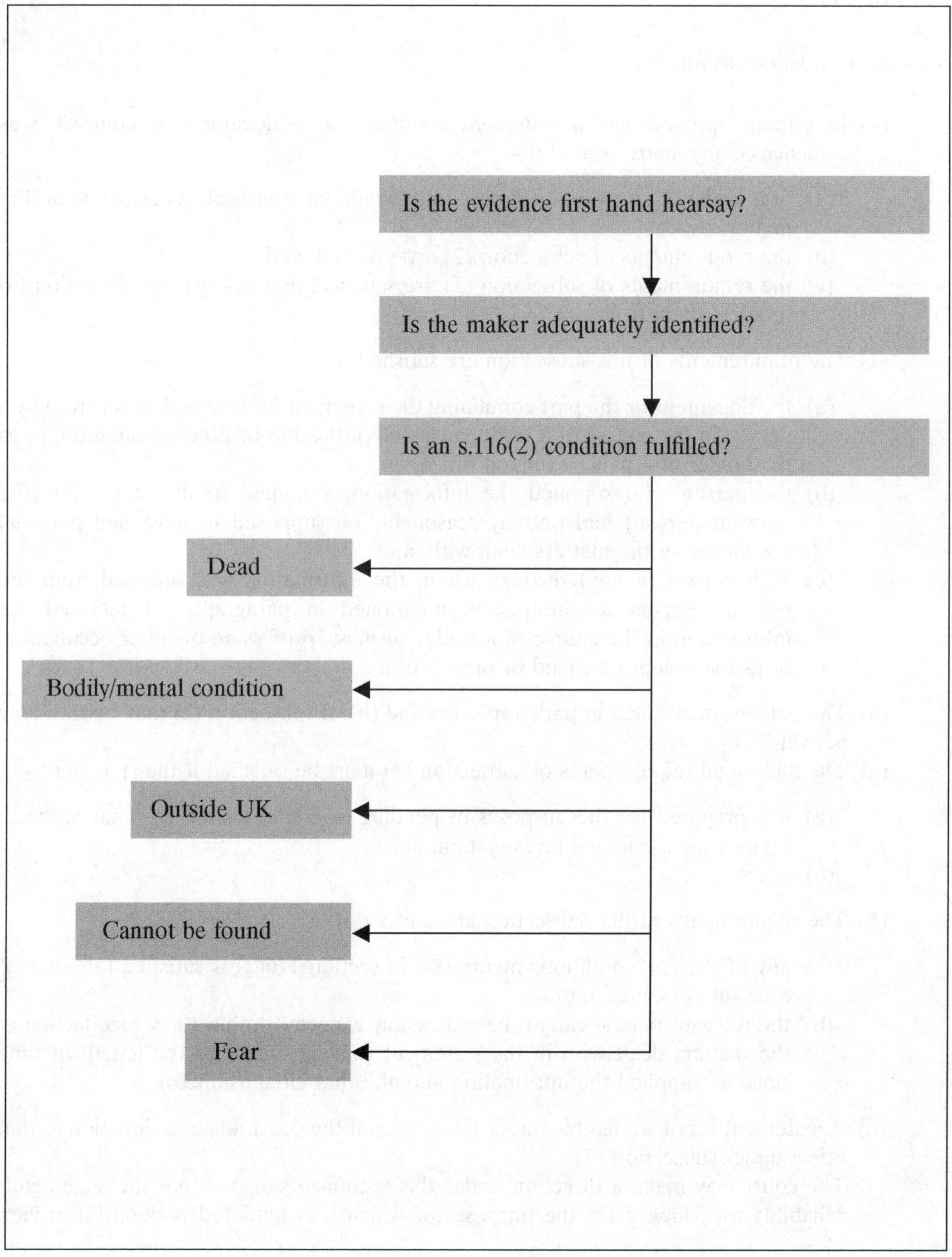

4.7.2 **Business and other documents admitted under Chapter II of Part 11, section 117**

Section 117 provides as follows.

'(1) In criminal proceedings a statement contained in a document is admissible as evidence of any matter stated if—

(a) oral evidence given in the proceedings would be admissible as evidence of that matter,
(b) the requirements of subsection (2) are satisfied, and
(c) the requirements of subsection (5) are satisfied, in a case where subsection (4) requires them to be.

(2) The requirements of this subsection are satisfied if—

(a) the document or the part containing the statement was created or received by a person in the course of a trade, business, profession or other occupation, or as the holder of a paid or unpaid office,
(b) the person who supplied the information contained in the statement (the relevant person) had or may reasonably be supposed to have had personal knowledge of the matters dealt with, and
(c) each person (if any) through whom the information was supplied from the relevant person to the person mentioned in paragraph (a) received the information in the course of a trade, business, profession or other occupation, or as the holder of a paid or unpaid office.

(3) The persons mentioned in paragraphs (a) and (b) of subsection (2) may be the same person.
(4) The additional requirements of subsection (5) must be satisfied if the statement—

(a) was prepared for the purposes of pending or contemplated criminal proceedings, or for a criminal investigation, but
(b) . . .

(5) The requirements of this subsection are satisfied if—

(a) any of the five conditions mentioned in section 116(2) is satisfied (absence of relevant person etc), or
(b) the relevant person cannot be reasonably expected to have any recollection of the matters dealt with in the statement (having regard to the length of time since he supplied the information and all other circumstances).

(6) A statement is not admissible under this section if the court makes a direction to that effect under subsection (7).
(7) The court may make a direction under this section if satisfied that the statement's reliability as evidence for the purpose for which it is tendered is doubtful in view of—

(a) its contents,
(b) the source of the information contained in it,
(c) the way in which or the circumstances in which the information was supplied or received,
(d) the way in which or the circumstances in which the document concerned was created or received.'

A document is defined in s.134 for the purposes of this chapter only as 'anything in which information of any description is recorded.'

This section closely resembles s.24 of the CJA 1988, and much of what follows is based on the courts' interpretation of that section.

Illustration

Suppose a railway accident investigator (Z) said to his assistant (A), from Z's own observation, 'at signal number 18 the live wire is short-circuiting to earth'. Suppose:

(i) Z has since died.
(ii) A did not see the live wire but simply wrote down what Z said at the scene.
(iii) A did not see the live wire, did not write anything down but waited until he arrived back at his office when he told his colleague X who told his colleague Y who wrote it down.

Questions

(a) Is A's oral evidence of what Z said admissible and, if so, under which section and subject to what conditions?
(b) Is A's document admissible and, if so, under which section and subject to what conditions?
(c) Is Y's writing admissible and, if so, under which section and subject to what conditions?

Figure 33—Explanatory table

Questions	Yes/No	Section	Conditions
A's oral evidence of what Z said?	Yes	116 (1)(a); (2)(a)	None. Z is identified; had personal knowledge of facts; and is dead.
A's document admiss-ible?	Yes	117	Provided subs.(2) satisfied; and possibly subs.(4) and therefore subs.(5) also (Z dead).
Y's writing admissible?	Yes	117	Provided subs.(2) satisfied especially re inter-mediaries; & possibly subs.(5) also (Z dead).

Due to the way in which the s.117(2) (like its predecessor) is drafted *Ockleton* ([1992] Crim. L.R. 15, 17) argued that in the Illustration above A's or Y's document might be rendered admissible, as a last resort, by A (or Y) mailing it to himself since it would have been received by someone in the post office service in the course of their job. This seems to have been a drafting error which has been perpetuated under s.117(2). On a literal reading of the words of the subsection, a document appears to be admissible under s.117 if received (by anyone) in the course of their job.

Section 117(4) & (5)

If the document was prepared for the purposes of pending or contemplated criminal proceedings, or for a criminal investigation (subs.(5)) the party seeking its admission must prove one of the five conditions mentioned in s.116(2) (absence/fear etc). Otherwise s.117 relies on the idea that people acting in a business capacity are more careful than when operating at a purely social level. Consequently apart from what is required under s.117(2) there are no pre-conditions to admissibility such as absence or fear in s.116 which must be strictly proved. The contents of the document may be contentious, and it may then be essential for the cross-examiner to be able to question the relevant person: *Price* [1991] Crim. L.R. 707. The issue was the contents of notes of a meeting between the defendant and his bank manager compiled by the latter who was not called to give evidence. In these circumstances the defendant has two options. First he might seek exclusion under the reliability conditions contained in subs.(7) where the burden of proof would be on him. Alternatively he might rely on his right fair trial under art.6 of the ECHR or seek exclusion of prosecution evidence under PACE s.78(1).

Section 117(2)(b) & (c): 'supplied' and personal knowledge

Although the relevant person need not be identified by name it must be shown that he had, or it may reasonably be supposed he had, personal knowledge of the 'matters dealt with' in the document. This will not be a problem where the person who supplied the information is the same as the person creating the document as contemplated by s.117(3). It involves accepting that a person might be said to supply information to himself notwithstanding that in *Derodra* [2000] 1 Cr. App. R. 41 Buxton L.J. said it was 'inapt to refer to a person as supplying information to himself'.

Can the document prove itself?

The question is whether the requirements of s.117(2) (knowledge, supply, intermediaries, profession) can be inferred from the documents themselves or whether, as with s.116(2) absence or fear must be proved by separate evidence. The answer is found in *Foxley* [1995] 2 Cr. App. R. 523. The defendant was convicted of corruption by having shown favouritism in the placing of contracts with foreign companies in exchange for money paid into a Swiss bank account by the companies concerned. The judge admitted company records and accounts which had been supplied by the companies to their own prosecuting authorities and forwarded to the English authorities. They were many years old. No oral evidence was called in support of the documents. Roch L.J. asked:

> 'is direct oral evidence required either from the officer of the appropriate authority in the foreign country that he has seized the documents in accordance with the laws of his

country or from an officer of the company that these were indeed documents from his company created in the course of business containing information supplied by a person who had or may reasonably be supposed to have had personal knowledge of the matters dealt with? In our judgment such direct evidence is not essential, although it will often be desirable . . . The court may, as Parliament clearly intended, draw inferences from the documents themselves and from the method or route by which the documents have been produced before the court.'

It may, nevertheless, be questioned whether the closing words of in s.117(2)(b) were complied with. (Professor Smith ([1995] Crim. L.R. 637) argued that the case has nothing to do with hearsay—the documents were not indicative that payment had been made but of the payments themselves.)

4.7.3 Multiple hearsay

You will recall the Illustration in para.4, in which we distinguished direct from hearsay evidence and then first hand from multiple hearsay. You may wish to refresh your memory now. T's evidence would be multiple hearsay because T heard the history of events from M who was told them by S to whom they happened. When we analysed that situation, we said the difference between first hand and multiple hearsay was significant. We will now see why.

Section 121 is headed 'Additional requirement for admissibility of multiple hearsay' and reads as follows.

> '(1) A hearsay statement is not admissible to prove the fact that an earlier hearsay statement was made unless—
>
> (a) either of the statements is admissible under section 117, 119 or 120,
> (b) all parties to the proceedings so agree, or
> (c) the court is satisfied that the value of the evidence in question, taking into account how reliable the statements appear to be, is so high that the interests of justice require the later statement to be admissible for that purpose.
>
> (2) In this section "hearsay statement" means a statement, not made in oral evidence, that is relied on as evidence of a matter stated in it.'

Subsection (1) creates an exclusionary rule in relation to multiple hearsay with exceptions (a)–(c) in subs.(1). Unless the exceptions apply, one hearsay statement cannot be proved by another. This section reinforces what we saw at para.4.7.1.1 above which is that s.116 is, in principle, limited to first hand hearsay.

4.7.4 Capability to make a statement: section 123

A hearsay statement is inadmissible if made, supplied or created by a person who (subs.(3)) is incapable of 'understanding questions put about the matters stated and giving answers which can be understood'. This is virtually the same test as that used in the YJCEA s.53 to determine competence as a witness and under s.54 to determine 'intelligible testimony' capability (see Ch.3, para.3.2).

4.7.5 Credit of the maker of the statement: section 124

In Ch.2, para.2.8.5 we saw that in principle a witness's answers in cross-examination on matters of credit are final and he cannot be impeached by contrary evidence. We noted exceptions such as previous inconsistent statements, bias and convictions and, when they apply, evidence to the contrary is admissible. Such contrary evidence is admissible where the witness does not give evidence: s.124(2)(a). In addition the court can (s.124(2)(b)) permit evidence to be given on an issue which would otherwise be collateral—in other words leave may be given to infringe the finality rule in collateral issues.

By way of illustration if the cross-examiner is permitted to ask a witness about some disreputable conduct falling short of a conviction, in normal cases the witness's answer would be final. Under s.124(2) the court has discretion to allow evidence of such conduct to be given where the relevant person does not give evidence.

4.7.6 Stopping a case where the evidence is unconvincing: section 125

Section 125(1) creates a catch-all power in respect of any offence where:

- after the close of the prosecution case;
- the case is based wholly or partly on a statement not made in oral evidence in the proceedings; and
- the evidence is important in the case; and
- is so unconvincing that a conviction would be unsafe.

In principle the section can apply to evidence admitted under the hearsay provisions of the Act including ss.114, 116 and 117. As we have seen, however, each of those sections carries at least one subsection enabling the court to exclude evidence otherwise admissible under it. It follows that the exact relationship of s.125 to other sections is a matter of speculation as its relationship to s.78(1) of PACE.

The court can direct either an acquittal or a re-trial but the defendant cannot be convicted of another possible offence such as common assault instead of an offence under s.47 of the Offences Against the Person Act 1861.

4.7.7 Discretion to exclude evidence: section 126

The section applies only where the evidence consists of a statement not made in the proceedings and where the court is satisfied—judged by the issue of 'waste of time'—that the case for admitting it is substantially outweighed by the case for excluding it. The court's power to exclude evidence under s.78(1) of PACE or at common law are expressly preserved by s.126(2). In *C & K* [2006] EWCA Crim 197 Pill L.J. referred [22] to s.126 as giving 'the court a general discretion to exclude evidence in criminal proceedings' but this is obviously wrong given its wording. It applies narrowly to 'waste of time.' It seems his Lordship read only the section headnote.

4.7.8 Overall considerations with regard to exclusion of hearsay evidence

The CJA 1988 mandated the court to consider the interests of justice before admitting hearsay. There is no similar provision in the CJA 2003 though there are some specific provisions such as those in ss.116(4) and 117(7).

Given the fair trial requirement of art.6 and the power to exclude under s.78(1) of PACE, what issues are likely to arise when the judge decides whether to admit hearsay evidence? As Waller L.J. observed in *Sellick* [2005] EWCA Crim 651 whether art.6 has been infringed is 'very fact sensitive'. In practice the following are factors are most likely to affect admissibility of hearsay evidence.

Article 6(3)(d)

'Everyone charged with a criminal offence has the following minimum rights;

(d) to examine or have examined witnesses against him and to obtain the attendance and examination of witnesses on his behalf under the same conditions as witnesses against him;'

Witness anonymity cases

In *Unterpertinger v Austria* (1986) 13 E.H.R.R. 175 the ECtHR said reading statements is not per se inconsistent with Art.6. It is the use made of them which is critical. One such use is where the State wishes to preserve anonymity of witnesses such as the identity of agents engaged in undercover operations. In cases brought against the Netherlands (*Kostovski* [1989] 12 E.H.R.R. 434; *Doorson* [1996] 22 E.H.R.R. 647; *Van Mechelen* [1997] 25 E.H.R.R. 647) the ECtHR held the State is entitled to protect its agents by adducing their anonymous evidence in documentary form. There must, however, be countervailing measures to ensure that the defence is able to question the evidence.

The cases arose in an inquisitorial system of criminal justice where a magistrate is instrumental in protecting the rights of the suspect and is centrally involved in the pre-trial procedures. This is not the situation in England. Anonymity may deny the opportunity to demonstrate demeanour as well as cross-examination on the witness's antecedents. According to the European Court in *Visser v The Netherlands* (App. 26668/96) the key issues in such cases include the extent to which anonymous evidence has been decisive in the proceedings and the reasons given by the judge as to why anonymity should be maintained. This decision must be considered in the light of the decision in *Davis* [2008] UKHL 36 which severely limits anonymity (see Ch.2).

Non anonymity cases

Irrespective of anonymity, the ECtHR has held that:

(i) where a conviction is based solely or to a decisive degree on documentary evidence from a person; and

(ii) the defence has had no opportunity either to cross-examine or have examined that person

the rights of the defence under art.6(3)(d) are violated: *Luca v Italy* (2003) 36 E.H.R.R.; *PS v Germany* (2000) 30 E.H.R.R. CD 301. In *Sellick* the Court of Appeal distinguished *Luca* on the ground that it was not concerned with witness intimidation by the defendant. At least two of the witnesses in *Sellick* did not give evidence because of fear and there is no reason why a defendant should be able to profit from his own wrongful act. In *Al-Khawaja* [2005] EWCA Crim 2697 the Court of Appeal upheld the decision to admit documentary evidence of the victim of an assault who had died before the trial commenced. The document was the principal evidence against the defendant. For the Court of Appeal the main issue was whether the trial overall was fair—cross-examination of the witness is but one aspect of it. The decision in *Sellick* seems correct in principle but it seems doubtful whether *Al-Khawaja* is consistent with *PS* or *Luca*. It was nevertheless cited with approval by Lord Phillips C.J. in *Cole, Keet* [2007] EWCA Crim 1924 [18] in a judgment in which his Lordship seemed intent on denying that part of *Luca* which holds that a trial cannot be fair in the absence of *both* conditions listed above.

Idle prosecutors

The prosecution cannot resort to documentary evidence where it has failed to take steps such as provision of a live television link or where it has indulged in subterfuge to conceal its failure: *Radak*. The Court of Appeal was critical of the prosecution which, it said, had known from the outset that the witness might not attend court and was now seeking to cover its 'culpability' by means which would impose significant unfairness on the defendant. The witness's evidence could have been taken on commission in the United States pursuant to statute. The Court concluded that the statement was not, in the interests of justice, admissible.

Judicial direction where documentary hearsay is admitted

It is clear that the judge's direction to the jury is crucial. In the unreported case of *McCoy* (December 10, 1999) (cited with approval in *Al-Khawaja*) the Court of Appeal said:

> 'If a statement of a critical witness is to be read to the jury, perhaps especially in an alibi case where identification is the true issue, it must be incumbent on the trial judge to ensure the jury realise the drawbacks which are imposed on the defence if the prosecution statement is read to them. It is not enough simply to say that counsel has not had the opportunity of cross-examining. The lay jury may not appreciate the significance of that fact. The judge must at least explain that it means they may feel quite unable to attach anything like as much weight to the evidence in the statement, as they might if it were tested in cross-examination; and where appropriate it would be necessary, certainly desirable, for the judge also to indicate to the jury by way of illustration the sort of matters that might well be put in cross-examination in the particular case.'

Al-Khawaja was said by Jack J. to be the first decision of the Court of Appeal on reading a statement because the witness had died. While placing great emphasis on art.6(3)(d) his

Lordship drew attention [26] to the strong public interest in the continuance of legal process where the sole witness to an alleged offence has died. The key is to ensure the issues in the above extract from *McCoy* are understood by the jury. It seems that the jury should be told to attach 'much less weight' to the documentary evidence which has not been the subject of cross-examination.

Other factors

(i) The quality of the evidence from the absent witness—is it compelling?

(ii) 'Forcing' the defendant to give evidence. The courts have rejected the argument that receiving hearsay evidence is unfair to the defendant because it 'forces' him to give evidence: *Cole* (1990) 90 Cr. App. R. 478. In *Moore* [1992] Crim. L.R. 882 the Court of Appeal held that there was no general principle against admissibility if the only way for the defendant to rebut the evidence in the statement was by giving evidence himself.

(iii) Disputed identification. Direct oral evidence of identification is subject to a mandatory warning (*Turnbull* (1976) 63 Cr. App. R. 132 see Ch.10, para.10.3.2). A hearsay statement containing such evidence is admissible (*Dragic* [1996] 2 Cr. App. R. 232) provided the judge addresses the *Turnbull* issues.

(iv) The relevant person's character. In *Lockley* [1995] 2 Cr. App. R. 554 it was held that where the relevant person had an established record of dishonesty the transcript of evidence from an earlier trial should have been excluded. The problem was compounded by an allegation that the witness's original statement had been made to police in circumstances where there was every inducement for her to lie. It is not, per se, a sufficient reason for excluding the statement that the relevant person was or may have been the defendant's accomplice (*James* [1996] 2 Cr. App. R. 38; *Gokal* [1997] 2 Cr. App. R. 266) but such circumstances require a clear explanation by the judge. It will also give the defendant an opportunity to attack the credit of the absent witness.

4.8 Summary

(i) A statement is capable of being hearsay only if it is tendered to prove the truth of its contents. We say that it is relied on 'testimonially'.

(ii) If relied on only to prove that it was made at all, the statement is direct evidence of that fact and is not hearsay.

(iii) If the production of the statement does not depend on human knowledge or input (e.g. laser bar-code reader) it is not hearsay.

(iv) There are four routes through which hearsay is admissible.

   (a) The exceptions preserved by s.118.
   (b) By agreement.

(c) Where the court is satisfied (s.114(1)(d) & (2) of the interests of justice.
(d) Under ss.116 & 117.

(v) The only major common law exception to the rule against oral hearsay in criminal proceedings is res gestae. This is preserved by s.118.

(vi) Under s.116 oral hearsay is admissible only if it first hand whereas under s.117 multiple hearsay in documents is admissible.

(vii) One hearsay document cannot prove another.

(viii) Where the prosecution relies on hearsay evidence it may be excluded under PACE s.78(1) if its admission would cause unfairness in the trial. Article 6 is to like effect though it is not limited to evidence on which the prosecution proposes to rely.

(ix) It is doubtful whether hearsay evidence should be admitted if it is the only evidence in the case and there has been no opportunity for examination of the relevant person though there may be an exception where the defendant has intimidated a witness.

Figure 34—End of chapter summary chart

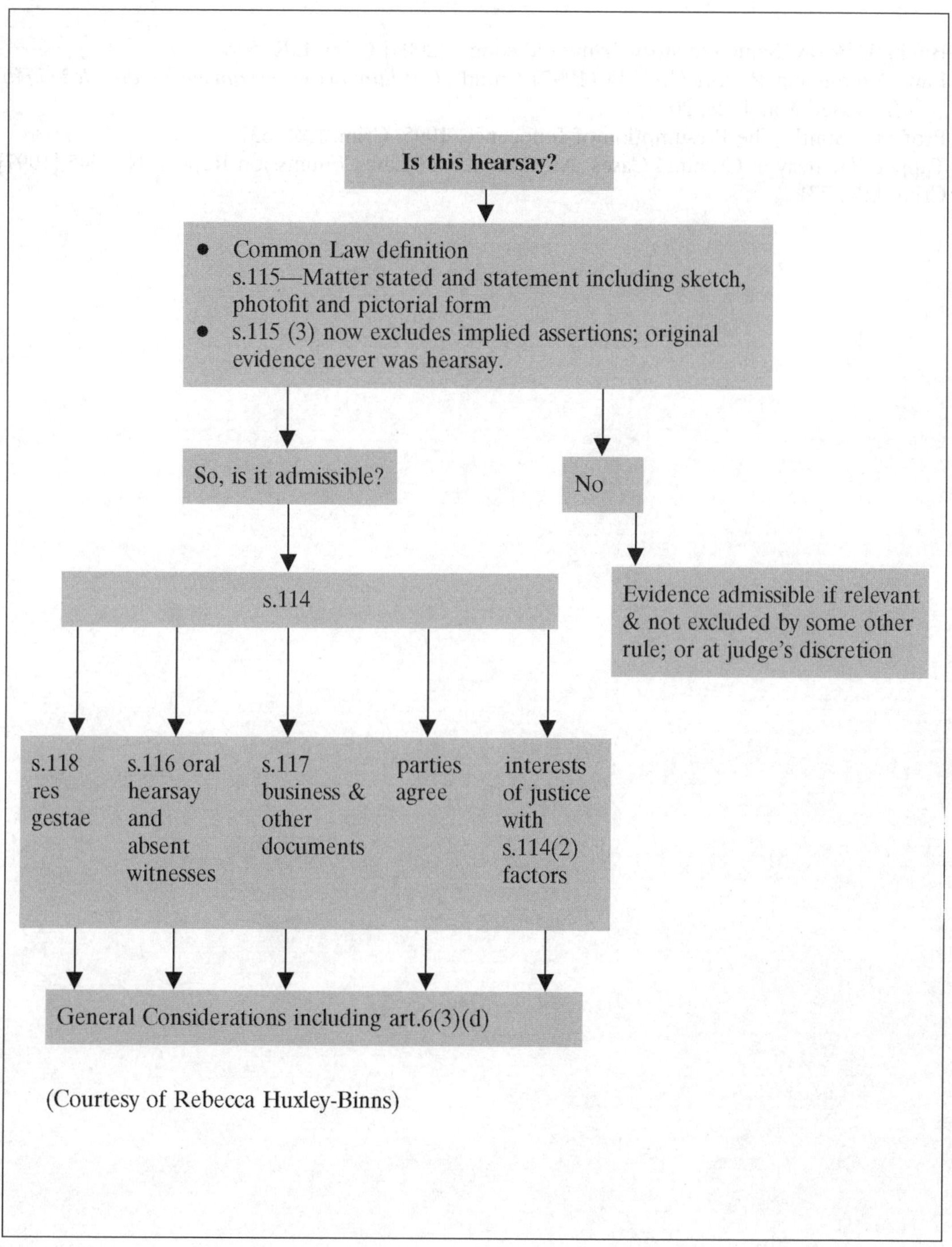

(Courtesy of Rebecca Huxley-Binns)

4.9 Further reading

Birch, 'Hearsay: Same old story, Same old song?' [2004] Crim. L.R. 556
Law Commission Report No. 245 (1997) Cmnd 3670 *http://www.lawcom.gov.uk/docs/lc245.pdf* (accessed March 28, 2008)
Professor Smith, The Presumption of Innocence, 1995, Crim. L.R. 637
Tapper, 'Hearsay in Criminal Cases: An Overview of Law Commission Report' No. 245 [1997] Crim. L.R. 771

5 Opinion

5.1 Introduction

When giving evidence a witness is supposed to testify only to the facts he perceived personally. He is debarred from giving evidence of his opinion—it is said that a 'witness must speak to the facts'. It is for the jury to draw inferences and reach conclusions from facts—not for the witness. By way of exception to the general principle, however, an expert witness may be asked for his opinion on matters calling for special knowledge (see para.5.3 below).

In theory, there is a clear distinction between evidence of fact and of opinion but, as Thayer wrote 'In a sense, all testimony to a matter of fact is opinion evidence . . . it is a conclusion formed from phenomena and mental impressions'. (*Preliminary Treatise on Evidence at the Common Law* (1898) p.524). This accounts in part for why non-expert evidence opinion is, in a narrow sense, admissible at common law, as we shall now see.

5.2 Non-expert opinion at common law

Keane (p.553) says that if a witness identifies the defendant as the culprit using the words 'he is the man I saw', strictly that is his opinion. In theory, a witness could be confined to describing the features of the person he saw leaving it to the court to draw an inference. The criminal courts would grind to a halt if that happened. In limited circumstances a witness may give a compendious account of what he perceived even where it involves opinion such as age: was the victim young or old?; or condition: was the carpet new? Other examples of this kind of evidence are speed, temperature, weather, handwriting, sanity, emotional and bodily conditions, intoxication. The facts on which such opinions are based will usually emerge through questions to the witness. It is impossible to draw up a closed list of issues falling in this area.

5.3 Expert opinion at common law

5.3.1 Expertise

The judge decides whether the witness is qualified 'through study, training or experience' to give evidence as an expert. This should be considered and approved before the witness gives evidence. In the trial of the jockey Kieron Fallon at the Old Bailey (September/December

2007) the defendant was charged with 'race fixing'—intentionally riding a horse not to win in order to accommodate bets on other horses. The trial collapsed when the 'expert' called by the prosecution admitted under cross-examination that he was not an expert on British horseracing. The witness said he was not familiar with the rules in the UK, was only giving his opinion on the riding and could not say what the outcome of a stewards' inquiry would have been. (*http://www.rte.ie/sport/racing/2007/1207/fallon.html*, accessed March 31, 2008.)

Whilst it is common for such a person to be professionally qualified, such qualifications are not required by law. In *Silverlock* [1894] 2 Q.B. 766 in order to prove certain documents were forged, the solicitor for the prosecution was called as an expert on handwriting. He had no professional qualification in the field but had made a very detailed study of the subject. Lord Russell held:

> 'there is no decision which requires that the evidence of a man who is skilled in comparing handwriting, and who has formed a reliable opinion from past experience, should be excluded because his experience has not been gained in the way of his business.'

In *Clare & Peach* [1995] 2 Cr. App. R. 333 the Court of Appeal acknowledged the possibility of a witness becoming an 'ad hoc' expert. The defendants were charged with violent conduct following a football match. There was monochrome video recording of the incident in which many members of the public were milling about. A police officer:

> 'had viewed the recording of the incident about 40 times. He had been able to examine it in slow motion, frame by frame, rewinding and playing as frequently as he needed. By studying the film in this way, he was able to follow the movements of individuals and see what actions they took. By comparing the individuals performing violent acts with the colour pictures taken before and at the match, he claimed to be able to identify not only the violent acts in the street but who was committing them.' (per Lord Taylor CJ).

It was held the officer had special knowledge which the jury did not possess and to 'afford the jury the time and facilities to conduct the same research would be utterly impracticable'. (per Lord Taylor). *Clare & Peach* is also authority as to matter which can be the subject of expertise—as to which we now turn.

5.3.2 Subject matter

As with non-expert evidence it is not possible to draw up a closed list of areas on which expert evidence is admissible. Matters requiring expertise change over time with changes in common knowledge. The scope of expertise ranges from scientific, technical and technological issues to matters of foreign law. Expert evidence is not available on the meaning of ordinary words used in general Acts of Parliament: *DPP v A&BC Chewing Gum* [1968] 1 Q.B. 159 though in this case it was held that expert evidence was admissible as to the likely effect on young people of articles alleged to be capable of depraving and corrupting under the Obscene Publications Act 1959. The case is, however, unusual and is probably confined to its own facts—if the articles in question had been aimed at adults the result of the case would almost certainly have been different. In contrast in *Stamford* [1972] 56 Cr. App. R. 398 it was held that whether an article sent through the post was 'indecent and obscene' was not a matter of expertise.

In *Stockwell* (1993) 97 Cr. App. R. 260 it was held that a jury could hear from an expert on facial mapping to support the contention that the defendant was the person seen on a security video. We encountered the case of *Clarke* [1995] 2 Cr. App. R. 425 on facial mapping in the Introduction (see para.5.3). You should refer back to it for the details of the technique. Citing *Turner* [1975] 60 Cr. App. R. 80 the defence was that expert evidence to explain the technique to the jury was inadmissible. Dismissing the appeal the Court of Appeal held the evidence fell into the category which was insufficiently intelligible to a jury without explanation.

Similarly, in *Skirving* (1985) 81 Cr. App. R. 9 the issue was whether it was admissible for an expert to depose as to the effects of cocaine and ingesting it in the way suggested in material published by the defendant. It was held, not unexpectedly, that the matters were not within the experience of the ordinary juror so the evidence was admissible to assist the jury to decide whether the article had a tendency to deprave and corrupt. Whether it actually did so was, nevertheless, exclusively for the jury.

In contrast, in *Land* [1998] 1 Cr. App. R. 301 it was held the jury could decide for itself whether the age of an unknown person depicted in a photograph was under 16 years for the purposes of s.1 of the Protection of Children Act 1978. Expert paediatric evidence to inform the jury of the different stages of puberty amongst adolescents from different racial origins and backgrounds was unnecessary because the court was as well equipped as any expert to draw such a conclusion.

Where the court is asked to admit evidence in an area where expertise is developing anew, the test accepted by the Court of Appeal in *Dallagher* [2003] 1 Cr. App. R. 195 is that found in *Cross & Tapper* (9th edn p.523) as follows:

> 'The better, and now more widely accepted, view is that so long as a field is sufficiently well-established to pass the ordinary test of relevance and reliability, then no enhanced test of admissibility should be applied, but the weight of the evidence should be established by the same adversarial forensic techniques applicable everywhere.'

A good example can be found in *Hoey* [2007] NICC 49 where Weir J. held that low copy number DNA (LCN DNA) profiling was not at the stage to meet the required standards of certainty. (LCN DNA involves invisibly tiny samples (as small as one millionth the size of a salt grain) being magnified sufficiently to be tested. The problem is that any damage to or rogue element in the microscopic sample is also magnified making the technique insufficiently certain in 2007 for proof beyond reasonable doubt.)

In *Dallagher* the Court of Appeal accepted the admissibility of ear prints even though the subject was in its infancy. Contrasting it with the stricter approach adopted in the United States in *Daubert v Merrell Dow Pharmaceuticals* 509 US 579 (1993) some commentators refer to *Dallagher* as a 'relaxed' rule of admissibility. Keane (564) says it carries dangers citing *Robb* (1991) 93 Cr. App. R. 161. A lecturer in phonetics was allowed to give evidence of voice identification using only auditory (voice quality, pitch and pronunciation) analysis. He accepted that world experts regarded auditory analysis as unreliable unless supplemented by acoustic analysis (voice frequency, resonance etc). The Court of Appeal held that his evidence was of significantly greater value than that of a layman. By the time of *O'Docherty* [2003] 1 Cr. App. R. 77 the Northern Ireland Court of Appeal held that time had moved on and refused to allow a conviction to be based solely on auditory analysis.

We shall meet the issue of developing expertise again in relation to evidence from medical experts (see below) where the courts have been very cautious. The important point is that the courts must remain the gatekeeper of admissibility. The admissibility of expert evidence is not, and must not become, an issue of expertise for experts.

The ultimate issue 'rule'

According to this 'rule' a witness may not be asked for his opinion on the issue between the parties because this would usurp the function of the jury. In criminal proceedings the rule is now honoured more in the breach than in the observance. In *A & BC Chewing Gum* Lord Parker said the rule had many inroads. Thus, strictly, an expert may not be asked if the defendant was suffering from diminished responsibility since that is for the jury to decide. In practice, it effectively happens (provided it is not done too blatantly) through the use of hypothetical questions.

The demise of the rule seems fairly imminent. It was considered along with other issues relating to expertise in *Stockwell*, where the Court of Appeal considered that it existed more in form than substance. Lord Taylor observed that counsel could bring an expert witness very close to expressing an opinion on the issue and that he should be allowed to do so.

Nevertheless, there are occasional signs of life in the rule, as in *Jeffries* [1997] Crim. L.R. 819. A police officer with specialist drugs knowledge could give expert opinion on drugs-related issues outside the knowledge/experience of the jury. However, she should not have been allowed to testify as to whether drugs paraphernalia found at premises related to the sale of drugs. Such evidence was, effectively, the same as expressing an opinion that the defendant was guilty.

Battle of experts and jury direction

The courts have encountered problems relating to what is sometimes called 'battle of the experts'. In *Cannings* [2004] EWCA Crim 01 the Court of Appeal held that where following full investigation into the circumstances of two or more unexplained infant ('cot') deaths in the same family reputable experts disagree as to the cause of death and a body of expert opinion concludes that natural causes cannot be excluded as a reasonably possible explanation, the prosecution of a parent should not be started or continued in the absence of additional cogent extraneous evidence supporting the suggestion of deliberate harm.

Cannings is not authority that a dispute between reputable experts should produce an acquittal. In *Cannings* there was, essentially, no *evidence*—only the inferences (based on coincidence of two deaths in the same family) which prosecution witnesses were prepared to draw—those same inferences being disputed by other reputable experts in the same field. This was sufficient for *Cannings* to be distinguished on the very different facts in *Kai-Whitewind* [2005] EWCA Crim 1092 where even though there was again fundamental disagreement between experts, there was some evidence on which a decision could be based.

The jury should be directed that they are not bound by expert opinion (*Fitzpatrick* [1999] Crim. L.R. 832) though the JSB Specimen Direction 33 requires the jury shall give 'the matter careful consideration' even if the evidence is unchallenged. The Direction also requires the jury to 'remember that this evidence relates only to part of the case, and that whilst it may be of assistance to you in reaching a verdict, you must reach your verdict having considered all the evidence'.

Evidence from medical experts

The principles outlined above apply to this area. The subject matter must be one of acknowledged expertise. In the context of mental conditions, the courts have held expert evidence can be received only in relation to mental illness or recognised psychiatric condition. In *Gilfoyle* [2001] Crim. L.R. 312 the Court of Appeal considered whether 'psychological autopsies' had, as a developing area of science or medicine, achieved acceptance by the scientific community as being able to provide accurate and reliable opinion. The court regarded the proposed evidence as 'unstructured and speculative' and 'not the stuff of which expert admissible evidence is made'. (per Rose L.J.). On the facts, the evidence would have attempted to indicate to the jury the level of happiness of the deceased.

Again the court will be guided by the principle of jury competence. In *Turner* (1975) 61 Cr. App. R. 67 Lawton L.J. said:

> 'the fact that an expert witness has impressive scientific qualifications does not by that fact alone make his opinion on matters of human nature and behaviour *within the limits of normality* any more helpful than that of the jurors themselves; but there is a danger that they may think it does.' (emphasis supplied.)

The defendant, who was not mentally ill, wished to call psychiatric evidence of the provoking effects on him of a confession of infidelity by his girlfriend, with whom he had had a deep emotional relationship. The Court of Appeal held the evidence was inadmissible. Similarly in *Camplin* [1978] 67 Cr. App. R. 14 Lord Simon held that in the law on provocation the jury could not hear an expert's opinion as to how he thought the defendant would react.

In *Chard* (1971) 56 Cr. App. R. 268 it was held that expertise was not admissible as to whether the defendant had the necessary mens rea for murder. The Court of Appeal held:

> 'where no issue of insanity, diminished responsibility or mental illness has arisen, and it is conceded on the medical evidence that the defendant is entirely normal, it is not permissible to call a medical witness to state how, in his opinion, the defendant's mind operated at the time of the alleged crime with regard to the question of intent.' (per Roskill L.J.).

However, in the Canadian case of *Lupien* [1970] 9 DLR (3d) 1 the opposite conclusion was reached on whether the defendant had the capacity to form mens rea, a somewhat different issue. The Court of Appeal held in *Smith* [1979] 3 All E.R. 605 that expert evidence was correctly admitted to show the unusual nature of the defendant's alleged automatism which involved sleepwalking.

In *Lowery v R.* [1974] A.C. 85 one defendant (D1) had said that he had tried to restrain his co-defendant (D2) from murdering a girl and was not the dominant partner. The question was whether D2 should have been allowed to call a psychologist to say that whereas D1 was aggressive and dominant, D2 was relatively less so. In the light of *Turner* it might seem such evidence would be inadmissible but the Privy Council held it was correctly admitted.

Why D2 should be allowed to bolster his case in this way is not clear. Although the evidence went towards rebutting D1's evidence, critics of the decision say it cannot be reconciled with *Turner*. Much depends on the purpose of calling the evidence. D1 had put his character in issue and perhaps the evidence merely went to rebut the claim of good character. However, in *Turner* Lawton L.J. confined *Lowery* to its 'special facts'. He said:

> 'We do not consider that it is an authority . . . that in all cases psychologists and psychiatrists can be called to prove the probability of the (defendant's) veracity.'

This statement may be designed to exclude such evidence entirely—after all, the credibility of witnesses is a matter for the jury not an expert. Alternatively, Lawton L.J. might have been seeking to exclude such evidence from an expert. *Lowery* was followed in *Randall* [2003] UKHL 69 Cr. App. R. 375 but the House of Lords expressly declined to consider doubts about expert evidence in this context.

The courts have applied the 'within the limits of normality' principle (Lawton L.J. in *Turner* (above)) by using the IQ limit of 70. In *Masih* [1986] Crim. L.R. 395 the defence wished to call expert evidence that the defendant (whose IQ was 72) was borderline sub-normal, immature, easily frightened and led by others, tended to wish to please and to conform, and would have difficulty in distinguishing truth from face value. The evidence was held to be inadmissible. Citing *Turner* and *Jordan* [1977] A.C. 699 the Court of Appeal held such evidence was admissible where the defendant's IQ was very low to enlighten the jury on what was abnormal and, consequently, outside their experience. This case was close to that line but the trial judge was correct and the appeal was dismissed.

Notwithstanding the decision on the facts, there are indications in the case of a slight mitigation of the rigour of *Turner*. There appears to be a slow movement towards a more relaxed approach as well as some recognition that terms such as 'normal' or 'ordinary' do not have a clearly understood meaning. In *Ward* [1993] 96 Cr. App. R. 1 the Court of Appeal accepted that expert evidence of 'a condition not properly described as mental illness, but a personality disorder so severe as to be characterised as mental disorder' was admissible. In *Strudwick* (1994) 99 Cr. App. R. 326 the Court of Appeal said:

> 'It is not suggested here that the appellant is suffering from a mental illness, but that is not in itself conclusive against the admission of this evidence. The law is in a state of development in this area. There may well be other mental conditions about which a jury might require expert evidence in order to understand and evaluate their effect on the issues in a case.'

It may also be necessary to distinguish the admissibility of such evidence in relation to defendant's confessions from where it is sought to rely on it in relation to joint trials as in *Lowery*. In the latter circumstances the courts have been increasingly conscious of the implications for a fair trial if evidence relating to the character of a co-defendant were excluded: *Randall*.

5.4 Facts on which expert evidence is given

Under s.30(1) of the CJA 1988 an expert report is admissible in criminal proceedings 'whether or not the person making it gives oral evidence' in the case. Under subs.(4) the report is evidence of any fact or opinion of which the person making it could have given oral evidence. If the maker of the report does not give evidence the report is admissible only with leave of the court. While valuable, the section would not permit a report to be admitted if it were based on the work of another as where a vehicle is examined by a mechanic with regard to its roadworthiness and an expert is called to give evidence as to whether, in his opinion, the condition of the vehicle caused an accident.

That gap is closed by s.127 of the CJA 2003. An expert can base his opinion on a statement prepared by another person provided that other person had, or may reasonably be supposed to have had, personal knowledge of the matters stated. Under s.127(3) the statement is evidence of any facts stated therein. This provision overcomes the problem in *Jackson* [1996] 2 Cr. App. R. 420 where an expert was called to give evidence in respect of blood typing. His witness statement said he had been assisted in his analysis by six assistants and that a full record of their work could be provided. It was held that his evidence depended on work of assistants which was hearsay. Evidence admitted under s.127 remains hearsay but is admissible as an exception. The court has power to disapply the section in the interests of justice (subs.(4)). It would then be necessary for all the facts to be proved by direct evidence.

Outside the statutory provisions, the law is that an expert is entitled to rely on both published and unpublished work in the field in question as the basis for his evidence even if he does not have personal knowledge of the facts in such material. In *Abadom* [1983] 1 All E.R. 364 the prosecution relied on evidence as the refractive index of glass—a measure as to how light is bent when it passes into a particular piece of glass. It was sought to show that glass broken at the crime scene and slivers found on the clothes of the defendant bore the same refractive index. An expert witness was questioned as to the frequency with which the particular refractive index occurred. He said it had been Home Office Central Research Establishment practice to collate statistics of the refractive index of broken glass which had been analysed in forensic laboratories over a period of years and that, having consulted these statistics, he found that this particular refractive index occurred in only 4 per cent of all the analyses which had been made. The Court of Appeal held not only that the evidence was admissible but that the witness was under a duty to consider any material that may be available in his field in coming to his conclusions. The evidence did not breach the hearsay rule. (It is surprising, therefore, to find that such evidence is preserved as a common law exception to the rule against hearsay by s.118(1) para.8 of the CJA 2003.)

5.5 Notice

The Criminal Procedure Rules require a party seeking to rely on expert evidence to give notice to the court and the other side. Rule 33 (at the time of writing) deals with the following matters.

Rule 33.1 Reference to an expert

Rule 33.2 Expert's duty to the court

Rule 33.3 Content of expert's report

Rule 33.4 Expert to be informed of service of report

Rule 33.5 Pre-hearing discussion of expert evidence

Rule 33.6 Failure to comply with directions

Rule 33.7 Court's power to direct that evidence is to be given by a single joint expert

Rule 33.8 Instructions to a single joint expert

As a matter of procedure, discussion is outside the scope of this work.

5.6 Summary

(a) Witnesses must speak to the facts.

(b) Expert evidence may be given about matters outside the experience of the jury.

(c) An expert may be allowed to give his opinion about such matters provided the facts underpinning it are proved or accepted by the court.

(d) The jury must give proper consideration to the opinion but are not bound by it.

(e) Expert opinion on issues relating to the defendant's mental make-up is admissible if it goes to matters outside the competence of the jury. The courts are slowly widening the range of such evidence while being cautious about accepting 'novel' developments.

5.7 Further reading

Jackson, 'The Ultimate issue Rule: One Rule Too Many' [1984] Crim. L.R. 7

McKay & Colman, 'Excluding Expert Evidence: A Tale of Ordinary Folk and Ordinary Experience' [1991] Crim. L.R. 800

Roberts, 'Towards the Principled Reception of Expert Evidence of Witness Credibility in Criminal Trials' (2004) 8 International Journal of Evidence & Proof

6 Confessions

All statutory references in this chapter are to the Police and Criminal Evidence Act 1984 (PACE) unless otherwise indicated.

6.1 Introduction

A confession is an out-of-court ('extra-judicial') statement either oral or written which is adduced as evidence of its contents and is, either in whole or in part, adverse to the interests of the person who made it. Although in most cases the confession will be adduced by the prosecution it can in some circumstances be adduced by a co-defendant. This is explained in detail below (see para.6.9.3). In either the standard situation when the confession is adduced by the prosecution, or the less usual situation where it is adduced by a co-defendant, the statement is hearsay. Suppose the prosecution relies on a confession made by the defendant to a police officer who narrates the confession to the court. The officer does so to prove the truth of the confession—you will recall in Ch.4, para.4.4.2, we called this relying on the statement 'testimonially'. The officer does not know whether the confession is true or false. It is therefore hearsay.

The common law was hostile to admitting hearsay statements but confessions were an established exception. This was justified on the basis that a person would not have confessed if the statement were not true but a better explanation was offered by Professor Smith ([1995] Crim. L.R. 280). He asserted the real reason is because a party to litigation cannot invoke the hearsay rule in respect of his own statement. If the raison d'être of the rule against hearsay is that the maker of the statement cannot be cross-examined, that cannot apply to admissions by the defendant who can always choose to give evidence and be cross-examined on what he said.

When you read the article bear in mind the following changes in the law.

(i) In *Hasan* [2005] UKHL 22 Lord Steyn [58] held that whether a statement is mixed or exculpatory (see para.6.2 below) is to be decided when it was made not when it was sought to admit it into evidence; and

(ii) as we saw in Ch.2 since the CJA 2003 previous statements by witnesses are evidence of their contents, not merely evidence of (in)consistency.

While in practice confessions are statements by detained persons to police officers the law casts a wider net to include confessions made to persons 'charged with the duty of investigating offences' (s.67(9)) such as officers of Customs and Excise: *Seelig & Spens* [1991] 94 Cr. App. R. 17; *Bayliss* (1994) 98 Cr. App. R. 235 (store detective may be within s.67(9)). This area is covered in detail in Ch.7, para.7.4).

Until PACE the law on confessions was governed by the common law under which a confession was excluded as matter of law (as opposed to discretion) if it had been obtained either (i) involuntarily or (ii) by oppression by either a threat or inducement from a 'person in authority'. Under s.76(2), voluntariness has ceased to be a criterion though a confession will still be excluded as a matter of law if obtained by oppression. However, the statutory meaning of 'oppression' is different from its common law meaning (see para.6.10).

At common law a confession is evidence of its contents only against the maker of it. D1's statement in which he makes admissions to an offence and which incriminates D2 is not evidence against D2 unless D2 by either words or conduct accepts the truth of D1's statement. There are common law and statutory exceptions to this rule which are dealt with below (see para.6.9). Notwithstanding the rule that D1's statement is not evidence against D2, its admission will often prejudice D2 even though the jury must be warned it is not evidence against him. The court has no discretion to exclude the statement only because of possible prejudice to D2 (*Lobban v R.* [1995] 2 All E.R. 602) and the only cure for such prejudice would be for the court to order separate trials of the defendants.

If the confession is the result of a tape-recorded interview the tape is, in principle, admissible as direct evidence of its contents and any transcript of it is also admissible at the judge's discretion without consent of either the prosecution or defence: *Rampling* [1987] Crim. L.R. 823. Tape recording of 'interviews' between police officers, and suspects is mandatory under PACE Code of Practice E 3.1 for indictable or either-way offences (see Ch.7, para.7.4).

6.2 The statutory meaning of 'confession'

By virtue of s.82(1), '"confession" includes any statement wholly or partly adverse to the person who made it whether made to a person in authority or not and whether made in words or otherwise.' The 'person in authority' rule is abolished.

'wholly or partly adverse to the person who made it . . .'

The defendant's statement may take one of three forms as follows.

Figure 35—Nature of defendant's statement

Type of statement	Explanation	Within the definition in s.82(1)?
Exculpatory	Contains nothing but denials in respect of the offence in question. Also known as 'self-serving.'	No
Inculpatory	Contains nothing other than admissions to the particular offence.	Yes
Mixed	Both serves and incriminates its maker in respect of a particular offence.	Yes

From this table you can see that a wholly exculpatory ('self-serving') statement is outside the statutory definition of a confession.

One test for deciding if a statement is 'mixed' is whether it contains anything 'adverse' to its maker—is it a statement 'against interest'? In *Garrod* [1997] Crim L.R. 445 Evans L.J. held that to be 'adverse' any admission must be significant in the sense 'that it is capable of adding some weight to the prosecution case on an issue' which is relevant to guilt. But whether we employ the 'adverse' or 'adding some weight' test it will not always be easy to decide whether a statement is 'mixed.' The statement will usually be mixed where its maker admits some ingredient of the offence though as Hooper L.J. said [15] in *Papworth and Doyle* [2007] EWCA Crim 3031:

> 'The fact that a defendant on trial for murder accepted in interview that the victim was dead is not likely to be a significant admission. Likewise, in the absence of an admission of an ingredient of the offence, it will be more difficult to conclude that the admissions which were made convert the statement into a mixed statement.'

Whether an admission of presence at the scene of a crime (an ingredient of most, though not all, offences) is significant (*Sharp* [1988] 86 Cr. App. R. 274) would therefore 'depend on the facts at the close of all the evidence.' (per Hooper L.J. in *Papworth* emphasis supplied). This statement appears to conflict with the view of Lord Steyn in *Hasan* [2005] UKHL 22. As we saw (para.6.1) his Lordship held [58] that whether a statement is exculpatory or mixed is to be decided with regard to the time when it was made not when it is sought to admit it into evidence. In other words the temporal test of 'adverse' is when the statement was made. By way of illustration, suppose the defendant made a statement in which he denied involvement in an offence. He gave an alibi which at trial is shown to be false. His statement does not thereby become adverse to him. *Hasan* was not cited in *Papworth*.

Murphy (p.313) notes that in *Aziz* the House of Lords suggested that a mixed statement 'which is not relied on by the prosecution at all' cannot have any evidential value. He cites *Garrod* and also *Western v DPP* [1997] 1 Cr. App. R. 474 that the test of a mixed statement is its content and not whether the prosecution is relying on any admissions contained in it. Murphy acknowledges that *Garrod* and *Western* are inconsistent with *Aziz* on this point but argues that they are preferable. Otherwise the prosecution controls the defendant's right to adduce the statement. (p.314) Although in *Hasan* Lord Steyn emphasised the 'unrestricted capability' of s.78(1) to exclude evidence including exculpatory or neutral statements this would not assist a defendant who wanted his statement to be admitted but did not wish to give evidence as in *Papworth*.

6.3 Judicial direction on confessions

Figure 36—Defendant's statement as evidence

Type of statement	Admissible?	As evidence of what?
Exculpatory	Yes	Only as evidence of D's reaction when first challenged: *Pearce* (1979) 69 Cr. App. R. 365
Inculpatory	Yes	Of its contents
Mixed	Yes	Of its contents

While a purely exculpatory statement is not evidence of its contents (*Storey* (1986) 52 Cr. App. R. 334) where it is relied on by the prosecution the jury should be directed it is evidence of how the defendant reacted (what was his attitude or explanation?) when first challenged or taxed with misconduct. The situation may be more complicated as where, for example, he made an exculpatory statement to the police but relies on the defence of duress at trial. We shall meet this again in Ch.8, (see para.8.2.4).

Where the statement is wholly inculpatory it is evidence of its contents and the jury will be so directed.

The direction in respect of a mixed statement is that 'all the components of a mixed statement are evidence of the facts stated, although their weight as evidence might differ widely': *Duncan* (1981) 73 Cr. App. R. 359 per Lord Lane approved by Lord Steyn in *Aziz* (above). His Lordship added that if the defendant has not given evidence the judge is entitled to comment adversely that the exculpatory passages have not been tested by cross-examination. Where the defendant has made a mixed statement pre-trial but does not give evidence he is nevertheless entitled to a good character direction (if applicable) under *Vye* [1993] 3 All E.R. 241 (See Ch.9, para.9.4).

6.4 The voir dire (from old French: 'to speak the truth')

Submission to exclude under s.76(2)

Where the defence intends to dispute the admissibility of a confession the prosecution should not mention it until the issue is resolved. The resolution is at a voir dire ('trial within a trial') from which the jury is excluded. In summary proceedings the magistrates are similarly required to hold a voir dire once the issue of admissibility is raised: *R. v Liverpool Juvenile Court* (1987) 86 Cr. App. R. 1. A voir dire proceeds in much the same way as a trial with evidence on oath and the usual examination of witnesses. Though the judge has no power to require him to testify (*Davis* [1990] Crim. L.R. 860) evidence from the defendant will normally be essential if a submission to exclude is to succeed.

If the defence submission succeeds the prosecution must not make any reference to the confession at all but this does not affect the possibility of co-defendants doing so. If the judge admits the confession the trial should proceed without the jury being told of the decision—otherwise the jury might think that the judge had disbelieved the defendant: *Mitchell* [1998] 2 Cr. App. R. 35.

The timing of the voir dire is in the hands of the defence. It may occur at the start of proceedings especially if the prosecution case depends wholly or mainly on the alleged confession. A successful submission to exclude might then result in dismissal of the case.

A submission to exclude under s.78(1)

Under s.78(1) the court has power to exclude any evidence on which the prosecution proposes to rely if its admission would lead to an unfair trial. The defence may use s.78(1) as a route to exclusion of any such evidence including (though not limited to) confessions. If, at summary trial, the defendant makes a submission for exclusion under s.78(1) there is no right to a voir dire. This is because issues which affect the fairness of the proceedings may well be much wider merely than those of admissibility within s.76(2); the court is entitled to look at all the circumstances of the case as the evidence unfolds. Hence, a submission under s.78(1) may properly be considered by magistrates only at the close of the prosecution case.

6.5 The burden and standard of proof at the voir dire

Under s.76(1) a confession may be given in evidence against a defendant only 'in so far as it is relevant to any matter in issue in the proceedings and is not excluded by the court in pursuance of this section'.

In order to make the issue of admissibility live, all the defence need do is 'represent' that the alleged confession was obtained in breach of s.76(2)(a) or (b). It was held in *R. v Liverpool Juvenile Court* that 'representation' is not the same as cross-examination. In addition the court may 'of its own motion' (s.76(3)) put the prosecution to proof as follows.

Figure 37—Section 76 of PACE

Section 76	**Content**	**Burden of proof**
2(a)	Oppression of the maker	On prosecution beyond reasonable doubt
2(b)	Circumstances rendering any confession unreliable	

6.6 The function of judge and jury

The judge

Section 76(2) applies when objection is taken that the confession was obtained either by oppression or in unreliable circumstances. The subsection provides as follows.

> 'If, in any proceedings where the prosecution proposes to give in evidence a confession made by an accused person, it is represented to the court that the confession was or may have been obtained
>
> (a) by oppression of the person who made it; or
>
> (b) in consequence of anything said or done which was likely, in the circumstances existing at the time, to render unreliable any confession which might be made by him in consequence thereof, the court shall not allow the confession to be given in evidence against him except in so far as the prosecution proves to the court beyond reasonable doubt that the confession (notwithstanding that it may be true) was not obtained as aforesaid.'

The judge's duty is to decide whether the prosecution has proved beyond reasonable doubt that the confession was not obtained in violation of s.76(2). This is a mixed question of law and fact. Where relevant, judges often admit psychiatric evidence about the defendant's mental make-up. It is on this evidence, rather than his own observation, that the judge should decide the issue of admissibility: *Silcott, The Times*, December 9, 1991 approved in *Ward* [1993] 2 All E.R. 577, 638–642 per Glidewell L.J. Police officers or general practitioners are not experts for this purpose: *Ham* (1997) 36 B.M.L.R. 169.

The purpose of the psychiatric evidence is to inform the judge of the defendant's condition at the relevant time. The issue is not whether he was suffering from a recognised mental condition but whether he was suffering from a personality disorder so severe as to render any confession unreliable: *Walker* [1998] Crim. L.R. 211.

The authorities (*Turner* (1975) 60 Cr. App. R. 80, *Ward* and *Heaton* [1993] Crim. L.R. 593) hold that such evidence is relevant where it gives the judge (and possibly the jury) insight into the defendant's personality which he would not otherwise have. In *O'Brien* [2000] Crim. L.R. 676 (a case on s.76(2)(b)) it was held the abnormal disorder must not merely be such as might render the confession unreliable but must, based on expert testimony, represent a substantial deviation from the norm. Expert evidence is not admissible on 'matters of human nature and behaviour within the limits of normality' on which the judge or jury is competent without the expert. In *Blackburn* [2005] EWCA Crim 1349 the condition known as 'coerced compliant confession' was held to be a suitable subject of expertise. Coerced compliant confessions occur when a suspect (whether or not innocent) confesses in the belief that it will result in a beneficial outcome for him.

Meaning of the words 'any confession which might be made by him . . .' in s.76(2)(b)

The judge's function is not to decide whether this confession is reliable—that is for the jury. In *R v Bow Street Magistrates' Court, Ex p. Prolux* [2001] 1 All E.R. 57 the Court of Appeal held that while the test of whether the confession is unreliable was in a sense hypothetical because of the word 'any', that word had to be understood as indicating 'any such' or 'such a' confession as the defendant made. So the test relates to any such confession which might be made in the prevailing circumstances. As we shall see, the truth of the actual confession is not relevant to this issue. In applying the test the judge must take some account of the content of the confession.

> 'Otherwise it would always be possible to think of some confession by the defendant that would be likely to be unreliable as a consequence of what was said or done.' (Allen 209).

No power to 'disadmit'

At common law (*Watson* (1980) 70 Cr. App. R. 273) the judge might, having ruled a confession admissible, subsequently change his mind and direct either an acquittal or that the jury should disregard it or order a new trial. In *Sat-Bhambra* (1989) 88 Cr. App. R. 55 it was held that *Watson* did not survive PACE. Judges cannot change their mind to 'disadmit' confession once ruled admissible. The House of Lords decision in *Mushtaq* [2005] UKHL 25 (see below) allows the jury to disregard a confession if they believe it to be unreliable.

The jury

If the judge decides the confession is admissible, the jury decides what weight to attach to it—a question of fact. Even when an unsuccessful submission for exclusion occurs, the defence may cross examine the police to the same effect as at the voir dire—to show the jury there was a breach of s.76(2). How should the jury be directed? In *Mushtaq* the House of Lords said the jury should be directed that if they decided the confession had been obtained in breach of s.76(2) they should disregard it. Lord Roger of Earlsferry said that exclusion of confessions is based on three factors:

(i) possible unreliability;

(ii) the privilege against self-incrimination; and

(iii) proper behaviour by the police towards suspects.

The second of these is an implied right within art.6 of the ECHR and must be fully respected by the court which is a public institution. It would breach the article to permit a jury to consider as part of its factual deliberations a confession which they considered had been obtained by oppression or in unreliable circumstances. (The House dismissed the appeal so the point of law as explained above is technically obiter.) You can read alternative directions to the jury in Specimen Direction 25 on the website of the Judicial Studies Board (*http://www.jsb.co.uk*, accessed March 31, 2008).

6.7 Questions at the voir dire and their subsequent use

Questions as to the truth of the confession

At the voir dire the prosecution is not permitted to ask the defendant whether the confession is true: *Wong Kam-ming v R.* [1979] 1 All E.R. 939 effectively overruling *Hammond* (1941) 28 Cr. App. R. 84. This is because such questions are not relevant to the admissibility of the confession within s.76(2). In making his decision on admissibility the judge can take account at the voir dire of any evidence already given in the trial: *Tyrer* (1990) 90 Cr. App. R. 446.

Using the defendant's voir dire evidence at the trial

Even if the defendant's evidence at the voir dire incriminates him in respect of the offence charged the prosecution cannot use his voir dire evidence at the trial proper either as part of its case in chief or as a previous inconsistent statement: *Wong Kam-ming* and *Brophy* [1982] 73 Cr. App. R. 287. This is because the effect of admitting the voir dire evidence at the trial would, in effect, be to force the defendant to give evidence at trial and it is his privilege not to do so notwithstanding s.35 of the CJPOA. (See Ch.8, para.8.2.6).

It has been argued that s.76 has altered the common law because the cases cited above apply only to 'judicial confessions' (those made in court at the voir dire), whereas s.76 is not limited to judicial confessions and applies to all confessions unless excluded by the court under s.76(2). Since the defendant's judicial confessions are never going to be excluded under s.76(2), the literal rule of statutory interpretation might suggest the restrictions imposed by *Brophy* and *Wong Kam-ming* no longer apply. This is a highly undesirable interpretation of the subsection because such change of ought not to be the consequence of 'side wind' but of express legislative provision.

The rule excluding voir dire evidence from the trial applies only to statements relevant to the voir dire. At the voir dire Brophy admitted in chief that he was formerly a member of an illegal organisation (IRA) in order to explain why, as he said, the police subjected him to unlawful interrogation. The police suspected that he would have undergone anti-interrogation training because they knew of his former membership. It was because this statement was relevant to his arguments at the voir dire that the House held that it could not be used at the trial. In other words, if Brophy had merely been 'bragging' in court at the voir dire then his admissions would not necessarily have been inadmissible at trial.

6.8 Editing the confession statement

The prosecutor's obligation is to present the whole statement to the court including those parts (exculpatory) favourable to the defendant: *Weaver* [1967] 1 All E.R. 277. Any matters which are simply prejudicial such as previous convictions or statements against other persons should be excluded. It was held in *Silcott* [1987] Crim. L.R. 765 that letters of the alphabet should be substituted for the names of co-defendants when reference to other parties cannot be expunged while leaving the confession intelligible and when such references are inadmissible.

In *Hay* (1983) 77 Cr. App. R. 70 the defendant was charged at separate trials with arson and burglary. He had made a statement under caution which was used at the arson trial but from which all references to the burglary had been expunged. He challenged the statement, called alibi evidence and was acquitted. At the subsequent trial for burglary it was held he was entitled to have the whole statement admitted, to be able to call the same alibi witnesses, and to prove the acquittal on the arson charge in order to show the issues between him and the prosecution.

You will find a Practice Direction (No. 24) on permissible editing on the website of the Ministry of Justice as follows (accessed March 28, 2008):

http://www.justice.gov.uk/criminal/procrules_fin/contents/practice_direction/pd_consolidated. htm

6.9 'Confession is evidence only against the maker of it'

6.9.1 Special rule for conspiracies or offences involving a common enterprise

The standard confessions rule

We saw in the Introduction that although a confession statement is hearsay it is, nevertheless, admissible in principle. We also saw that at common law it can be used by the prosecution as evidence only against the maker of it. A statement by D1 in which he incriminates D2 is not evidence against D2.

Common law special rule for acts in furtherance of a conspiracy

The special common law rule is that the acts and/or statements of a party to a nominate conspiracy (D1) are admissible against conspirators (D2 and others) provided the object conspired to has either not occurred or is ongoing. The rule applies both on a charge of conspiracy and where the charge implies a common purpose. Murphy (275), argues that the rule has nothing to do with hearsay but is 'non-hearsay evidence of common design'. The law is said to rest on the principle of agency, but this was doubted by Professor Smith ([1996] Crim. L.R. 386) who implied that the argument is circular. If the acts or statements of conspirator D1 are admissible to prove the conspiracy against D2 because D1 is deemed to be D2's agent, it can only be because there is already a conspiracy between them.

If the object conspired to has been accomplished by the time of the acts or statements which are sought to be admitted, the acts or statements cannot have been done in furtherance of the conspiracy and will not be admissible as evidence against the other alleged parties under the special rule. They would be governed by the standard rule as stated above.

By way of illustration, suppose the prosecution wished to prove D1 had said to D2 that D3 had 'gone out to collect some housebreaking items'. D1's statement points to something already done so can hardly be said to be 'in furtherance' of the offence in question. Although this is technically correct, the courts have taken a fairly relaxed view about the meaning of the words 'in furtherance' of the object conspired to and it seems probable that the court would admit the evidence: *Jones, Williams & Barham* [1997] 2 Cr. App. R. 119. In *Blake & Tye* (1844) 6 Q.B. 126 it was alleged that B had conspired with T who was not called as a witness. It was held that the prosecution should not have been allowed to lead evidence of a stub from T's chequebook showing payment to B of half of the proceeds of the alleged offence because by the time the cheque was written, the fraud in question was completed. On the other hand, evidence from T's daybook was admissible because it was completed during the course of the fraud although B was no more connected with that than he had been with the chequebook.

This issue of 'connection' (or lack of it) is very important. Where the evidence in question is a document, then provided the document can be shown to have been prepared in furtherance of the conspiracy, the prosecution does not need to show that the defendant(s) against whom it is admitted knew of its existence, even less that he (they) were parties to it: *Devonport & Pirano* [1996] 1 Cr. App. R. 221. The evidence in question was a document showing the distribution of the proceeds of a fraud compiled by a party to the fraud without the knowledge of any of his fellow conspirators. In the Commentary to *Jenkins* [2003] Crim. L.R. 1008 Professor Smith wrote:

> 'the rule whereby a statement made by a conspirator in pursuance of a conspiracy becomes admissible against other conspirators only comes into play when there is at least prima facie evidence of the conspiracy from elsewhere.'

This is the basis of the decision in *Donat* (1986) 82 Cr. App. R. 173 which holds that where the prosecution relies on a document created by D1 as evidence against D2 etc. the document must be excluded if there is no other evidence of common purpose. The document may be adduced before that other evidence under the principle of conditional admissibility. The 'other' evidence must be independent (non-hearsay) evidence additional to that of D1 that D2 etc. was party to conspiracy: *Governor of Pentonville Prison Ex p. Osman* [1989] 3 All E.R. 701.

Charges implying a common purpose

The special rule applies in modified form where the charges imply a common purpose, but there is no nominate conspiracy charge: *Gray* [1995] 2 Cr. App. R. 100. In its modified form the rule is limited to evidence which shows the involvement of each defendant in the commission of the substantive offence(s). The special rule cannot be extended to cases where individual defendants are charged with a number of separate offences and the terms of a common purpose are either not proved or are ill-defined: *Murray* [1997] Crim. L.R. 506.

Figure 38—Summary table

Confessions standard rule		
Confession by D1	Evidence against D1?	Evidence against D2, 3 etc.?
	Yes	No
Confessions special rule		
Confession by D1	Evidence against D1?	Evidence against D2, 3 etc.?
	Yes	Yes if but only if: nominate charge of conspiracy *or* charge implies common purpose; and D1's acts/statement made in furtherance of common purpose; and independent evidence of common purpose

The case of Hayter [2005] U.K.H.L. 6

Hayter is a difficult case and controversial decision which Murphy (422) says extends the special rule. D1, D2 and D3 were jointly charged with murder. The only evidence against D3 was his own out-of-court confession that he shot and killed the deceased. The confession alleged that D2 was a 'middle man' (a recruiter and paymaster) between D3 and the person who instigated the killing (D1—the victim's wife). There was some low level circumstantial evidence of D2's involvement in the offence but the prosecution accepted it did not provide a case to answer against him. The case raised two questions as follows. (i) Was D3's confession admissible in respect of D2 at all? (It was accepted that if the answer to this question was 'no' then the judge must direct the acquittal of D2.) (ii) If so, did any conditions attach to admissibility?

(i) By a majority the House held in the affirmative (ii) While the jury must not use any part of D3's confession evidentially against D2, nevertheless if they decided D3 was indeed the killer, that conclusion was relevant in deciding whether to convict D2.

Although on the face of it the reasoning of the majority in *Hayter* appears to lean heavily on the effect of s.74 of PACE, in *Persad v State of Trinidad and Tobago* [2007] UKPC 51 Lord Brown [24] said s.74 had 'informed and reinforced the reasoning of the majority' rather than constituting 'its essential underpinning'. Section 74 (see Ch.4, para.4.6) allows the prosecution to prove that A has been convicted of an offence on some previous occasion when to do so is relevant to an issue in the current trial of B. In *Hayter*, if D3 had been separately tried and convicted in earlier proceedings, the fact of his conviction would have been admissible at the later trial of D2. The majority view was that the outcome should be the same as if there had been separate trials. To put the matter briefly, the majority distinguished the content of the confession from the finding of guilt based on it.

In a powerful dissenting speech Lord Rodger of Earlsferry argued [47] the Crown was asserting the 'power of the jury to turn inadmissible into admissible evidence and to convict (D2) by evidence which is inadmissible against him'. Lord Steyn countered this [20] as follows:

> 'if one postulates . . . that D3 made no out of court confession but that his guilt was established by an eye-witness, a fingerprint or circumstantial evidence the judge would have been entitled to direct the jury that they may take into account their finding that D3 was guilty of murder in considering the case against D2.'

This is of course true but none of the types of evidence referred to by Lord Steyn carry the inherent risks associated, for good reason, with hearsay.

The limits of *Hayter* were considered in *Persad* (above). Lord Brown made it clear [16] that *Hayter* does not apply unless the defendants are charged with a joint offence for which they are allegedly jointly liable. In *Persad*, the victim had, during a robbery, been raped by one man and buggered by another. In a statement to the police D1 admitted the rape and said D2 had buggered the victim. In his own statement to the police, D2 denied entering the premises where the offences occurred alleging it was D1 and D3 who had gone inside. D3 denied presence at the scene. Since D2's statement was exculpatory in respect of the rape and buggery (unlike D3's statement in *Hayter* where he admitted the killing) it was inadmissible against D3. As an exculpatory statement with regard to the sexual offences, D2's statement was less likely to be true so could not be evidence against D3 with regard to the count of buggery.

Here is a table which explains the two cases.

Figure 39—*Hayter* Explanatory table

Case	Charge	Cast in order of appearance	Outcome
Hayter	Jointly charged with murder of V		
D1		Instigator	Guilty on basis of evidence she sought the killing
D2 only appellant		Middle man	Guilty if but only if findings of guilt against D1 and D3 are used as factual building blocks against him
D3		Hit man	Guilty on the basis of his out-of-court confession to his girlfriend

Figure 40—*Persad* Explanatory table

Case	Charges	Jointly charged?	Defendant	Decision
Persad				
D1	Robbery Rape Buggery	No	Admits robbery Admits rape Denies buggery —says D2 did it	
D2	Robbery Rape Buggery		Admits robbery Denies rape Denies buggery	
D3 only appellant	Robbery Rape Buggery		Denies robbery Denies rape Denies buggery	D2's exculpatory statement re sexual offences inadmissible against D3. Appeal re buggery allowed

6.9.2 The effect of the Criminal Justice Act 2003 section 114(1)(d) (the 'safety valve')

We saw in Ch.4, (para.4.7.1) that under the CJA 2003 s.114(1)(d) the court can admit hearsay evidence, where to do so is in the interests of justice provided the court has addressed the issues arising under s.114(2). Suppose D1 has made a statement (whether oral or written and whether formally or informally made) which wholly or partly exculpates D2. Suppose further that the statement is not admissible under the special common law just covered (see para.6.9.1), and that PACE s.76A (see para.6.9.3) is inapplicable because D1's statement does not amount to a confession within PACE s.82(3).

In *McLean* [2007] EWCA Crim 219 the Court of Appeal held that subs.(1)(d) is wide enough to allow the reception of such a statement. If admitted under the subsection 'the jury is by law entitled to consider it, to determine its weight and to make up its mind whether or not it can rely upon it.' (per Hughes L.J. [20]). In other words, the statement becomes evidence in the case without restriction on its use. In *Y* [2008] EWCA Crim 10 Hughes L.J. said [52]:

> '... what may be admitted under section 114(1)(d) is a hearsay statement; the nature of the vehicle which carries that statement (and whether it is associated with a confession or otherwise) is certainly relevant to whether it is in the interests of justice to admit it, *but it is irrelevant to whether section 114(1)(d) is capable of applying to it*. A bare accusation against someone, whether associated with a confession by the maker or not, is *capable* of falling within section 114(1)(d). It follows that if such an accusation is in fact associated with a confession by the maker, it cannot *ipso facto* become incapable of falling within section 114(1)(d).' (emphasis supplied.)

His Lordship emphasised [57]:

> '. . . the existence of section 114(1)(d) does not make police interviews routinely admissible in the case of persons other than the interviewee, and . . . the reasons why they are ordinarily not admissible except in the case of the interviewee are likely to continue to mean that in the great majority of cases it will not be in the interests of justice to admit them in the case of any other person.'

6.9.3 **Section 76A**

> (1) In any proceedings a confession made by an accused person may be given in evidence for another person charged in the same proceedings (a co-accused) in so far as it is relevant to any matter in issue in the proceedings and is not excluded by the court in pursuance of this section.
>
> (2) If, in any proceedings where a co-accused proposes to give in evidence a confession made by an accused person, it is represented to the court that the confession was or may have been obtained—
>
> (a) by oppression of the person who made it; or
>
> (b) in consequence of anything said or done which was likely, in the circumstances existing at the time, to render unreliable any confession which might be made by him in consequence thereof, the court shall not allow the confession to be given in evidence for the co-accused except in so far as it is proved to the court on the balance of probabilities that the confession (notwithstanding that it may be true) was not so obtained.

The issue with which s.76A is concerned is as follows. Suppose one defendant (D1) makes a confession

(i) which is excluded by the court under either s.76(2) or s.78(1); or

(ii) on which the prosecution does not seek to rely because they accept it was obtained in breach of s.76(2) or would lead to an unfair trial under s.78(1): *Myers* [1998] 1 Cr. App. R. 153; and

(iii) D2 wishes to adduce D1's statement as part of his defence.

Under s.76A (introduced by s.128 of the CJA 2003) D1's statement is admissible unless excluded by the court in pursuance of the section. As noted above (para.6.1) D2 might wish to rely on D1's statement where D1 shoulders the blame for an offence for which he is being jointly tried with one or more co-defendants as in *Myers*. Where D2 is allowed to adduce D1's confession, he may do so either by cross-examination of the officer to whom it was made or, if the officer is not called as a witness by the prosecution, by calling the officer as a witness. While capable of going merely to credit as a previous inconsistent statement, its principal value would be as evidence of its contents.

The section has no application when D1 has pleaded guilty. He is no longer standing trial with D2 and so becomes a compellable witness for D2: *Finch* [2007] EWCA Crim 36. If in such circumstances D1 proved hostile, D2 could argue for admission of D1's confession under s.3 of the CPA 1865 and s.119 of the CJA 2003.

Subject to the difference relating to the standard of proof (balance of probability), subs.(2) replicates the test of admissibility found in s.76(2)(a) and (b). Reference should be made to the relevant sections below (paras 6.10 and 6.11) for their meaning. The effect of the s.76A is that if D1's confession is excluded by the judge under either part of s.76(2) as part of the prosecution's case, it will not be admissible for D2 either. However, if D1's confession is excluded by the court under s.78(1) it would be admissible for D2 provided it did not also fail the test in s.76(2). It is possible to envisage circumstances where the prosecution might be the incidental beneficiary of the admission of D1's statement even where it had been excluded as part of the prosecution case.

6.10 Oppression

As we have seen the common law excluded confessions obtained by oppression. 'Oppression' remains a ground of exclusion under PACE but its meaning has changed as a result of the Court of Appeal's decision in *Fulling* (1987) 85 Cr. App. R. 136. The defendant said that she had been interviewed three times over two days during which she said nothing until she confessed to an offence. She alleged this followed a break in the interviews during which the police told her that for the previous three years, her lover had been having an affair with the woman who was in the next cell. Her evidence was that this caused her such distress that she wanted to leave the police station and hence made the confession. She argued her statement should have been excluded under s.76(2)(a).

On appeal Lord Lane held that PACE is a codifying statute citing Lord Herschell in *Bank of England v Vagliano Bros* [1891] A.C. 107, 144–145 that:

> 'the proper course is in the first instance to examine the language of the statute and to ask what is its natural meaning, uninfluenced by any considerations derived from the previous

state of the law, and not to start with inquiring how the law previously stood, and then, assuming that it was probably intended to leave it unaltered, to see if the words of the enactment will bear an interpretation in conformity with this view. If a statute, intended to embody in a code a particular branch of the law, is to be treated in this fashion, it appears to me that its utility will be almost entirely destroyed, and the very object with which it was enacted will be frustrated. The purpose of such a statute surely was that on any point specifically dealt with by it, the law should be ascertained by interpreting the language used instead of, as before, by roaming over a vast number of authorities in order to discover what the law was, extracting it by a minute examination of the prior decisions. . .'

Ignoring the partial definition of oppression in s.76(8) that it includes 'torture, inhuman or degrading treatment and the use or threat of violence (whether or not amounting to torture)' the Court turned to the Oxford English Dictionary. It found assistance in the third meaning given by the dictionary as follows:

> 'Exercise of authority or power in a burdensome, harsh, or wrongful manner; unjust or cruel treatment of subjects, inferiors, etc.; the imposition of unreasonable or unjust burdens.'

Lord Lane said:

> 'one of the quotations given under that paragraph runs as follows: "There is not a word in our language which expresses more detestable wickedness than oppression."'

The Court further held that 'oppression' always involved impropriety by the interrogator. The appeal was dismissed the Court adding that although no such submission had been made, the conduct in question was not within s.76(2)(b) either. Lord Lane's judgment has been subject to well-deserved criticism and not-a-little derision.

- The new definition is objective in nature so prevents the court considering the detainee's characteristics—is he a hardened criminal or an innocent abroad? Section s.76(2)(a) requires the prosecution prove the confession was not obtained by oppression. Whether it was will usually depend in part on the detainee's characteristics.
- Conduct can be oppressive without being deliberate or conscious though the judgment implies such conduct is always required.
- The opening words of the test reintroduce 'the person in authority' rule which was abolished by s.82(1).
- The use of the word 'wrongful' is misleading. A breach of the PACE Codes of Practice is 'wrongful' and while some such breaches might conceivably be oppressive, the overwhelming majority never could. Mere wrongful conduct is not a sufficient for oppression.
- The range of conduct now covered (from power exercised (by a jobs-worth?) in a burdensome manner to 'detestable wickedness') is so wide as to be meaningless.

Subsequent decisions indicate that 'rudeness' and 'discourtesy' will not, without more, be oppressive (*Emmerson* (1991) 92 Cr. App. R. 284); neither will mere trickery as to whether a conversation is being tape-recorded: *Parker* [1995] Crim. L.R. 233. On the other hand in *Paris, Abdullahi & Miller* (1993) 97 Cr. App. R. 99, the police were allowed to 'shout, hector and bully' the suspects—who were represented by a solicitor—'without interruption'. The length of the sessions and their tenor would have been oppressive to a person of normal mental capacity but Miller had an IQ of 75, a mental age of 11 and a reading age of 8. Miller denied murder over 300 times in sessions which were not so much interviews as opportunities for the police repeatedly to put their theory of events to the suspect.

> 'Short of physical violence, it is hard to conceive of a more hostile and intimidating approach by officers to a suspect. It is impossible to convey on the printed page the pace, force and menace of the officer's delivery.' (per Lord Taylor).

6.11 Circumstances rendering any confession unreliable

We saw in the Introduction (para.6.1) that a confession would be excluded at common law if it had not been made 'voluntarily' i.e. not obtained 'by fear of prejudice or hope of advantage held out or excited' in effect by the person to whom it was made: *DPP v Ping Lin* [1975] 3 All E.R. 175, 183 (per Lord Hailsham). Much case law built upon such issues as threats of more serious ('maximising') or less serious ('minimising') charges, threats or promises in respect of offences to be taken into consideration; or informing or not informing other people (e.g. employer, family); or promises to 'put in a word' with the judge.

By way of example in *Northam* (1967) 52 Cr. App. R. 97 a suspect on bail for one offence confessed to another offence after asking whether that other could be taken into consideration. He was subsequently convicted of the other offence but the conviction was (reluctantly) quashed on the ground of inducement. *Northam* was followed in *Zaveckas* (1970) 54 Cr. App. R. 202 and illustrates the technicality of the common law approach to inducements. Technicality was one reason for replacing the common law test of voluntariness with what we shall refer to as unreliability under PACE s.76(2)(b). While the same kind of threats or promises which caused exclusion at common law will operate similarly under s.76(2)(b) the law now casts its net far wider than did the common law. It is not limited to threats or promises and takes account of all relevant circumstances including those unknown to interviewing police officers.

6.11.1 Causation and the meaning of 'unreliability'

The relevant part of s.76(2)(b) reads:

> 'in consequence of anything said or done which was likely, in the circumstances existing at the time, to render unreliable any confession which might be made by him in consequence thereof.'

In *Crampton* (1991) 92 Cr. App. R. 369 Stuart-Smith L.J. helpfully told us that 'unreliable' means 'cannot be relied on as being the truth'. Murphy (289) says:

> 'It is submitted that the role of the court is to consider whether the circumstances, considered as a whole, disclose any reason to doubt that it would be safe to leave the confession to the jury for their consideration.'

The confession must, however, have been made 'in consequence' of things said or done so if the defendant's motive for making a statement was entirely self-generated it cannot have been made in consequence of anything said or done. The extract from Murphy must be read in the light of this principle of 'externality' established by the case of *Goldenberg* (1989) 88 Cr. App. R. 285. The defendant was a heroin addict who had been in custody for five days and was charged with conspiracy to supply diamorphine. He asked for an interview at which he confessed. The fact that he might have done so because he hoped to get bail was treated as irrelevant. The Court of Appeal also held that merely holding an interview could not amount to something 'said or done' and that the confession was admissible.

Murphy (p.290) argues that the decision in *Goldenburg* is illogical. If the police lawfully detain a person known to them to be an addict who confesses to obtain bail, the confession is excludable. However, if the police do not know the suspect is an addict, the same facts do not give rise to the possibility of exclusion. Murphy also accuses the Court of Appeal of inconsistency citing *Everett* [1988] Crim. L.R. 826 where the Court took account of the defendant's mental state, and *Effik* (1992) 95 Cr. App. R. 427 and *Walker* [1998] Crim. L.R. 211 where the Court took account of the effect of ingesting drugs prior to interview.

Once the externality required in *Goldenburg* is demonstrated, all of the defendant's characteristics plus the surrounding circumstances can be taken into account in deciding whether to exclude the confession. Externality need be neither unlawful nor improper and must be considered in the overall circumstances in which the confession came to be made including any self-generated motive. Once unlawful or improper conduct by the police intrude, exclusion becomes more likely. Externality may result from the answer to a question from the detainee such as in *Zaveckas*: 'If I make a statement will I get bail?' In *Howden-Simpson* [1991] Crim. L.R. 49 the question was whether police would charge only one or two offences if the defendant admitted his involvement in a large number of others. Such questions should be left to be answered by the custody officer rather than the officer in the case.

Delaney (1989) 88 Cr. App. R. 388 illustrates the combination of personal characteristics and improper conduct by the police on exclusion. The defendant was 17 years of age, educationally sub-normal, with a low IQ and psychologically unsuited to sustained questioning because he was subject to quick emotional arousal. The police failed to make contemporaneous notes of the interview (Code C11.3 and 11.14), and admitted they had tried to minimise the gravity of the offence (assault on a girl aged three years) and had suggested that such an offender needed psychiatric help rather than punishment. The Court of Appeal held the confession should have been excluded. (The case stresses the importance of a record of what was said or done as evidence of what induced the confession.)

McGovern (1991) 92 Cr. App. R. 228 is in a similar vein. The defendant was pregnant, aged 19 years with a low IQ (73) and a mental age of 10. She was ill prior to the interview and distressed during it. She was improperly denied legal advice and the police also breached recording requirements. The Court of Appeal held the confession should have been excluded.

'Discretionary' exclusion

Where the defendant's mental state (broadly defined) is the *only* issue relevant to exclusion, the submission should be brought under s.78(1) because the confession will not have been the 'consequence of anything said or done'. *Harvey* (1988) Crim. L.R. 241 illustrates the point. The defendant was of low intelligence and suffered from a psychopathic disorder. Although there was no impropriety, her confession was excluded because it may well have been brought about when she heard her lover confess. There was expert evidence that her admissions were probably motivated by a 'child-like' desire to take blame.

The courts have accepted that confessions made during hypoglycaemic (*Powell* [1980] Crim. L.R. 39), hysterical (*Isequilla* [1975] 1 All E.R. 77) or schizophrenic episodes (*Miller* (1986) 83 Cr. App. R. 192) are excludable under the discretion.

Exclusion under s.78(1) is also appropriate where improper or unlawful conduct by the police is contemporaneous with, or follows, the statement. The statement would not have been made 'in consequence of anything said or done'. This would occur for example, where there is a failure to record the statement in accordance with Code C or to offer for signature any notes that were taken: *Delaney* and *McGovern* (above); *Chung* (1991) 92 Cr. App. R. 314.

6.12 Confessions by Mentally Handicapped Persons: section 77(1)

> '(1) Without prejudice to the general duty of the court at a trial on indictment to direct the jury on any matter on which it appears to the court appropriate to do so, where at such a trial—
>
> (a) the case against the accused depends wholly or substantially on a confession by him; and
>
> (b) the court is satisfied—
>
> (i) that he is mentally handicapped; and
>
> (ii) that the confession was not made in the presence of an independent person,
>
> the court shall warn the jury that there is special need for caution before convicting the accused in reliance on the confession, and shall explain that the need arises because of the circumstances mentioned in paragraphs (a) and (b) above.
>
> (2) (Applies subs.(1) to summary proceedings).'

While the section is self-standing, failure by the police to observe its stipulations (as well as those in Code C11.15—11.20 and 'Notes for Guidance' 11C–E) may lead to exclusion of the confession under s.76(2) rendering its provisions irrelevant. Under Code C1.4 if a police officer:

> 'has any suspicion or is told in good faith that a person of any age may be mentally disordered or otherwise mentally vulnerable, in the absence of clear evidence to dispel that suspicion the person shall be treated as such for the purposes of this Code.'

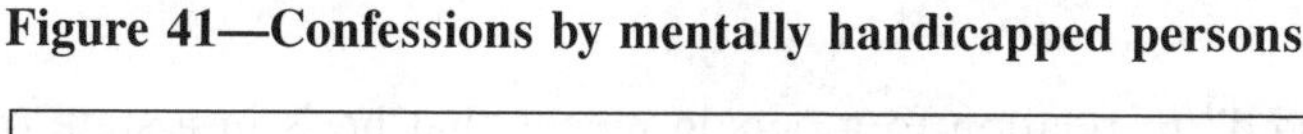

Figure 41—Confessions by mentally handicapped persons

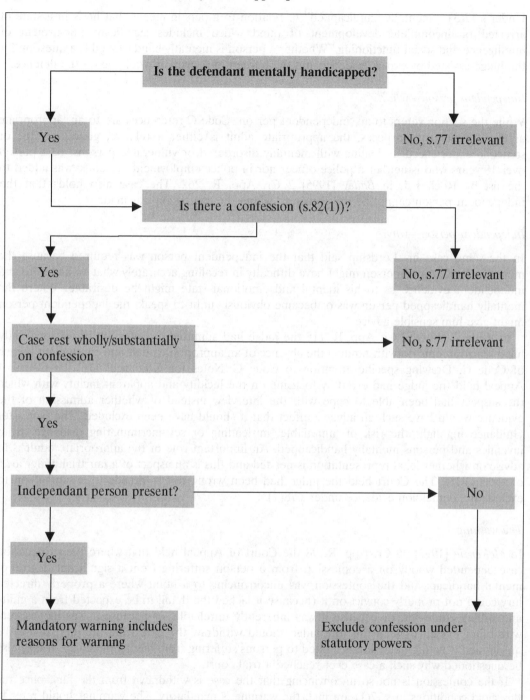

Is the defendant mentally handicapped?

Yes

No, s.77 irrelevant

Is there a confession (s.82(1))?

Yes

No, s.77 irrelevant

Case rest wholly/substantially on confession

No, s.77 irrelevant

Yes

Independant person present?

No

Yes

Mandatory warning includes reasons for warning

Exclude confession under statutory powers

'Mentally handicapped'

Under s.77(3) '"mentally handicapped" in relation to a person means that he is in a state of arrested or incomplete development of mind which includes significant impairment of intelligence and social functioning.' Whether a person is mentally handicapped is a question for the judge assisted by expert evidence and the burden of proving it would be on the defence.

Independent person—who?

While the section refers to an 'independent person' Code C references are to an 'appropriate adult'. For current purposes, the appropriate adult is either a relative, guardian, etc.; or someone experienced in dealing with mentally disordered or vulnerable persons; or a person over 18 years who is neither a police officer nor in police employment. 'Friends' was added to the list by Roch L.J. in *Bailey* [1995] 2 Cr. App. R. 262. The case also holds that the independent person cannot be the person to whom the confession was made.

Independent person—why?

In the same case his Lordship said that the independent person was required because the mentally handicapped person might have difficulty in recalling accurately what he had said, and independent evidence as to his mental and emotional state might be desirable. Where the mentally handicapped person was or became obviously unfit to speak, the independent person might give him sensible advice.

In *Aspinall* [1999] 2 Cr. App. R. 115 the judge had admitted a confession of an apparently lucid schizophrenic notwithstanding the absence of an appropriate adult and consequent breach of Code C. Drawing specific attention to Code C 'Notes for Guidance' 11C the Court of Appeal held the judge had erred by focusing on the lucidity and apparent facility with which the suspect had been able to cope with the interview instead of whether admission of the evidence would have such an adverse effect that it should have been excluded. The Notes for Guidance highlight the risk of 'unreliable, misleading or self-incriminating evidence' from juveniles and persons mentally handicapped. An important role of the appropriate adult is to advise on whether legal representation is needed and this is an aspect of a fair trial under art.6 of the ECHR. The Court held the judge had been wrong not to accede to a submission to exclude the confession evidence under s.78(1).

The warning

In *McKenzie* [1993] 96 Cr. App. R. 98 the Court of Appeal held that where the prosecution case depended wholly on a confession from a person suffering from a significant degree of mental handicap; and the confession was unconvincing to a point where a properly directed jury could not properly convict on it (because it lacked the detail to be expected from a guilty and willing confessor, or because it was inherently unreliable, or because it was inconsistent with other evidence) then the trial judge should withdraw the case from the jury. It may be questioned why this statement is limited to persons suffering from mental handicap. It may also be questioned why such a case ever reached a trial court.

If the confession is not so unconvincing that the case is withdrawn from the jury, once the threshold conditions in s.77(1) are met, the warning is mandatory. The warning should refer to the risk of 'unreliable, misleading or self-incriminating evidence'; should include reference to the defendant's mental characteristics, and should explain the role of the (absent) independent adult.

6.13 Summary

(a) A confession is a statement either wholly or partly against the interest of the person making it.

(b) Subject to exceptions, a confession is evidence only against the person who made it.

(c) Admissibility of a confession in the hands of the prosecution is governed by PACE s.76(2). The prosecution must prove the admissibility conditions otherwise the confession must be excluded.

(d) Admissibility of a confession is a matter for the judge at a voir dire. The weight to be given to a confession is for the jury.

(e) A confession may be excluded by the court in exercise of judgment under s.78(1) of PACE.

(f) There is a limited range of circumstances where a co-defendant may be permitted to adduce the defendant's confession even if the prosecution cannot.

Figure 42—Chapter summary flow chart

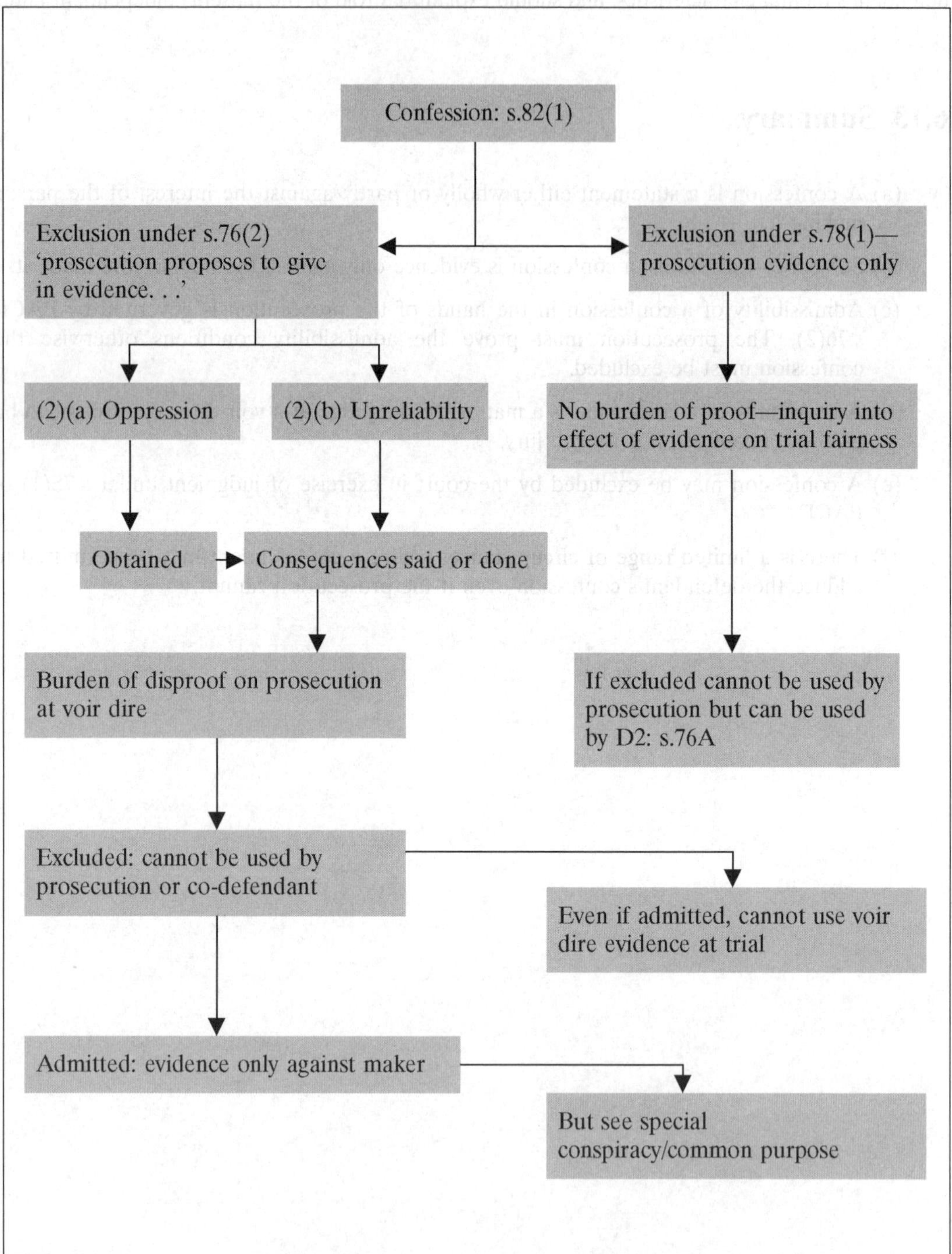

6.14 Further reading

Mirfield, Allen [1985] Crim LR 569, 572
Pattenden, Murphy 'Should Confessions be Corroborated?' (1991) 107 L.Q.R. 317
Smith, 'Proving Conspiracy' [1996] Crim. L.R. 386
Smith, 'More on Proving Conspiracy' [1997] Crim. L.R. 333
Smith, Professor [1995] 'The Presumption of Innocence' Crim. L.R. 280
Criminal Law Revision Committee 11th Report Cmnd 4991
Royal Commission on Criminal Procedure Cmnd 8092

7 Evidence Illegally, Improperly or Unfairly Obtained

All statutory references in this chapter are to the Police and Criminal Evidence Act 1984 (PACE) unless otherwise indicated.

7.1 Introduction

There are occasions when we read in the papers or hear on television that the police obtained evidence that a person had committed an offence by secretly tape-recording (some might say 'bugging') an interview room at a police station when a solicitor and a suspect believed they were having a private conversation or, having intelligence that a passenger on an aircraft is a courier smuggling a large quantity of drugs, the police and customs facilitate his arrival into the country arresting him only when he meets his contact. Conduct or operations like these give rise to a number of questions.

- What are the pros and cons of obtaining evidence in this way?
- Should the courts entertain prosecutions where evidence has been obtained in this way?
- If they do, do the judges have discretion to exclude it?
- If they do, how should the judges exercise the discretion?

These kinds of issues are covered in para.7.2.

A further matter can be raised. Suppose a covertly-made tape recording revealed the whereabouts of stolen property or the commission of other offences. If the court decided to exclude the evidence of the tape recording, does it follow that evidence of the finding of the property or other offences would or should also be excluded? This question is considered in para.7.3.

The next part of the chapter (para.7.4) deals with how the courts have dealt with breaches of the Codes of Practice under PACE particularly in respect of Code C which deals with the protection and rights of suspects in custody. This is followed (in para.7.5) by an outline of police powers of arrest and detention conditions.

Before we go any further it is vital to understand that this chapter is concerned with the exclusion of admissible evidence, in other words, evidence which passes the relevance test and which is not subject to any evidential rule of exclusion—you must bear this in mind all the way through the chapter. References to evidence 'improperly' obtained should be read as covering evidence obtained in breach of the law, of Codes of Practice or through some other means which, it is alleged, would give rise to an unfair trial.

7.2 Exclusion of evidence improperly obtained

7.2.1 Common law exclusion

The courts could have decided that if the police (or other State agencies) act improperly, any evidence subsequently obtained should be excluded—the 'fruit of the forbidden tree' principle. Why did they not do so?

Where the evidence, albeit obtained improperly, is relevant to the prosecution's case why should the courts burden themselves with a strict principle that improper means would automatically lead to exclusion? Would any breach of the law, regulations or unfairness, even though minor, lead to exclusion? Suppose that some improperly obtained evidence revealed a conspiracy to murder. Is such evidence also to be excluded because it was the consequence of minor impropriety? The law is often concerned with balancing means and ends and this is an example of the problem. It may have been such considerations which led Crompton J. in *Leathem* (1861) 30 L.J.Q.B. 205 to say: 'It matters not how you get it; if you steal it even, it would be admissible in evidence'.

His Lordship's statement needs to be viewed with caution. In the first place as we saw in Ch.6, the common law limited how confessions might properly be obtained from suspects. Second, in *A v Secretary of State for the Home Department (No. 2)* [2005] UKHL 71 the House of Lords reversed the decision of the Court of Appeal ([2005] 1 W.L.R. 414) which had upheld the power of UK administrative tribunals and the Special Immigration Appeals Commission to receive evidence obtained by official torture in foreign countries without the involvement of British authorities when reviewing the use of Control Orders under UK anti-terrorist legislation. Lord Bingham said:

> 'principles of common law, standing alone, compelled the exclusion of third party torture evidence as unreliable, unfair, offensive to ordinary standards of humanity and decency and incompatible with the principles which should animate a tribunal seeking to administer justice.'

The United Kingdom is signatory to International Conventions which prohibit the use of torture.

Notwithstanding what Crompton L.J. said in *Leathem* the superior courts claimed discretion to exclude (admissible) evidence where they considered its *use* would prejudice a fair trial. While the judges did not seek to discipline the police by excluding improperly obtained evidence (they did not see that as their role) they nevertheless claimed to be guardians of the use of such evidence in court. The leading common law authority on the discretion to exclude is *Sang* [1979] 69 Cr. App. R. 282 where the House of Lords unanimously agreed (ratio) there was no discretion to exclude the evidence of an agent provocateur, even assuming that the defendant would not otherwise have committed the offence. The simplest way of explaining *Sang* is that since there is no defence of entrapment in the substantive criminal law, it was inappropriate for the law of evidence, which is part of the adjectival law, to exclude evidence obtained in such circumstances by means of exclusionary discretion.

The case revealed some agreement but also wide disagreement between the judges in the House as to the basis and extent of the common law discretion to exclude admissible evidence. The agreement was that judges can always exclude evidence the prejudicial effect of which outweighs its probative value. The detail of the disagreement need not detain us though put shortly it was between, on the one hand, those judges who considered the discretion to exclude improperly obtained evidence existed only in specific and well established areas of the law of evidence and, on the other, those who took the view that the overall duty of a judge is to obtain a trial fair to both sides. For the latter group the discretion could not be limited to the well established areas.

In the years between *Sang* and the implementation of s.78(1) the narrower approach gained ascendancy. As we shall see below, later cases considered the relationship of *Sang* to s.78(1). In *Smurthwaite, Gill* [1994] 1 All E.R. 898 Lord Taylor C.J. reiterated that the common law does not recognise a defence of entrapment and that a 'purely evidential provision in a statute' cannot be taken to have altered that part of *Sang*. Nevertheless, he acknowledged that s.78(1) could lead to 'entrapment' evidence being excluded in the exercise of discretion and, in this sense, s.78(1) 'clearly turns the common law position on its head.' This is not to say that *Sang* has been over ruled but whatever its status as authority, s.82(3) expressly preserves the common law power of 'a court to exclude evidence (whether by preventing questions being put or otherwise) at its discretion'. Currently the only clear use of s.82(3) is where prosecution evidence has been admitted and the judge subsequently decides it should be excluded. Since s.78(1) refers to refusing prosecution evidence 'to be given' it is now too late to employ s.78(1) but s.82(3) comes to the rescue.

7.2.2 Section 78(1)

> 'In any proceedings the court may refuse to allow evidence on which the prosecution proposes to rely to be given if it appears to the court that, having regard to all the circumstances, including the circumstances in which the evidence was obtained, the admission of the evidence would have such an adverse effect on the fairness of the proceedings that the court ought not to admit it.'

The key issues arising from s.78(1) are as follows.

(i) It applies to evidence on which the prosecution (not the defence) proposes to rely. As we just saw, s.78(1) cannot be used (to 'dis-admit') once the court has admitted it.

(ii) The section does not refer to fairness to either of the parties but simply to 'fairness'. In *Christou* (1992) 95 Cr. App. R. 264 Lord Taylor said the concept of fairness under the section and at common law was identical.

(iii) It applies to *any* evidence (though only on which the prosecution proposes to rely) so embraces admissions or confessions—there is overlap with s.76(2). It seems, however, that in contrast to s.76(2) where causality is crucial, no third party act or omission need be proved before exclusion can be ordered under s.78(1): *Brine* [1992] Crim. L.R. 122.

(iv) It refers to 'proceedings' not to 'trial'. The word 'proceedings' seems to have been a deliberate choice—contrast ss.77 and 79 where the word used is 'trial'. 'Proceedings' is clearly wider than 'trial' and encompasses everything from questioning a person whether or not they are detained: *Christou* 285 (per Lord Taylor).

(v) While the subsection appears to be based on discretion rather than on rules, appearances are deceptive. Once the judge decides the evidence would have the necessary adverse effect on the fairness of the proceedings, then it must be excluded. This process is a judgment not discretion: *Middlebrook, The Times*, February 18, 1994. 'May', it appears, means 'shall'.

(vi) The adverse effect required must be more than minimal—the word 'such' makes this clear while not setting a particular threshold. In s.101(1) of the CJA 2003 words such as 'important' and 'substantial' are employed as the threshold test of admissibility of evidence of bad character. Is 'such' the PACE equivalent? 'Such' does convey the idea that fairness is not 'all-or-nothing' but a matter of degree and is relative to other issues in the proceedings. There is no laundry list of items comprising 'fairness'—the courts must take account of all relevant circumstances from differing points of view.

(vii) It applies only to criminal proceedings including extradition proceedings in a criminal cause or matter: *R. v Governor of Brixton Prison Ex p. Levin* [1998] 1 Cr. App. R. 22. Lord Hoffmann said that there could be little room for the exercise of discretion in such proceedings because extradition is based on reciprocity of international obligations which would be adversely affected if the courts were to superimpose discretions based on local notions of fairness.

(viii) In *R. v Governor of Brixton Prison Ex p. Saifi* [2001] 1 W.L.R. 1134 Rose L.J. held it was inappropriate to refer to either party as having evidential or proof burdens under the section. Each party simply tries to persuade the court to its point of view and so with regard to proof or evidential burdens, s.78(1) is neutral [52]. Where there is a dispute as to the facts (*Bryce* (1992) 95 Cr. App. R. 320) the court must first satisfy itself as best it can as to the facts before making judgments on abuse of process or exclusion of evidence.

(ix) Most commentators agree that the words of the subsection were designed to widen the common law—particularly the phrase 'including the circumstances in which the evidence was obtained.' PACE came into force in January 1986. Initially the judges seemed to harbour doubts about the scope of s.78(1). In *Mason* (1987) 86 Cr. App. R. 349 Watkins L.J. said the section 'does no more than to restate the power which the judges had at common law before the Act was passed'. This view was confirmed in *Chalkley* [1998] 2 Cr. App. R. 79 where the Court of Appeal upheld the narrower view of the House of Lords in *Sang*. The judgment is comprehensively savaged by Dennis (pp.98–99) who asserts that *Chalkey* is inconsistent with other decisions of the same court and that Auld L.J. wrongly introduced a test of reliability of the evidence into the decision whether to exclude it. Arguing that evidence produced by the worst excesses of conduct may be of excellent quality, Dennis says that *Chalkley* is wrongly decided on this point too. We shall return to a consideration of *Chalkley* at para.7.2.4.4.

Article 6 of the European Convention on Human Rights

As we saw in Ch.1 under s.3 of the HRA courts are required to interpret all primary and subordinate legislation in a way which is compatible with the ECHR. Article 6, like s.78(1), is based on fairness but refers to a 'hearing' rather than 'proceedings.' It reads as follows:

> '1. In the determination of his civil rights and obligations or of any criminal charge against him, everyone is entitled to a fair and public hearing within a reasonable time by an independent and impartial tribunal established by law. Judgment shall be pronounced publicly but the press and public may be excluded from all or part of the trial in the interests of morals, public order or national security in a democratic society, where the interests of juveniles or the protection of the private life of the parties so require, or to the extent strictly necessary in the opinion of the court in special circumstances where publicity would prejudice the interests of justice.
> 2. Everyone charged with a criminal offence shall be presumed innocent until proved guilty according to law.
> 3. Everyone charged with a criminal offence has the following minimum rights;
>   (a) to be informed promptly, in a language which he understands and in detail, of the nature and cause of the accusation against him;
>   (b) to have adequate time and facilities for the preparation of his defence;
>   (c) to defend himself in person or through legal assistance of his own choosing or, if he has not sufficient means to pay for legal assistance, to be given it free when the interests of justice so require;
>   (d) to examine or have examined witnesses against him and to obtain the attendance and examination of witnesses on his behalf under the same conditions as witnesses against him;
>   (e) to have the free assistance of an interpreter if he cannot understand or speak the language used.'

The function of the ECtHR is to ensure a fair trial but the Court does not lay down rules on the admissibility of evidence—this is regulated by national law: *Schenk v Switzerland* (1988) 13 E.H.R.R. 242. The Court cannot therefore exclude evidence which is admissible under national law even where it was obtained improperly under national law—its obligation is to determine whether the trial was fair.

The role of the Court of Appeal

In *O'Leary* (1988) 87 Cr. App. R. 387 the Court of Appeal said it is for the trial judge to decide whether the evidence 'would' have the unfair effect on the trial stated in s.78(1). Only if the Court of Appeal is satisfied that his decision is '*Wednesbury* unreasonable' (*Associated*

Provincial Picture Houses v Wednesbury Corporation [1948] 1 K.B. 223) will the Court of Appeal substitute its own judgment for that of the judge. *Mason* is an example of such a substitution. The police lied to a suspect and his solicitor whose advice was based directly on the effect of the lie.

7.2.3 **Abuse of process—staying the proceedings**

Staying is a common law power (*Connelly v DPP* [1964] A.C. 1254) which, until fairly recently, mainly related to claims of undue delay in bringing cases to trial. When a defendant makes a successful application to have proceedings terminated as an abuse of process, the prosecution is stayed. Strictly, therefore, an application to stay does not raise evidential issues because no evidence is heard. The finding of abuse of process acts as a remedy for the defendant. In *Loosely* [2001] UKHL 53 the House of Lords said that the doctrine of abuse of process has two strands as follows:

'(i) Protection of citizens from being lured into acts forbidden by law and then being prosecuted for them. Lord Nicholls described [1] this as 'misuse of state power and an abuse of the process of the courts . . . unattractive consequences, frightening and sinister in extreme cases . . .'

(ii) 'The integrity of the criminal justice process' (per Lord Hoffman [36]) which must not be compromised by accepting prosecutions based on manifestly unacceptable practices by law enforcement officers. Ashworth says this strand is about the courts as the guardians of the rule of law and human rights' ([2002] Crim. L.R. 161, 163).

There is overlap between staying for abuse of process and exclusion under s.78(1) which applies later in the proceedings. Where an application to stay succeeds proceedings are halted, whereas even if a submission under s.78(1) succeeds, the prosecution may be able to proceed without the excluded evidence. However, trials do not always develop logically and evidence sufficient to stay the proceedings may emerge once the trial is underway. If so an application to exclude under s.78(1) is effectively an application to stay and should be approached by the judge as though it were.

Where conduct of the investigating agency is grossly improper, a stay may be appropriate even if there is substantial incriminating evidence not tainted with impropriety. In *Grant* [2005] EWCA Crim 1089 Laws L.J. said [55] even where there is gross impropriety the courts must take account of the need to protect the public from serious crime and this 'may militate in favour of a refusal to stay'. His Lordship also held [45] that the burden of proof of abuse of process lies on the defendant on a balance of probability. The police had covertly recorded conversations between the defendant and his solicitor in the station exercise yard. The tape yielded nothing that was relied on by the prosecution at trial or which undermined the defence but the court quashed the defendant's conviction holding it to be a deliberate violation of the right to professional legal advice and an affront to the integrity of the justice system. At [57], citing *S v Switzerland* 14 E.H.R.R. 670 and *Niemietz v Germany* 16 E.H.R.R. 97, his Lordship said:

'We are quite clear that the deliberate interference with a detained suspect's right to the confidence of privileged communications with his solicitor, such as we have found was done here, seriously undermines the rule of law and justifies a stay on grounds of abuse of process, notwithstanding the absence of prejudice consisting in evidence gathered by the crown as the fruit of police officers' unlawful conduct.'

7.2.4 **Entrapment**

Dictionary definitions of 'entrapment' include:

- 'to catch as in a trap; to ensnare; to entangle';
- 'the luring, by a police officer, of a person into committing a crime so that he may be prosecuted for it'.

We will start this discussion with an outline of the facts from a small selection of decided cases. You might consider whether you would admit the evidence as well as the reason for your decision.

The facts

In *H* [1987] Crim. L.R. 47 a woman made a complaint of rape against her boyfriend who was interviewed under caution, and released pending further enquiries. The woman then instigated a series of telephone conversations with the man which, with the assistance of the police, were tape-recorded, though she denied it when asked by him. The prosecution sought to use the tapes in evidence.

In *Christou* in an area plagued by robberies, the police set up a spoof jeweller's shop and video-taped (amongst other persons) thieves selling the proceeds of their robberies to undercover police officers. The prosecution sought to use the tapes in evidence.

In *Bryce* an undercover police officer, in two conversations, asked how 'warm' (i.e. recently stolen) a Saab motor car was and received allegedly incriminating replies. The prosecution wished to use the replies in evidence. There was no recording of the alleged conversations.

In *Williams v DPP* [1993] 3 All E.R. 365, with authorisation, police parked a van containing (dummy) cigarette packets in a street having a high incidence of vehicle theft. The appellants were arrested when they stole the packets.

The decisions

H: evidence excluded. The whole venture (a telephone 'sting') was designed to obtain evidence of admissions to an offence when it was by no means clear that one had been committed.

Christou: evidence admitted. Any trick had been applied by the defendants to themselves. The argument that this device bypassed Code C on questioning was untenable—the Codes were not designed to apply to such circumstances.

Bryce: evidence excluded. The questions went directly to the heart of criminality and guilty knowledge in particular.

Williams: evidence admitted—the police had neither incited, counselled nor procured the commission of an offence.

Whatever decision you came to about admission of the evidence, you may well also have found you had different reasons for your decisions. This is partly explained by the wide variety of factual circumstances in the cases. As we saw above, 'fairness' does not lend itself to a tick box or laundry list approach—it is the circumstances of individual cases which decide the decision to admit or exclude. The fairness of the proceedings can be violated in a variety of ways. As we shall see in the next section trial courts have not been left without some guidelines on admissibility when deciding admissibility under s.78(1).

7.2.4.1 **A test of entrapment**

Notwithstanding some inconsistency, the courts have generally treated interference with the right to confidential legal advice as serious enough to lead to exclusion: *Mason* (above). There has been forthright condemnation as in *Toseland* (unreported), *The Times* January 30, 2002 where Newman J. termed police conduct a 'flagrant breach of the law' adding that the police had:

> 'made a mockery of the caution. They undermined and infringed the statutory right of a defendant to confer with a solicitor in private. His right is meaningless if the officers wait for him to go out with his solicitor so they can . . . listen to what he declined to mention.'

Other than in the area of legal advice, however, the initial approach was case-by-case, weighing the factual issues involved and it was not until *Smurthwaite, Gill* that the Court of Appeal attempted to give guidance on the limits of acceptable conduct and where lines might be drawn. In that case Lord Taylor C.J. asked:

- does the evidence consist of admissions to a completed offence or does it consist of the actual commission of the offence;
- how active or passive was the officer in obtaining the evidence;
- has there been any abuse by officers of their role? Even if there has been, in *Marshall & Downes* [1988] 3 All E.R. 683 the Court of Appeal held that the presence or absence of improper conduct is not a single issue determining exclusion;
- how complete and convincing is any record that was or should have been made of the events (see *Bryce* above); is there any corroboration of the events?

Ashworth ([2002] Crim. L.R. 161, 162) is critical of the list as 'general and descriptive', and says it may be difficult to use it as a guide to conduct. There are simply too many factual variables to make it useful. The active/passive question has also attracted comment. It tends to suggest a distinction between an act and an omission and, as such, is at best unhelpful and probably plain misleading. What Lord Taylor C.J. may have had in mind was that undercover officers may well 'go along' with certain events to maintain their cover (passive) as opposed to instigating/causing an offence (active). In *Loosely* Lord Hoffman [69] said:

> 'undercover officers who infiltrate conspiracies to murder, rob or commit terrorist offences could hardly remain concealed unless they showed some enthusiasm for the enterprise. A

good deal of active behaviour in the course of an authorised operation may therefore be acceptable without crossing the boundary between causing the offence to be committed and providing an opportunity for the defendant to commit it.'

The key issue in entrapment cases is causing/providing an opportunity and it is around this idea that this part of the test needed to be formulated.

7.2.4.2 **Conjoined appeals: *Loosely*; Attorney General's Reference No. 3 of 2000 [2001] UKHL 53**

Loosely

Loosely (L) and another defendant (H) were charged with supplying heroin to an undercover police officer (R). The police had mounted an undercover operation because of concern about the trade in Class A drugs in the area. One focus of the operation was a public house where a man provided R with L's first name and phone number and suggested R should telephone L if he wished to obtain drugs. R phoned L and said: 'Hello, mate, can you sort us out a couple of bags?' to which L replied, 'Er yes, I'll sort you out, mate'. At L's flat a price of £30 for half a gram of heroin was agreed. L and R then drove to H's flat in R's car. L left the car, taking £30 from R. He returned a few moments later saying that he had 'the stuff'. On return to the L's flat L took a package from his mouth, took a small quantity of the contents for himself, giving the remainder to R. The package was found to contain 152 milligrams of heroin at 100 per cent purity. This was repeated on two further occasions in the next seven days.

Having heard evidence at a voir dire from R and the officer in charge of the operation the judge declined either to stay the indictment as an abuse of process or to exclude the evidence pursuant to s.78(1). L changed his pleas to guilty.

The Court of Appeal dismissed L's appeals against conviction but certified the following point of law of general public importance for the opinion of the House.

> 'Should the judge have refused to admit the evidence of (R) because the role played by (R) went beyond mere observation and involved asking (L) to supply him with heroin, a request to which, on the judge's findings, (L) readily agreed?'

Attorney General's Reference No. 3 of 2000

The defendant (D) was charged with supplying or being concerned in the supply of a class A drug. Undercover police officers had approached S and asked if he wished to purchase contraband cigarettes. S took the officers to D and during conversation the officers asked D if he could supply them with some 'brown'. Further conversation followed in which D was persuaded by the officers to supply them with heroin. He indicated that he was 'not into heroin' himself and also that since the police were obtaining cheap cigarettes for him 'a favour was a favour.' The trial judge stayed the prosecution on the ground that the police had no reasonable grounds to suspect that D was involved in the supply of class A drugs and had gone too far in inducing such supply by the offer of cheap cigarettes. D was acquitted but the Attorney General referred a point of law to the Court of Appeal in the following terms.

> 'In a case involving the commission of an offence by (D) at the instigation of undercover police officers, to what extent, if any, have (i) the judicial discretion conferred by s.78 of

(PACE); and (ii) the power to stay the proceedings as an abuse of the process of the court been modified by Article 6 of the European Convention for the Protection of Human Rights and Fundamental Freedoms and the jurisprudence of the European Court of Human Rights?'

On appeal the House held neither the power to stay nor the power to exclude under s.78(1) have been modified by art.6, and that the two national powers are in conformity with the article. Lord Hoffman answered in curious terms [81] ('To this question I would give the same answer as the Court of Appeal, namely that no modification is required'.) which tends to make us wonder whether he had read it.

Judgment on the conjoined appeals—the 'unexceptional opportunity' test

The House accepted as the key test a distinction made by Lord Bingham C.J. in *Nottingham City Council v Amin* [2000] 1 Cr. App. R. 426. The defendant was charged with plying for hire without a licence. Two special constables in plain-clothes had hailed his cab in an area for which he was unlicensed and he had conveyed them for a fare. Lord Bingham drew a distinction between where:

(i) the defendant commits a crime only because he had been 'incited, instigated, persuaded, pressurised or wheedled into committing it by a law enforcement officer' (police cause the offence); and

(ii) the officer gave the defendant a chance to break the law (opportunity/'virtue testing') and the defendant freely took it in circumstances where he would have behaved the same way if it had been offered by anyone else.

Moon [2004] EWCA Crim 2872 is an example of police causing the offence. An undercover police officer posing as an addict suffering withdrawal symptoms approached the defendant on four occasions to supply her with drugs. The Court of Appeal held the defendant had no disposition towards dealing and the officer had caused the crime to be committed.

In *Amin* the police acted in the same way as any member of the public wanting a cab would have done. This is the 'unexceptional opportunity' test. Lord Bingham emphasised (436) that the key issue was whether the defendant had a fair trial overall and not the fairness of any subordinate process in isolation. What this is supposed to mean on the facts is anybody's guess.

Applying the test to the facts of the conjoined appeals the House affirmed Loosely's convictions—the officers had done no more than present themselves as customers for drugs. In the *Reference* the police had gone much further, instigating an offence the defendant would not otherwise have committed. In the words of Lord Nicholls [23] the police had created 'crime artificially'. The judge had been correct and the Court of Appeal wrong.

7.2.4.3 **The 'unexceptional opportunity' test in practice**

Some statutory provisions such as the Trade Descriptions Act 1968 s.27 and the Criminal Justice and Police Act 2001 s.31 authorise 'test purchases'. Test purchasers are appropriately trained law enforcement officers who seek 'by means of authorised activity, to establish the nature and/or availability of a commodity or service, the possession, supply or use of which involves an offence'. (*Undercover Operations Code of Practice* issued jointly by all UK police authorities and HM Customs and Excise). The statutory provisions do not extend to drugs purchases.

> 'No doubt a test purchaser who asks someone to sell him a drug is counselling and procuring, perhaps inciting, the commission of an offence. Furthermore, he has no statutory defence to a prosecution.' (Per Lord Hoffman in *Loosely* [70])

Outside the statutory areas, the unexceptional opportunity test should work well in straightforward virtue testing cases such as *Amin* or *London Borough of Ealing v Woolworths Plc* [1995] Crim. L.R. 58. The latter was a prosecution under the Video Recordings Act 1984 s.11 where the test purchaser was a boy of 11 years. The magistrates concluded that the Trading Standards Department had acted 'ultra vires' and excluded the evidence under s.78(1). The Divisional Court held that the boy had not entrapped the respondent; had not acted as an agent provocateur; nor incited, aided or abetted the commission of an offence by the respondent. There was no pressure on the shop assistant. To prevent evidence being gathered in this way would 'emasculate the enforcement of a sensible piece of legislation'. The Court added that the Act had been passed for the protection of young people (though it did not consider whether giving evidence in such cases might have an adverse effect on young people).

Three unresolved problems

First, the test applies only to 'unexceptional opportunities' to break the law. What is the definition of such opportunities? How do we distinguish them from the 'exceptional'? According to Lord Hoffman in *Loosely* [55] unexceptional opportunities seems to be limited to 'regulatory offences committed with ordinary members of the public'. Is there an intermediate category between the exceptional and the unexceptional? In *Jones* [2007] EWCA Crim 1118 a message seeking girls between 8 and 13 years for sex for payment was written on the toilet door of a train. Following a complaint by a member of the public an undercover police officer engaged the defendant in mobile phone text messages in which the officer said she was both under 13 and a virgin. The defendant was arrested at a meeting. The defendant argued he had been entrapped by the police into committing offences under the Sexual Offences Act 2003 in relation to inciting sexual conduct with a girl under 13 years. The Court of Appeal, applying the unexceptional opportunity test, dismissed the appeal. Although the officer had taken part in a pretence it did not go beyond providing the defendant with the opportunity to commit the incitement offence. The police certainly did not instigate the offence. As expressly acknowledged by Thomas L.J. [32], the case went far beyond the sphere of regulatory offences—the offence under s.8(2) of the Sexual Offences Act 2003 carries a maximum of life imprisonment.

Secondly, since, by definition, the test applies only to the unexceptional, what should be the correct test for staying or exclusion of evidence in the exceptional crimes such as contract-killing, conspiracy to rob or large-scale drug dealing? Part of the answer to this question is provided by the House in *Loosely*, where it was accepted that it must sometimes be necessary to employ proactive conduct or to engage in some kind of subterfuge. Additionally, in *Teixeira de Castro v Portugal* (1999) 28 E.H.R.R. 101 the ECtHR held there are two key elements in entrapment cases. First there must be proper supervision of this type of operation following a decision to target a particular person. Secondly, predisposition is crucial—it must be shown that the defendant had a pre-disposition towards such a crime—normally from his previous convictions. In *Loosely* the House of Lords accepted the first principle but declined the second partly on the ground that it can operate unfairly against those with previous convictions but in respect of whom there are no current suspicions. Lord Nicholls [21] said the difficulty with using predisposition as a criterion is that:

> '. . . whenever the defendant's predisposition to commit the crime is established there cannot be a defence of entrapment . . . but surely it is going too far to say that a person who is ready and willing to commit a certain kind of crime can never be entrapped into committing it. As Lamer J observed in *R v Mack* (1988) 44 CCC (3d) 513, 551, it is always possible that, notwithstanding a person's predisposition, in the particular case it was the conduct of the police which led the defendant into committing the crime. In other words, the existence or absence of predisposition in the individual is not the criterion by which the acceptability of police conduct is to be decided. Predisposition does not make acceptable what would otherwise be unacceptable conduct on the part of the police or other law enforcement agencies. Predisposition does not negative misuse of state power.'

The House preferred reasonable suspicion to predisposition. Reasonable suspicion helps to ensure the police act in good faith and not merely on personal characteristics. For example, knowledge that a person is a drug addict would be insufficient to suspect them of dealing. Lord Nicholls [28] said that suspicion may not be of a person but may attach itself to premises: 'sometimes suspicion may be centred on a particular place, such as a particular public house'.

Thirdly the unexceptional opportunity test seems to require no more of the police than it would of an ordinary member of the public—hailing a cab in the street. However, by virtue of the *Undercover Code of Practice* referred to above test purchases must:

(i) be authorised by an officer of the rank of superintendent who must:

  (a) be satisfied that such a purchase is 'required in support of an investigation into a criminal offence' in respect of commodities or services; and that
  (b) reasonable grounds exist to suspect that such an offence is being committed.

Point (i) goes some way towards the supervision issue in *Texeira de Castro*, though the Code is limited to authorisation (stopping short of supervision), and the authorisation remains non-judicial. Points (ii) and (iii) would seem to rule out random virtue testing. There is no indication in the judgment in *Amin* that there was any reason to suppose that Mr Amin personally was committing licensing offences or that such offences were being committed in the City of Nottingham. If this is so, then the decision must plainly be wrong in the light of *Loosely*. The *Woolworth* case may well be similar. It also throws the decision in *Williams* into question. You will recall that the police, with authorisation, parked a transit van containing dummy cigarette packets in a street having a high incidence of vehicle theft. They had no idea of whom, if anyone, might attempt to interfere with the load and had certainly not 'targeted' any particular individuals. Professor Smith ([1993] Crim. L.R. 776) noted that the police certainly 'procured' the commission of an offence: if no one had attempted to steal the cigarettes, the police would have regarded the exercise as a 'failure'. In *Loosely*, Lord Hoffman [65] upheld this decision but on the single ground of authorisation. This is a virtue testing case but one where the police went much further than a member of the public possibly could. The temptation to crime is so great that, arguably, it amounts to instigation. In his judgment in *Williams* Farquharson L.J. described the police activity as an 'entirely legitimate enterprise . . . and of permissible character for the detection of crime'. This view may now be doubted. One well-known way for the police to prevent and detect crime is to put officers on the beat.

7.2.4.4 **Private entrapment**

The discussion so far has been concerned with improper activities by law enforcement officials. This has become known as 'executive lawlessness'. Do the principles outlined above apply to entrapment by private individuals (sometimes known as 'commercial lawlessness')? In *Shannon* [2001] 1 Cr. App. R. 168 the defendant had supplied drugs to a newspaper journalist posing as an Arab Sheik in a 'sting' designed to obtain evidence of drugs offences by him. The report indicates that the journalist acted on an informant's tip-off to the effect that the defendant was supplying drugs in show business circles but not why such suspicions were not referred to the police. The Court of Appeal rejected an instigation argument based on *Teixeira* though the facts seem hardly distinguishable. *Shannon* received tacit approval from Lord Nicholls [12] in *Loosely*. However, if the same principles govern both public and private entrapment, the question is whether *Shannon* seems more aligned with the *Attorney General's Reference* or with *Loosely*. The court did not deal with the issue of the lack of supervision of such operations—are newspaper journalists the new law enforcers and, if so, to what safeguards are they required to attend? The Court of Appeal approved its own previous decision in *Chalkley* though as we have seen its authority is dubious. As in *Chalkley*, the Court of Appeal in *Shannon* put much (misplaced) emphasis on the reliability of the evidence at the expense of the approach in *Smurthwaite*.

Shannon's application to the European Court of Human Rights was rejected as inadmissible (App. No. 67537/01) though the Court added that 'it cannot be excluded that evidence obtained as a result of entrapment by a private individual may render proceedings unfair'. On the facts there was no evidence of entrapment. (See *http://www.timesonline.co.uk/tol/news/uk/article716329.ece* (accessed March 31, 2008) for other fascinating activities of 'fake sheiks' in relation to the former England football manager Sven-Goran Eriksson and other high profile personalities.)

7.3 Facts discovered in consequence of inadmissible confessions

Suppose a suspect is questioned and makes a statement which is ruled inadmissible. Can it be shown either that property was found at a place mentioned by him in that statement or it was found 'as a consequence of what the suspect said'? The answers are provided by s.76(4)–(6) which read as follows:

> '(4) The fact that a confession is wholly or partly excluded in pursuance of this section shall not affect the admissibility in evidence—

(a) of any facts discovered as a result of the confession; or
(b) where the confession is relevant as showing that the accused speaks, writes or expresses himself in a particular way, of so much of the confession as is necessary to show that he does so.

(5) Evidence that a fact to which this subsection applies was discovered as a result of a statement made by an accused person shall not be admissible unless evidence of how it was discovered is given by him or on his behalf.
(6) Subsection (5) above applies—

(a) to any fact discovered as a result of a confession which is wholly excluded in pursuance of this section; and
(b) to any fact discovered as a result of a confession which is partly so excluded, if the fact is discovered as a result of the excluded part of the confession.'

The effect of these provisions is that the prosecution can adduce evidence of any fact discovered in consequence of an inadmissible confession (s.76(4)) but unless the defendant gives evidence to this effect, the prosecution cannot show that the evidence came from his confession if the confession is inadmissible (s.76(5)). Evidence can be admitted from the admissible part of a partly excluded confession (s.76(6)(b)). The purpose of s.76(4)(b) is shown by *Voisin* [1918–19] All E.R. Rep. 491. The dismembered body of a woman was found in a parcel together with a piece of paper on which were written the words 'Bladie Belgiam'. The defendant was in police custody in respect of the offence but had not been cautioned. He was asked if he would be willing to write the words 'Bloody Belgian' and voluntarily wrote it 'Bladie Belgiam'. It was held that the words were admissible to prove the way in which the defendant wrote. This was followed in *Nottle* [2004] EWCA Crim 599. It was alleged the defendant had a grievance against a person named Justin and that he had scratched the words 'Fuck you Jutin' on some cars owned by Justin's father. When invited by the police to write the words in question he wrote 'Jutin' on 12 occasions.

Apart from the limited purpose of subs.(6)(a), the confession is not evidence of its contents.

7.4 Section 78(1) and the courts' approach to breaches of the PACE Codes of Practice

In this section, we are concerned with the possible exclusion of evidence due to breaches of the Codes of Practice under PACE. This is the full list of Codes with outline explanation of content from the Home Office website.

Figure 43—Content of PACE codes

Code	Content
A	The exercise by police officers of statutory powers to search a person or a vehicle without first making an arrest. It also deals with the need for a police officer to make a record of a stop or encounter.
B	Police powers to search premises and to seize and retain property found on premises and persons.
C	Requirements for the detention, treatment and questioning of suspects not related to terrorism in police custody by police officers.
D	Main methods used by the police to identify people in connection with the investigation of offences and the keeping of accurate and reliable criminal records.
E	Tape recording of interviews with suspects in the police station.
F	Visual recording with sound of interviews with suspects. There is no statutory requirement on police officers visually to record interviews. However, the contents of this code should be considered if an interviewing officer decides to make a visual recording with sound of an interview with a suspect.
G	Powers of arrest under section 24 the Police and Criminal Evidence Act 1984 as amended by section 110 of the Serious Organised Crime and Police Act 2005.
H	Requirements for the detention, treatment and questioning of suspects related to terrorism in police custody by police officers.

http://police.homeoffice.gov.uk/operational-policing/powers-pace-codes/pace-code-intro/ (accessed March 28, 2008).

As we noted (see para.7.2.2 above) s.78(1) is sufficiently wide to cover confessions so there is overlap with s.76(2). While many of the cases under s.78(1) are concerned with exclusion of confessions for Code breaches, the subsection extends to exclusion of any evidence on which the prosecution proposes to rely. There is, therefore, scope to seek exclusion (for Code breaches) of non-confession evidence where its admission would adversely affect the fairness of the proceedings. A breach of Code D with regard to identification procedures would be one example; breach of Code B followed by finding of incriminating objects (*Stewart* [1995] Crim. L.R. 550) would be another. Where the submission is for exclusion of a confession, s.76(2) is advantageous in that it is rule-based as well as being explicit as to the burden of proof. Generally (see para.7.7.2(viii)) no issue as to the burden of proof will arise under s.78(1) which is concerned with persuading the court to a point of view. If there is a dispute as to some factual issue the burden should be on the party alleging it to raise and prove it. Section 78(1) can cover issues arising after the confession was made—s.76(2) cannot be used in this way.

To whom do the Codes apply?

Section 67(9) extends the Codes of Practice to persons other than police officers, who are 'charged with the duty of investigating offences or charging offenders' In *Joy v Federation against Copyright Theft* [1993] Crim. L.R. 588 it was held that whether a person was charged with the duty of investigating offences was a question of fact and that the duty could arise by statute, at common law or through an employment contract. The magistrates had erred in holding that a person employed by the respondents was not covered by s.67(9) only because he was employed by a private company.

In *Smith* (1994) 99 Cr. App. R. 233 Neill L.J. likened 'investigating' to the sort of conduct required of a police officer. It does not follow that a person is 'charged with the duty of investigating offences' only because he receives information in the course of his employment which indicates that an offence has been committed. Decisions on this matter are fact-specific as the following table indicates.

Figure 44—Duty of 'investigating offences'

Case	Job	Codes Apply?
Okafor [1994] 3 All E.R. 741 *Sanusi* [1992] Crim. L.R. 43	Officers of Customs & Excise	Yes
Bayliss (1994) 98 Cr. App. R. 235	Store detective	Yes
RSPCA v Eager [1995] Crim. L.R. 59	RSPCA inspector	Yes
Director of Serious Fraud Office, Ex p. Saunders [1988] Crim. L.R. 837	Officers of the Serious Fraud Office	Yes
Seelig, Spens [1991] 4 All E.R. 429	Department of Trade & Industry inspectors during an investigation under Companies Acts	No
DPP v G, The Times, 24. November 1997	Head teacher interviewing teacher re possible assault on pupil	No
Twaites (1990) 92 Cr. App. R. 106	Company internal investigators	Yes
Dudley Metropolitan Borough Council v Debenhams Plc August 16, 1994	Trading standards officers	Yes
Devani [2007] EWCA Crim 1926	Prison employee monitoring CCTV in meetings between solicitor and prisoner Prison officer	No Yes

Exclusion

The Codes are concerned with procedural fairness and are designed to offer protection to a suspect during the investigative process. In *Walsh* (1989) 91 Cr. App. R. 161 Saville J. said the main object of PACE and the Codes was to achieve fairness, and to preserve and protect suspects' legal rights. Protection for the police against unjustified allegations is also important. If breaches of Codes were 'substantial and significant then the standards of fairness set by Parliament have not been met'.

If the police or others charged with a duty of investigating offences act in bad faith the evidence is likely to be excluded: *Alladice* (1988) 87 Cr. App. R. 380 (improper denial of access to solicitor). In *Canale* [1990] 91 Cr. App. R. 1 Lord Lane referred to 'flagrant, cynical and deliberate' breaches of Codes by the police which lead to confessions which should have been excluded by the judge. Acting in good faith does not necessarily mean evidence will be admitted. Exclusion is not automatic but the word 'such' in s.78(1) emphasises that the whole issue is a balancing exercise.

Key issues under Code C:

Right not to be held incommunicado and access to legal advice

The right not to be held incommunicado is provided by s.56 and the right to legal advice is provided by s.58. Codes C5 and 6 respectively contain provisions on these rights. The rights arise in respect of all offences and can be restricted in relation to indictable offences only. A suspect can waive his right to legal advice but such waiver is effective only if written (C3.5). The prosecution must justify refusal of access on one of the grounds in s.58(8) each of which starts 'will'. Improper refusal will usually (*Samuel* [1988] 87 Cr. App. R. 232; *Parris* (1988) 89 Cr. App. R. 68) though not invariably (*Alladice*; *Dunford* (1990) 91 Cr. App. R. 150) result in exclusion of a confession. The suspect's characteristics including his sophistication and knowledge of the legal system are relevant. Dunford was an experienced criminal, knew of his right to silence and not to sign the custody record, so breach of s.58 did not lead to exclusion of the confession. His solicitor's presence would not have made it less likely that he would have confessed.

'Interview'

The police may not question a person they suspect of having committed an offence except under caution if his answers are to be admissible in court: C10.1. The interview may, but need not, follow arrest: C11.1A. Tape recording of interviews is mandatory (Code E.3) for indictable and either-way offences. If not tape-recorded, notes must be made of any 'interview' wherever held: C11.7.

The Act and Codes apply only to 'interviews' which are defined in Code C11.1A as 'the questioning of a person regarding their involvement or suspected involvement in a criminal offence or offences' The interview is the point at which the protection of the Codes engages. Problems have arisen as to whether 'a few questions near to the scene of a crime' constitute an interview: *Weekes* (1993) 97 Cr. App. R. 222. If questioning has reached a stage where the Code safeguards are needed 'fairness demands . . . the provisions of the Code should be implemented'. (per Farquharson L.J.). The test is whether the questioning is designed to obtain admissions to an offence.

In *Ward* (1994) 98 Cr. App. R. 337 after arrest, and while still at the scene, a police officer's question 'Do you mean by that you were driving?' was held to be an interview. Similarly in *Miller* [1998] Crim. L.R. 209 the single question 'Are those ecstasy tablets?' was held to constitute an interview.

Tainting

Tainting refers to the possibility of exclusion of a subsequent, properly conducted interview because of the 'hang-over' effects of a previous improperly conducted interview. Exclusion is not invariable. The courts look at each case and ask what was the breach; how fundamental was it to the particular suspect; when was it, and how long did its effects last; did a solicitor at a second interview know of the previous breach etc.; what were the arrangements at the subsequent interview(s) and did they enable the suspect to exercise an informed and independent choice to repeat or retract their previous statements; was the breach deliberate? As might be expected, decisions cut both ways. The interviews were excluded in *McGovern* [1991] 92 Cr. App. R. 228 and *Gillard and Barrett* [1991] Crim. L.R. 124 but admitted in *Y* [1991] Crim. L.R. 917.

7.5 Summary

(a) In this chapter we have been concerned with the courts' power to exclude admissible evidence.

(b) The 19th century judges ruled that the courts were not concerned with the way in which evidence was obtained, only the use to which it was to be put in court.

(c) *Sang* is the leading common law authority on judicial discretion to exclude admissible evidence but its authority was weakened by fundamental disagreements in the obiter dicta. It has been overtaken by s.78(1) which is based on 'fairness' and permits the courts to take account of the way in which the evidence was obtained.

(d) Evidence obtained following improper conduct by the police may result in an application for a stay for abuse of process or an application to exclude on the ground of fairness under either s.78(1) or art.6 of the ECHR.

(e) Section 78(1) applies only to evidence on which the prosecution proposes to rely. In this respect it is similar to s.76(2). The section can cover evidence of any type, including admissions and confessions. There is overlap with s.76(2) in respect of the latter.

(f) Entrapment is not recognised as a defence in the criminal law but may be a ground for the exclusion of evidence under s.78(1).

(g) Exclusion for breach of the Codes of Practice is discretionary.

(h) Article 6 of the European Convention on Human Rights embodies the same test of fairness as s.78(1). The protection they afford extends to the whole criminal process starting with questioning prior to arrest.

(i) The ECtHR has repeatedly held that its function is not to validate or invalidate national legislation but to determine whether on the facts of a particular case, the defendant received a fair trial.

7.6 Summary of Police Powers of Arrest and Detention under PACE and Codes of Practice

Where in the course of an investigation a police officer has (reasonable: *James* [1995] Crim. L.R. 650) grounds to suspect a person has committed an offence, he must caution him and record that fact. The terms of the caution are contained in Code C10.5 as follows.

> 'You do not have to say anything. But it may harm your defence if you do not mention when questioned something which you rely on later in court. Anything you do say may be given in evidence.'

The officer may continue to question the suspect thereafter. Unless that person is under arrest, the officer who cautions him must also say that he is under no legal obligation to remain with the officer.

Offences are either:

(a) indictable; or
(b) summary; or
(c) either way; or
(d) recordable.

An offence is non-recordable *only* if it is not punishable by imprisonment and is not is not listed in the Schedule to the National Police Records (Recordable Offences) Regulations 2000 (as subsequently frequently amended).

Powers of arrest are contained in s.24.

Where the offence is indictable there are limitations, on some of the defendant's rights as well as enlargement of some police powers particularly extended periods of detention and access delays (ss.56 and 58). Taking of intimate and non-intimate samples (ss.62, 63 and 63A–C) is lawful only for a recordable offence.

The officer must tell the suspect of the fact of arrest and the grounds, even if obvious. Failure to do so will render the arrest unlawful, though subsequently telling the suspect renders the arrest lawful from that point.

On arrest, the police officer must caution the suspect and record the fact.

The police officer may then search the suspect if he has reasonable grounds to believe that he has with him any article which might represent evidence relating to an offence. The officer may search the premises where the arrest took place for evidence relating to the offence for which the suspect was arrested.

There is a further power to search, after arrest, the premises occupied or controlled by the suspect to look for evidence relating to that offence or connected with or similar to that offence, provided the officer has reasonable grounds for suspecting the evidence is on the premises. The search must be authorised in writing by an officer of at least the rank of inspector. Any relevant evidence may be seized and retained by the officer.

If the arrest is not valid, any search of the suspect or his premises will be unlawful, but this will not necessarily lead to exclusion of incriminating evidence discovered because the court may still admit it: s.78(1).

Following arrest, the suspect should be taken to a designated police station which has facilities for the detention of persons arrested.

At the police station, the suspect should be brought before a custody officer who must decide:

(a) whether there is evidence to charge the suspect and if there is he must be charged; or

(b) to detain him for questioning without charge or for the purpose of securing or preserving evidence relating to the offence for which he is under arrest. If any part of this applies, then the custody officer must open a custody record in respect of the detained person.

The duty of the custody officer is then to tell the detainee of the following rights (as well as to provide him with written notice to like effect):

(a) the right to know the reason for his detention, s.37(5); and

(b) the right to have someone informed of the fact of his arrest and place of detention if he so requests, and that he may be allowed to speak on the telephone to one person named by him, again if he so requests, s.56; and

(c) the right of access to free legal advice, if he so requests, s.58; and

(d) the right to consult the Codes of Practice.

Exercise of the right under (b) and (c) may be delayed for up to 36 hours on the written authority of a superintendent but only when the suspect has been arrested for an indictable offence (s.42(1)).

The consent of the custody officer is required (Code C12.1) before a person can be interviewed and, if a solicitor is on his way to the station then any such interview must not start until the solicitor arrives: Code C6.6 which also contains exceptions.

Once charged, Code C16.5 applies and the detainee must not be asked any further questions relating to that offence other than under the proviso to Code C16.5.

7.7 Further reading

Ashworth, 'Redrawing the Boundaries of Entrapment' [2002] Crim. L.R. 161

Choo, 'What's the Matter with s.78?' [1999] Crim. L.R. 929

Mirfield, 'Silence, Confessions and Improperly Obtained Evidence' (OUP 1997)

Ormerod and Birch, 'The Evolution of the Discretionary Exclusion of Evidence' [2004] Crim. L.R. 767

8 Silence

All statutory references in this chapter are to the Criminal Justice and Public Order Act 1994 (CJPOA) unless otherwise indicated.

8.1 Introduction

The common law drew a distinction between in-court and out-of-court silence which the CJPOA maintains. John Lilburn (1614–1657) is said to be mainly responsible for establishing the right to in-court silence, refusing to answer questions relating to charges of publishing heretical books partly because they were put to him in Latin rather than in English. Lilburn, a seventeenth century Leveller, told his judges that they were trying 'to ensnare me, foreseeing the things for which I am imprisoned cannot be proved against me'. He was pilloried but eight years later his appeal against punishment was allowed by the House of Lords who held it was 'contrary to the laws of nature and the Kingdom for any man to be his own accuser'.

At common law, it is not an offence to fail to answer questions whether from the police or anyone else, but there are statutory exceptions. Some agencies such as the Serious Fraud Office have extensive powers of investigation of offences and it can often be either an offence or a contempt of court not to answer their questions. We saw in Ch.2, para.2.2. that such answers are not generally admissible against the defendant in subsequent proceedings.

If a person voluntarily answers questions his answers are, subject to the law on confessions (see Ch.6), admissible in court. Two issues arise at common law where a person fails to answer questions, deny an allegation or give evidence in court.

(i) Is his failure virtually equivalent to the unspoken words 'You are correct' or 'I agree'? This explains why this area of law is said to be concerned with 'inferential confessions' from silence.

(ii) Is the judge entitled to comment at all on a person's failure to respond or to give evidence? If so, what should be the terms of any such comment?

The answers are as follows. The common law allows inferences to be drawn from a failure to respond to an accusation (or a statement/question akin to an accusation) but *only* where the parties are speaking 'on even terms' and where the circumstances objectively call for a reaction. We discuss this in detail at para.8.2.4. The common law also allowed the judge limited comment on a defendant's failure to respond or give evidence, but does not permit him to tell the jury they can draw an inference of guilt from silence. However, as you will see in the table below, this part of the law has been superceded by s.35 of the CJPOA.

While the common law continues to apply when the parties are on even terms, under CJPOA in four circumstances the jury may be directed they can draw adverse inferences.

Figure 45—Summary of sections 34–37 CJPOA

Section	Summary of content—failure to
34	mention facts when questioned by a police officer
35	give evidence or answer questions in court
36	account for objects, substances or marks on or about him
37	account for his presence at a particular place

Since the statutory position is now by far the most common, we shall study it first followed by the position at common law. Before we do, there are two points which should be borne in mind about the relationship of the statutory provisions to art.6 of the ECHR. The first is that juries do not have to give reasons for their verdicts so control over any adverse inferences the jury draws from the defendant's silence (either in-court or pre-trial) is limited to the judicial direction before they retire. Whether this is sufficient in terms of a fair trial is open to question.

Secondly, it is clear the courts have reservations about drawing inferences from silence because of possible breach of the privilege against self-incrimination. In *Beckles* [2004] EWCA Crim 2766, reiterating comments of the Court of Appeal in *Brizzalari* [2004] EWCA Crim 310, Lord Woolf discouraged 'too ready reliance by prosecutors on s.34' which is aimed primarily (he said) at ambush defences and/or possible defences following a 'no comment' interview. The volume and cost of the case law generated mainly by s.34 should make us wonder 'whether the game is worth the candle'. (Commentary to *Taylor* [1999] Crim. L.R. 77 by Professor Birch.)

8.2 CJPOA

8.2.1 Section 34—Effect of accused's failure to mention facts when questioned or charged

'(1) Where, in any proceedings against a person for an offence, evidence is given that the accused—

(a) at any time before he was charged with the offence, on being questioned under caution by a constable trying to discover whether or by whom the offence had been committed, failed to mention any fact relied on in his defence in those proceedings; or

(b) on being charged with the offence or officially informed that he might be prosecuted for it, failed to mention any such fact, being a fact which in the circumstances existing at the time the accused could reasonably have been expected to mention when so questioned, charged or informed, as the case may be, subsection (2) below applies.'

Under subs.(2), the court, in determining whether there is a case to answer and the court or jury, in determining whether the defendant is guilty of the offence charged, may draw such inferences from the failure as appear proper.

Key issues in s.34(1)

In the following table every question must be answered 'yes' before adverse inferences are permissible.

Was D questioned under caution?

Was questioning from police officer?

Was officer seeking to ascertain whether/by whom an offence had been committed?

Did D fail to mention a fact?

Did D subsequently rely on the fact?

Could D reasonably have been expected to mention the fact?

Although each question and answer is important, the key issue is 'subsequent reliance'. It is not failure to mention facts per se which makes the section bite—it is failure plus reliance. So if the defendant admits in cross-examination the truth of a fact relied on by the prosecution, no adverse inference should be drawn even though he did not mention it at interview: *Betts & Hall* [2001] EWCA Crim 224. Kay L.J. illustrated this as follows:

> '. . . if a defendant were to admit for the first time at trial that a fingerprint was his but say that he could offer no explanation for it being found where it was, he would have relied on no fact.'

In *Dervish* [2001] EWCA Crim 2789 the defendant gave a no comment interview and made no comment when charged but did rely on facts in his defence. The interview was excluded by the judge. It was held that although adverse inferences could not be drawn under s.34(1)(a) they could nevertheless be drawn under s.34(1)(b).

The object of s.34 is to ensure early disclosure of the defence not the scrutiny and testing of it by the police: *Knight* [2003] EWCA Crim 1977. In order to avoid the section biting, some defendants hand interviewing officers a prepared statement then refuse to answer questions at interview. The section cannot engage if the defendant does not rely on any facts other than those in the statement (*Ali* [2001] EWCA Crim 863) but otherwise it might. If there are significant differences between the content of the prepared statement and the defendant's evidence at trial it might be proper to draw an inference under s.34 or it might be possible to invoke common law and treat the statement as a lie: *Turner (Dwaine)* [2003] EWCA Crim 3108. There is a special form of jury direction (a *Lucas* Direction) in relation to lies which we consider at para.8.2.5. Although using a prepared statement may avoid s.34 inferences: (i) if the statement is wholly exculpatory it is not admissible as evidence of its contents (see Ch.6, para.6.2); and (ii) it will not avoid s.35 inferences if the defendant fails to give evidence or answer questions in court (see para.8.2.6).

No responses, no evidence

Section 34 does not apply where the defendant simply puts the prosecution to proof: *Bowers* [1998] Crim. L.R. 817. Rose L.J. said 'the jury must resolve two questions: first that the defence relied on a particular fact and secondly, that he had failed to mention it when questioned'. We shall deal with these two issues separately.

Reliance

In spite of what was said by Rose L.J., whether or not there has been reliance must be a matter for the judge. If there has been no reliance, the judge must not merely invite the jury not to draw an inference, he must instruct them directly not to do so: *McGarry* [1999] 1 Cr. App. R. 377 per Hutchinson L.J. This goes much further than *Bowers* where Rose L.J. said that such a direction 'might have been preferable'. The 'no reliance—no inference' aspect of *Bowers* was approved in *Webber* [2004] U.K.H.L. 1 where the House of Lords, relying on the unreported Northern Ireland case of *Devine* referred to 'probing the prosecution case' as different from relying on a fact.

A fact relied on may be established either by the defendant himself in evidence, by a witness in his behalf, or by a prosecution witness, either in examination in chief (though only if adopted by the defence) or in cross-examination: *Bowers*. The Court of Appeal dismissed the argument that the defendants had not relied on any fact only because they had not given evidence—it is not how the fact came to be proved but whether or not it is relied on. The court approved the view of the Court of Appeal for Northern Ireland in *McLernon* [1992] N.I. 168 that if defence counsel suggests to a prosecution witness a fact which assists the defence, and the witness accepts it, there is reliance.

In *Webber* the House of Lords approved *McLernon* but added two further dimensions. The appellant had made positive suggestions to prosecution witnesses—suggestions which were rejected. The House held that this was more than 'probing' and amounted to reliance. If, in marginal cases, the judge is unsure whether counsel is doing more than probing, Lord Bingham said that clarification should be sought in the jury's absence. The House further held that where a co-defendant adopts as part of his defence suggestions put to a prosecution witness in cross-examination by the defendant that also amounts to reliance by the co-defendant. Here is a summary of the position.

Figure 46—Reliance on a fact

D relies on a fact when or if	
D	gives evidence of the fact himself
D	calls witnesses who give evidence of the fact
D	cross-examines prosecution witnesses (PW) to establish the fact
D	relies on the fact under cross-examination by the prosecution
D2	accepts as part of his case suggestion made by D1 to PW

Reliance on a fact

As we have seen, the heading to s.34 states 'failure to mention facts'. It is perhaps surprising, therefore, that the caution does not use the word 'fact' but says 'it may harm your defence if you do not mention when questioned *something* which you later rely on in court'. (Emphasis supplied). In *Webber* the House made it clear both that reliance triggers the section and it is reliance on a fact—not a 'matter', or an 'issue' or theories or failure to answers questions, but a fact. Although *Webber* does not break much new ground, it is an excellent review of this part of the law.

Failure to mention a fact

This should be a simple matter: either he did or he did not mention the fact in question. If he did not but offered some explanation for the failure, it is inappropriate for a judge to indicate to the jury his own view of that reason. In *Gowland-Wynn* [2001] 1 Cr. App. R. 41 the judge said he thought the defendant's reasons 'quite extraordinary'. Despite an otherwise impeccable direction on inferences, the Court of Appeal quashed the conviction.

Facts unknown

The prosecution must canvass the defendant as to whether he knew the fact at the time of interview or charge. If the defendant did not know the particular fact, or did know it but was not questioned about it, the section does not bite. In *Nickolson* [1999] Crim. L.R. 61 the defendant was asked in cross-examination whether he could account for semen staining on the victim's nightdress. He suggested that it could have been picked up on the nightdress after he had masturbated in, and then left, the bathroom. He had not been questioned about the staining at interview because the existence of the staining was not then known. It was held that no inference should have been drawn from his failure to mention his explanation. In the first place he had not been questioned about it. Second, his answer was more in the nature of speculation to the question 'Can you think of any way how..?' than reliance on a fact.

Advance disclosure issues

Under the Criminal Procedure and Investigations Act 1996 s.3(1) the prosecution is required to make primary disclosure of its case to the defence following which, under s.5(5) for trials on indictment, the defence must give a statement to the court and the prosecutor. The statement must contain the general nature of the defence and must also state where issue is taken with the prosecution and why. Where the defendant fails to give a statement, gives it late or departs from it at trial (s.11(2)), adverse inferences can be drawn (s.11(5)) with regard to guilt but not in deciding whether there is a case to answer. The prosecution can cross-examine the defendant on any differences between the defence in the statement and what he says at trial (*Hayes* [2004] All E.R. (D) 315) for which leave of the judge is not required: *Tibbs* [2000] 2 Cr. App. R. 309.

'Trying to discover whether or by whom the offence had been committed'

Under Code of Practice C11.6 and 16.1 an interview should cease once the officer believes there is sufficient evidence to charge. Thereafter the officer is no longer 'trying to discover whether or by whom the offence had been committed'. It follows that no inference should be drawn from any 'no comment' interview or responses after this point: *Gayle* [1999] Crim. L.R. 502. Although the facts of *Gayle* may defeat s.34(1)(a) it is by no means clear that they also defeat s.34(1)(b)—silence on being charged.

'Circumstances existing at the time could reasonably have been expected to mention'

This phrase that allows the court to take account all of the defendant's characteristics (the test is subjective), his sobriety, health, command of English as well as such matters as the time of day and what facts were known to him or were disclosed to him by the police. The jury decides whether it would have been reasonable for the defendant to mention the fact when questioned.

Legal Advice

Can a defendant reasonably be expected to have mentioned facts when either (i) he has asked for but not yet received legal advice; or (ii) when a lawyer has advised a 'no comment' interview.

(i) The proper time for legal advice

Following the decision of the ECtHR in *Murray v UK* (1996) 22 E.H.R.R. 29 ss.34, 36 and 37 of CJPOA were amended so no adverse inferences may be drawn when the defendant was at an authorised place of detention and was not allowed an opportunity to consult a lawyer prior to questioning. The decision in *Murray* is based on art.6(3) of ECHR:

> 'Everyone charged with a criminal offence has the following minimum rights:
>
> (c) to defend himself in person or through legal assistance of his own choosing or, if he has not sufficient means to pay for legal assistance, to be given it free when the interests of justice so require;'

The decision underlines the importance of access to legal advice at the start of questioning. In *Murray* access was delayed for 48 hours and in *Averill v UK* (2001) 31 E.H.R.R. 36 for 24 hours. Under Code C6.6 questioning a suspect who wants legal advice before he has received it would generally be a breach of the Code. The amendments to the CJPOA cover neither street interviewing nor any questioning of suspects by police while exercising their powers to search premises under s.18 of PACE before taking a suspect to a police station. Such conduct may amount to an attempt to circumvent Code C, especially the entitlement to legal advice which arises only at interviews at police stations.

(ii) The nature of the advice and its consequences

If in court the defendant explains his refusal to answer questions from the police merely on the basis of legal advice, he does not thereby waive professional legal privilege. Such explanation is unlikely on its own to persuade the court not to draw adverse inferences. So it will often be necessary for the solicitor to be called to narrate the advice and this will amount to waiver of the privilege: *Bowden* [1999] 2 Cr. App. R. 176.

In *Condron* (2001) 31 E.H.R.R. 1 the defendants' solicitor advised them not to answer questions because he thought they were unfit to be interviewed. Though the judge had drawn the jury's attention to the defendants' explanation he had left it open to the jury to draw adverse inferences *even if* they were satisfied as to the defendants' explanation for their silence—presumably in the sense that the jury did not consider it reasonable to fail to mention the fact(s) at that stage. The summing up was thus defective. At [61] the ECtHR held:

> '. . . as a matter of fairness, the jury should have been directed that if it was satisfied that the applicant's silence at the police interview could not sensibly be attributed to their having no answer or none that would stand up to cross-examination it should not draw an adverse inference.'

At [62] the Court said that this direction was more than merely 'desirable' as the Court of Appeal had held. As part of its judgment the ECtHR said:

> 'the very fact that the (defendant) is advised by his lawyer to maintain his silence must also be given appropriate weight by the domestic court. There may be very good reasons why such advice may be given.'

This forceful statement reflects the Court's view that the right to silence is 'at the heart of a fair procedure under Article 6' and is at odds with dicta in some English decisions which down play the importance of legal advice. The cases turn on whether it is sufficient to prevent an inference that the defendant 'genuinely' relied on legal advice or whether the word 'reasonably' brings something to the direction. In *Hoare & Pierce* [2004] EWCA 784 Auld L.J. said [54]:

> 'legal entitlement is one thing. A (defendant's) reason for exercising it is another. His belief in his entitlement may be genuine but it does not follow that his reason for exercising it is. . .'

In *Beckles*, Lord Woolf said [46]:

> 'if the jury consider the defendant genuinely relied on the advice, that is not necessarily the end of the matter. It may still not have been reasonable for him to rely on the advice, or the advice may not have been the true explanation for his silence.'

His Lordship added:

> 'it is possible to say that he acted genuinely on the advice. However, the fact that he did so because it suited his purpose may mean that he was not acting reasonably in not mentioning the facts.'

The JSB Direction No. 40 para.5 (Defendant's Failure to Mention Facts when Questioned or Charged—s.34, CJPOA 1994) includes the following direction.

> 'If, for example, you considered that he had or may have had an answer to give, but genuinely and reasonably relied on the legal advice to remain silent, you should not draw any conclusion against him. But if, for example, you were sure that the defendant had no answer, and merely latched onto the legal advice as a convenient shield behind which to hide, you would be entitled to draw a conclusion against him, subject to the direction I have given you.'

While this may, as Note 5 to the direction says, reconcile the conflicting decisions it does not address the substantive issue of whether legal advice should be sufficient per se to avoid the drawing of inferences. As Murphy puts it (p.335):

> 'It is submitted that more weight should be given not only to the professional opinion of solicitors, but also to the effect likely to be produced on suspects by being given legal advice. It would surely only be rarely that a suspect, already in a stressful situation being detained at a police station and interrogated by police officers, would consider accumulating the additional stress of rejecting his solicitor's advice.'

8.2.2 **Failure to account for objects, substances or marks (section 36), or presence at the scene (s.37)**

Differences between s.34 and ss.36 and 37

(i) Whereas s.34 refers to facts not mentioned by the suspect ss.36 and 37 refer to his failure to account for facts already known to the police and which may already be evidence of involvement in crime.

(ii) For the same reason as in (i) above, neither ss.36 nor 37 contain any limitation in relation to facts which the defendant could reasonably have been expected to mention when asked.

(iii) Sections 36 and 37 apply only to constables and to officers of customs and excise. Contrast s.34(4) which refers not only to constables but also to persons charged with the duty of investigating offences or charging offenders. We considered the meaning of this phrase in Ch.7 para.7.4.

Overlap

Suppose a person is asked to account for marks of paint on a jemmy in his garage and he says nothing. At trial, he explains he had been helping demolish a building. Section 34 could apply because of a failure to mention a fact he subsequently relies on and s.36 because of a failure to explain the paint mark.

Given the width of s.34 there seems to be no good reason for the existence of ss.36 and 37.

8.2.3 **A prima facie case**

Under ss.34(2), s.36(2) and s.37(2) failure to mention facts, account for marks etc., or presence may be taken into account when deciding either the issue of guilt or whether there is a case to answer. While failure to answer questions etc. may be added to other evidence, s.38(3) provides that neither guilt nor a case to answer can depend *solely* on adverse inferences from silence under these sections.

In *K.S. Murray v DPP* (1993) 97 Cr. App. R. 151 Lord Mustill defined a prima facie case as when:

> 'the prosecutor has erected a case which, absent rebuttal, the fact-finder may (but will not necessarily) accept as proved. At this stage the trial is in a state of balance. The fact-finder waits to see whether in relation to each essential ingredient of the offence the direct evidence, which it is at least possible to believe should in the event be believed and whether inferences that might be drawn from such evidence should actually be drawn. Without this level of evidence, there is nothing for the adverse inference to bite on.'

The JSB Direction No. 40 para.3 suggests the jury must be sure that 'apart from his failure to mention those facts, the prosecution's case against him is *so strong* that it clearly calls for an answer by him.' (Emphasis supplied.) Such a direction surely raises the question of why inferences are necessary at all if the case is otherwise 'so strong'. Be that as it may, the Court of Appeal has insisted that inferences should not be drawn unless the other evidence clearly calls for an explanation: *Petkar, Farquhar* [2003] EWCA Crim 2668 (per Rix L.J. [51]).

A submission of 'no case' is normally made at the close of the prosecution case—'half time'. If at that time the defendant has not relied on any fact in his defence, the prosecution will have to establish its case without the assistance of statutory inferences. This is consistent with treating inferences from silence as additional to evidence produced by the prosecution—'corroboration in all but name'. (Birch, 'Suffering in Silence' [1999] Crim. L.R. 774).

8.2.4 The meaning of sections 34(5): 36(6) and 37(5): the common law

Section 34(5) preserves the common law rule that a person's reaction when an allegation of misconduct is made against him is admissible evidence from which an adverse inference might be drawn. We considered this in Ch.6, (see para.6.2). Sections 36(6) and 37(5) preserve the same common law in relation to objects, substances and marks and presence at a particular place respectively.

The authoritative statement of common law is found in the speech of Lord Atkinson in *Christie* [1914] A.C. 545 at 554:

> '. . . the rule of law undoubtedly is that a statement made in the presence of an accused person, even on an occasion which should be expected reasonably to call for some explanation or denial from him, is not evidence against him of the facts stated save in so far as he accepts the statement, so as to make it his own. If he accepts the statement in part only, then to that extent alone does it become his statement. He may accept the statement by word or conduct, action or demeanour, and it is the function of the jury which tries the case to determine whether his words, action, conduct or demeanour at the time when a statement was made amounts to an acceptance of it in whole or in part . . .'

As we saw at para.8.1, drawing adverse inferences at common law requires both that the parties are on 'even terms' and, as the extract from Lord Atkinson's speech makes clear, circumstances such that a reaction is called for. Although there is dicta in *Chandler* [1976] 3 All E.R. 105 that a person can be on even terms with a police officer, the better view is against it (Murphy, p.320). The even terms principle derives from *Mitchell* (1892) 17 Cox C.C. 508 where Cave J. said:

> 'undoubtedly, when persons are speaking on even terms and a charge is made and the person charged says nothing, and expresses no indignation and does not repel the charge, that is some evidence to show that he admits the charge to be true.' (Emphasis supplied.)

The defendant was charged with procuring an unlawful miscarriage. A magistrate was taking a deposition from the victim when she became too ill to continue. She subsequently died. The issue was whether the unfinished deposition could be admitted as a statement (in effect an allegation of an offence) in the presence of the defendant. He was legally represented but his solicitor had had no opportunity to cross-examine the woman. For that reason, the deposition was excluded. The reference to 'charged' and 'charge' in the extract above is not to formal charging by the police—it means an accusation or allegation. The form of what is said is less important than its substance—see *Parkes v R.* [1976] 3 All E.R. 380 below.

The mere presence of the police will not of itself violate even terms. In *Horne* (1990) Crim. L.R. 188 following a 'glassing' in a restaurant, the police found the defendant hiding in a car park, took him inside seating him opposite the victim who said 'take that bastard away, he's the one who glassed me'. This was followed by silence from Horne, a subsequent denial by him and finally an admission. It was held that his silence was capable of amounting to an acknowledgement of the truth of the accusation. The parties were on even terms notwithstanding the police presence.

Jury direction at common law

The jury must be told they cannot simply infer guilt from silence. First, the prosecution must demonstrate the defendant accepted the whole or at least part of the accusation or allegation. He may do so by silence, by a short, unconvincing denial ('I am innocent': *Christie*), or by conduct, or by a combination but it is only that part of the allegation which he accepted that is the platform for the next stage. Second the prosecution must demonstrate (*Chandler* 105, 111) that an inference of guilt should follow from acceptance. In *Chandler* Lawton L.J. referred to the 'intellectual process' which must be followed.

> 'Some comment on the (defendant's) lack of frankness . . . was justified, provided the jury's attention was directed to the right issue, which was whether in the circumstances (his) silence amounted to an acceptance by him of what (was) said. If he accepted what had been said, then the next question should have been whether guilt could reasonably be inferred from what he accepted. To suggest as the judge did that (the defendant's) silence could indicate guilt was to short circuit the intellectual process which has to be followed.'

The case of *Parkes* affords a good example of the principles in operation. The defendant was charged with murder of a girl by knifing. He was found holding a knife by the dying girl's mother. She twice asked him why he had killed her daughter. He made no reply but when said she would detain him until the police arrived he attempted to stab her. The defendant's guilty reaction indicated acceptance of the mother's statement and was something from which an inference of guilt was proper.

The importance of not jumping straight to an inference of guilt can be demonstrated as follows. Suppose the defendant is alleged to have assaulted another and fails to respond. We might infer acceptance of the allegation but an inference of guilt is not inevitable as where the defendant subsequently says he acted in self-defence.

Is a reaction called for?

Whether a reply would be expected depends on all the circumstances including the physical and mental make-up and situation of the defendant. Munday ('Cum Tacent Clamant', p.454) suggests it is more profitable to focus on whether a reaction is called for than on the even terms doctrine. Citing *Parkes* he says these were circumstances when a 'normal person would have said something' and the even terms test hardly contributes much to the analysis.

However, in *Collins* [2004] EWCA Crim 83 Thomas L.J. referred to the even terms doctrine as part of the common law. Its value is as a test for distinguishing 'civilian' allegations and accusations on the one hand from questioning by the police on the other—especially where the questioning is not under caution. In response to a question from the police (it is not clear from the report whether the caution had been given) the first defendant (D1) told a lie which the second defendant (D2) did not correct. The Court of Appeal, allowing the appeals, said that D2's failure to correct the lie could in principle amount to adoption of D1's statement provided there was proper exploration of D2's reaction to D1's statement.

Figure 47—Summary of position at common law

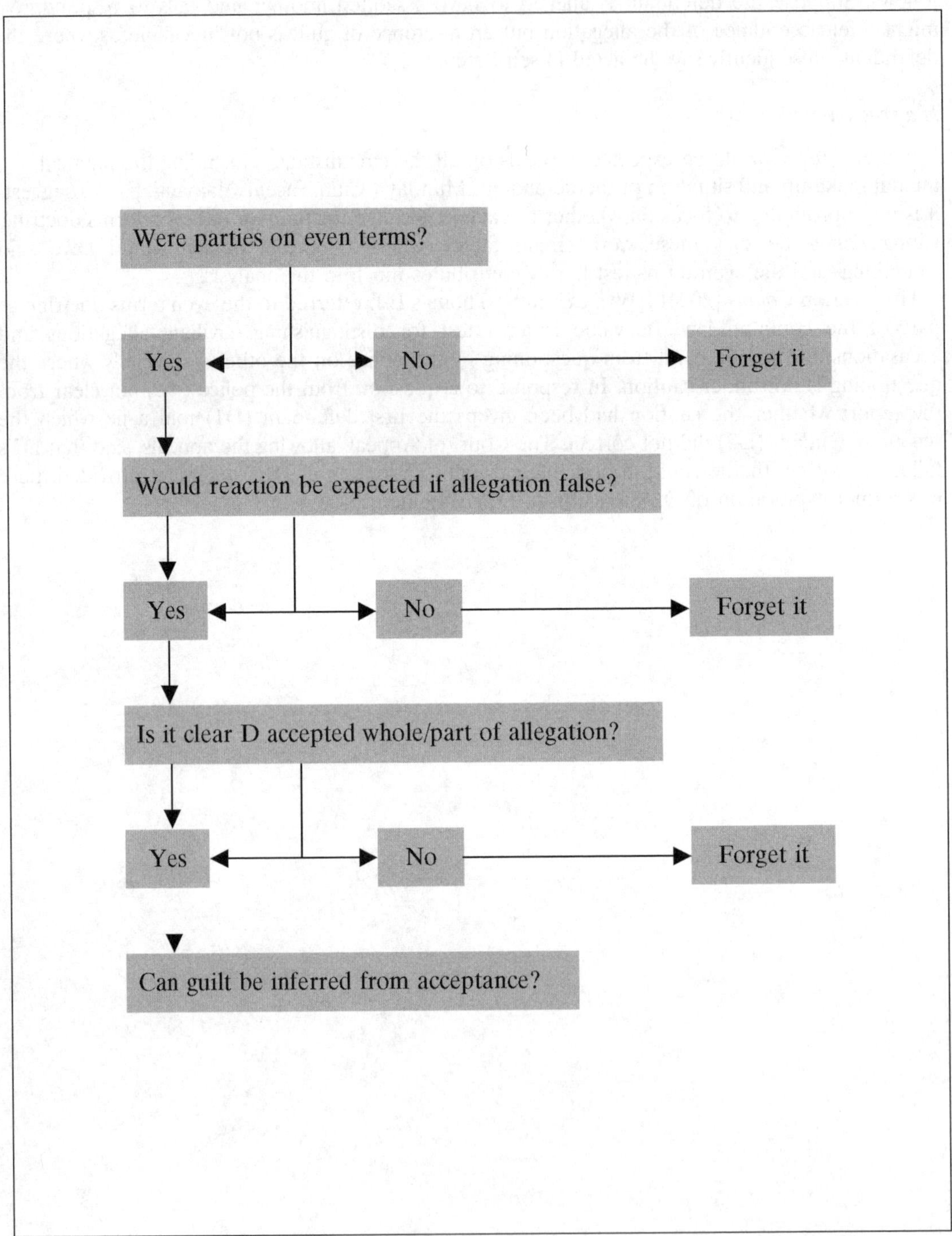

8.2.5 **Common law adverse inferences from lies**

Suppose the defendant admits his answers to the police in interview were untrue e.g. in court he admits an alibi was false. Can the prosecution rely on his lie as evidence of guilt? The answer is a provisional 'yes'. In *Lucas* [1981] 73 Cr. App. R. 159,163 the Court of Appeal laid down guidelines in the form of a jury direction as to when the defendant's lies can be used in this way. In *Burge, Pegg* [1996] 1 Cr. App. R. 163 the Court of Appeal identified four circumstances in which the *Lucas* warning should be given. They form the basis of the JSB Specimen Direction No. 27.

When should a Lucas direction be given?

Direction No. 27 Note 1 states:

> 'If the inevitable consequence of the jury having found that the defendant has told lies is that he is guilty of the offence charged no separate direction is required.'

Otherwise the situation is as follows.

(i) Where the defendant raises a defence of alibi. The direction is:

> 'Even if you conclude that the alibi is false, that does not itself entitle you to convict the defendant. The prosecution must still make you sure of his guilt. An alibi is sometimes invented to bolster a genuine defence.'

Another way of putting this is that even if the jury is satisfied the alibi witnesses are untruthful, they must also be satisfied that the prosecution has proved its case.

(ii) If corroboration or supporting evidence (see Ch.10) is required and attention is drawn to lies as capable of supplying it.

(iii) If the prosecution relies on a specific issue as one on which the defendant has lied and which is, therefore, evidence of guilt.

(iv) Where the judge considers the jury might rely on such a lie even though the prosecution did not. (The decision to warn in this event should follow consultation with counsel.)

The Lucas direction

The judge should remind the jury of the burden of proof and say that lies are not per se evidence of guilt. The jury should also be told (*Sharp* [1993] 3 All E.R. 225 and *Bey* [1993] 3 All E.R. 253) that people lie for many reasons, e.g. to bolster a weak defence or to protect someone else, etc. If the jury thinks there is or might be an innocent explanation for lies, then it should take no notice of them. 'Innocent' is used relatively. In *Bullen* [2008] EWCA Crim 4 the defendant lied first as to whether he had held a bottle at all and secondly as to whether he has been left with a broken bottle in his hand. The jury should have been instructed the lie might simply have been an attempt to distance himself from responsibility for murder rather than from involvement in the events leading to the death of the victim which he admitted.

As *Bullen* illustrates it is crucial that the judge directs the jury on the exact factual issue to which it is alleged the lie is relevant. In *Taylor* [1998] Crim. L.R. 822 the defendant was charged with murder and admitted that he had killed the deceased during a loss of temper. He also admitted lies to the police when questioned door-to-door. As in *Bullen* the jury needed to be sure the lies went to the charge of murder rather than mere involvement in the death of the deceased which Taylor admitted anyway. His conviction for murder was reduced to manslaughter.

When does the prosecution rely on a lie?

A *Lucas* direction is not required simply because of a head-on conflict of evidence between prosecution and defence or if the lie goes *only* to the issue of the defendant's credit or only because of inconsistencies in statements made by the defendant either pre-trial or in evidence: *Barnett* (2002) 166 J.P. 407. In *Landon* [1995] Crim. L.R. 338 Hobhouse L.J. said:

> 'The *Lucas* situation only arises where . . . due to some change in evidence or account by the defendant, there is scope for drawing an inference of guilt from the fact that the defendant has, on an earlier occasion, told lies, or on some other matter, told lies at trial.'

Figure 48—Reliance on a lie

Fact situation	Reli-ance	Reason
(a) In a prosecution for handling stolen goods, the defendant gives different and incompatible reasons for his possession of the goods.	No	Because the standard explanation in handling cases is a denial of knowledge or belief that the goods were stolen. The prosecution would assert that this explanation was untrue but it 'would be absurd to suggest that every case of handling required a *Lucas* direction': *Barnett* (supra).
(b) In a prosecution for burglary the defendant says he was elsewhere.	No	Because this is simply a direct and irreconcilable conflict of evidence between the parties. In *Harron* [1996] 2 Cr. App. R. 457 Beldam L.J. said this is not a situation where there is a difference between the issue of guilt and the issue of lies.

8.2.6 In-court silence

> 'If all criminals of every class had assembled, and framed a system after their own minds is not this rule the very first which they would have established for their security? Innocence never takes advantage of it. Innocence claims the right of speaking, as guilt invokes the privilege of silence.' (Bentham, Treatise on Evidence, p.241)

8.2.6.1 Section 35 'Effect of accused's silence at trial'

Under subs.(3):

> 'Where this subsection applies, the court or jury, in determining whether the accused is guilty of the offence charged, may draw such inferences as appear proper from the failure of the accused to give evidence or his refusal, without good cause, to answer any question.'

Procedure

Under subs.(2) the court must satisfy itself at half time that the defendant is aware that failure to give evidence or (if he does give evidence) to answer questions without good cause may result in adverse inferences being drawn. He is presumed to be without good cause unless (subs.(5)) he can claim privilege or the court exercises discretion to allow him not to answer.

Exercise of discretion must be evidentially based. It will not be evidentially based where it consists of the defendant's counsel giving explanations to the jury as to why his client had not given evidence (*Cowan* [1996] 1 Cr. App. R. 1) or, in the context of police questioning, why the defendant had not answered questions. The Court of Appeal held the:

> 'rule against advocates giving evidence dressed up as a submission applies . . . it cannot be proper for a defence advocate to give to the jury reasons for his client's silence at trial in the absence of evidence to support such reasons.'

This position was endorsed in *Condron* [1997] 1 Cr. App. R. 185 a case on s.34.

It will be evidentially based where the defendant's physical or mental condition 'makes it undesirable for him to give evidence' (subs.(2)). In *Friend* [1997] 2 Cr. App. R. 231 the Court of Appeal focused on the defendant's chronological (14 years) rather than his mental age (approximately 9 years) holding the latter was not per se a reason for exercising discretion. The judge should assess the extent of any mental handicap or lack of maturity from all of the evidence, including conduct before and after the offence, but excluding the commission of the offence itself, at least where it is disputed. The defendant had been able to give a coherent account in police interviews. While he was virtually illiterate with the reading skills of a boy of 6 years, he was not suggestible.

8.2.6.2 **Section 35 and a prima facie case**

What we said about the nature of a prima facie case (see para.8.2.3) applies here. Since the court will not know at half-time whether the defendant will give evidence (and is not entitled to ask) unlike ss.34, 36 and 37, failure to give evidence cannot be taken into account in deciding whether there is a prima facie case. The JSB Specimen Direction (No. 40 para.4) requires that 'the prosecution's case is so strong that it clearly calls for an answer by him' and 'that the only sensible explanation for his silence is that he has no answer, or none that would bear examination'.

8.3 Summary

(a) The common law and CJPOA live alongside each other.

(b) The former relates to all circumstances other than those covered by ss.34–38 of the Act.

(c) The even terms doctrine, expectation of reaction and acceptance are the key issues at common law.

(d) Silence can be part of a prima facie case under CJPOA ss.34, 36 or 37 but not under s.35.

(e) Access to legal advice is the pre-requisite to drawing adverse inferences under CJPOA. Thereafter the message is 'no reliance, no inference'.

(f) Careful direction of the jury is vital if the CJPOA provisions are to withstand fair trial challenges under art.6.

8.4 Further reading

Birch, 'Suffering in Silence: A Cost Benefit Analysis of s.34 of the Criminal Justice and Public Order Act 1994' [1999] Crim. L.R. 769

Dennis, 'Silence in the Police Station: The Marginalisation of s.34' [2002] Crim. L.R. 25.

Jackson, 'Silence and Proof: extending the boundaries of criminal proceedings in the United Kingdom' (2001) 5 E. & P. 145.

Leng, 'Silence pre-trial, reasonable expectations and the normative distortion of fact-finding' (2001) 5 E. & P. 240.

Munday, '*Cum Tacent Clamant*: Drawing Proper Inferences from a Defendant's Failure to Testify' [1996] C.L.J. 32.

Pattenden, 'Inferences from Silence' [1995] Crim. L.R. 602.

9 Evidence of Character

9.1 Introduction

All statutory references in this chapter are to the Criminal Justice Act 2003 unless otherwise indicated.

The character provisions in the Act are contained in Pt 11, Ch.1 which embraces ss.98–113 inclusive.

9.2 Jury trial, indictments and cross-admissibility

An indictment is a written accusation that a named person has committed offences. The indictment states the charges (known as 'counts') against a defendant. There can be one count or a large number of them. In the latter case, not all of the counts need be of exactly the same type, e.g. they need not all be burglary or theft, though they could be. Counts alleging different offences may be put into the same indictment provided the court is satisfied that there is a sufficient nexus between them. The same jury will then hear evidence on all the counts.

Severing the indictment

If the court decides there is insufficient nexus, each count will be heard by a different jury—the indictment will have been 'severed'.

No cross-admissibility between counts

Provided the indictment is not severed, the same jury will hear all of the evidence relating to all of the counts in the indictment. However, when it comes to making a decision on whether the defendant is guilty of each individual count, the jury will be directed not to take into consideration in deciding guilt on count 1 anything which it has heard which is relevant only to count 2 until it starts to consider count 2, at which point the jury must forget evidence relating only to count 1. There is no cross-admissibility between counts.

Cross-admissibility permitted

Where the court holds both that there is sufficient nexus to allow more than one count in the indictment *and* there is what is known as admissible similar fact or extraneous act evidence (SFE/EAE) in the case the jury can take into account, in deciding the defendant's guilt on count 1, evidence which it has heard relating to count 2 and counts 3, 4, 5 etc. This is known as 'cross-admissibility'. This is covered in diagrammatic form now.

Figure 49—Cross-admissibility

Count	Indictment severed	Not severed No SFE/EAE	Not severed SFE/EAE present
1	Each count heard by different jury	All counts heard by same jury. Evidence on count 1 not to be taken into account on count 2. And similarly between counts 2 and 3 etc.	All counts heard by same jury. Jury instructed that evidence on count 1 is admissible on count 2, 3, etc. And similarly that evidence on count 2 is admissible on counts 1, 3 4 etc.
2	Each count heard by different jury		
3			
4			
etc.			

The meaning of similar fact or extraneous act evidence (SFE/EAE) is explained below (para.9.4.2.3).

9.3 The meaning of 'character'

Suppose you were asked to write a reference for Alice and were asked to comment on her 'character'. What would you understand was wanted of you? The dictionary definition includes the following: 'the sum of the peculiar qualities which constitutes individual personality'. So your reference would probably have dealt with whether Alice was honest, trustworthy, reliable, etc. Has she always held down a job? Does she pay her bills on time? Is she a devoted worker for charity? We might have thought about any rumours we had ever heard about her or, e.g., if we knew that she had a commendation for bravery for assisting in an emergency.

The common law has long been concerned with character—usually but not exclusively that of the defendant. Three questions arose at common law:

1. what was meant by 'character' evidence;
2. was such evidence admissible; and, if so,
3. how might the jury use it?

The answer to the first question is that at common law 'character' (whether good or bad) means both reputation—what a person is believed to be—and disposition—what a person actually is. Although there has been recent statutory reform in this area of law, evidence of the defendant's good character and its value are untouched by the reform and we shall deal with this in the section immediately below. Bad character, in the sense of disposition, is often proved by evidence of previous convictions. However, the two-word phrase 'bad character' has been given a special statutory meaning under the Criminal Justice Act 2003 and we shall need to consider it separately.

We need to postpone discussion of the second and third questions for the time being.

9.4 The defendant's character

9.4.1 Good character

A defendant has always been entitled to prove that he is of good character—that he was of good general reputation and that he had no convictions. Historically he could do this by calling character witnesses or by cross-examining prosecution witnesses. When he was made a competent witness by the CEA he could also give evidence of character himself. Strictly speaking he is limited to proving good character by evidence of good general reputation only (*Rowton* (1865) Lee. & Ca. 520; *Redgrave* (1981) 74 Cr. App. R. 10) though in practice the courts permit evidence of good specific disposition.

Figure 50—Proving good character

D proves good character by	Giving evidence himself	Calling character witnesses	Cross-examining prosecution witnesses	Limitation: evidence of good general reputation only

Where the defendant is of good character the judge is required to direct the jury on its evidential value. He should say that a person of good character is more likely to be telling the truth. This requirement ('a rule of practice' per Lord Steyn in *Aziz* [1995] 2 Cr. App. R. 478, 486) derives from the case of *Vye* [1993] 97 Cr. App. R. 134. The direction is in two parts referred to in the case as the first and second 'limbs'. There are specimen directions in respect of good character (Direction 23) and they can be found on the JSB's website (*http://www.js.board.co.uk* assessed March 28, 2008). The judge is under no obligation to give a direction unless good character is specifically raised by the defence: *Barrow v R.* [1998] A.C. 846.

In *Campbell* [2007] EWCA Crim 1472 Lord Phillips C.J. (obiter) appeared to wish to downgrade the mandatory nature of the *Vye* direction. In what can only be described as an extraordinary statement [21–23] he said the good character direction:

> 'is an extreme example of the way that directions that are desirable . . . have become treated as mandatory requirements of law.'

His Lordship described this as a 'lamentable state of affairs', regarding the *Vye* direction as an example of something the judge was required to tell the jury but something the jury could have somehow operated for themselves 'by the application of common sense'. The pros and cons of mandatory directions may need to be addressed but, if so, it should be done in a mature and orderly way taking account of the accumulated wisdom of those long experienced in jury trial both as advocates and judges.

The first limb in Vye

This is also known as the credibility direction and is mandatory where the defendant has given evidence or where he has made out of court admissions to the police. It is not required where any such statement is purely exculpatory: *Aziz* (above) per Lord Steyn. The dictionary definition of 'credibility' is 'the quality of being believed or trusted'. 'Credibility gap' is defined as 'a disparity between claims or statements made and the evident facts of the situation or circumstances to which they relate'. It is not difficult to imagine a jury employing this definition to the defendant's advantage or otherwise.

The JSB Direction is that good character is a factor to be taken into account when the jury is considering the defendant's statements or evidence. The credibility gap may, of course, persuade them to convict notwithstanding previous good character.

The second limb direction in Vye

This is known as the propensity direction and is mandatory whenever the defendant is of good character. It does not depend on whether he has made pre-trial statements or given evidence in the proceedings. The jury must be told that good character has probative value, a person of good character is less likely to have committed the offence than is someone of bad character. The jury should understand that good character is not itself a defence.

How should the judge express the direction?

The judge must direct the jury by affirmative statements (*Lloyd* [2000] 2 Cr. App. R. 355) rather than by a series of rhetorical questions ('is it not less likely that he would be involved in offences of this kind given his clear character?'). *McLoughlin* (unreported) June 5, 1998 holds that dealing with character in the latter way was 'deficient and that it mattered' (per Auld L.J.). *Lloyd* also underlines the importance of the good character direction when the character of the complainant is bad and there is no other evidence.

Modification of the Vye *direction*

It may be necessary to adjust the direction. Lord Steyn gave a practical example in *Aziz* (above). Suppose a defendant of good character is charged with theft from his employer. Under cross-examination from a co-defendant, evidence emerges that the defendant has systematically cheated the employer for some years. What should the judge do? Lord Steyn said that 'a good starting point is that a judge should never be compelled to give meaningless or absurd directions'. In limited circumstances, such as these, a judge has discretion not to give a *Vye* direction where to do so would, on the facts, make no sense.

The courts tend to overlook minor offences, those committed a long time previously or those which are unconnected with the current offence: *Gray* [2004] EWCA Crim 1074 (previous driving offences on a charge of murder). *Durbin* [1995] 2 Cr. App. R. 84 illustrates the benevolence of the courts in this respect. The defendant had two spent convictions for offences of dishonesty (one had become spent just before trial,) gave the police a false account of his movements immediately prior to the events in question and subsequently admitted that he had been engaged in smuggling goods across European frontiers. It was held that he was entitled to both limbs of the *Vye* direction modified to take account of facts known to the jury which tended to militate against his claim to be of good character.

Where the defendant is known by the judge to be of bad character he may decline to give either limb of *Vye* notwithstanding such evidence was not disclosed to the jury. In *Lawson* [2006] EWCA Crim 2572 Hughes L.J. said [40]:

> '...we do not accept the proposition that if a defendant has a history of bad character which the judge holds not to be capable of having substantive probative value . . . so the application to adduce evidence of it fails, then it follows that the defendant is entitled to a conventional good character direction. The good character direction is appropriate to those who are, or . . . may be treated as if they are . . . without known bad character of any kind.'

Two defendants: one of good, and the other of bad, character

A defendant of good character is entitled to the *Vye* directions even though the absence of such direction in respect of the other defendant tells the jury something. The problem for the second defendant is that the jury may decide there is no smoke without a fire. In such circumstances he may decide to be 'up front' about his criminal record.

Figure 51—The effect of *Vye*

The effect of *Vye* where D of good character			**Mandatory**
First limb	Credibility	Good character taken into account re pre-trial statements and/or evidence. D more likely to be telling the truth.	Yes unless no pre-trial statements or evidence; no if pre-trial statements are exclusively exculpatory.
Second limb	Propensity	D less likely to have committed offence.	Yes.

9.4.2 Bad character of the defendant

9.4.2.1 Introduction

Meaning of bad character at common law

We saw above that the defendant is limited to showing he is of good character by evidence of good general reputation. The prosecution was entitled to rebut this claim by evidence of bad general reputation. This common law rule is preserved by s.118(1) para.2.

Section 99(1) of the CJA 2003 provides that, subject to some savings in s.118(1), 'the common law rules governing the admissibility of evidence of bad character in criminal proceedings are abolished'. When we examine s.101(1)(d) below we shall discover the importance of the word 'rules' in s.99(1).

The prosecution can and usually will seek to rebut a claim to good character by evidence of bad specific disposition i.e. that the defendant has previous convictions. If the defendant does have previous convictions, it is probable that the prosecution will seek to admit them under the provisions of the CJA 2003 and it this which we consider next.

Meaning of bad character under the Criminal Justice Act 2003

Section 98 defines 'bad character' as evidence of, or a disposition towards, misconduct 'other than evidence which:

(a) has to do with the alleged facts of the offence with which the defendant is charged; or
(b) is evidence of misconduct in connection with the investigation or prosecution of that offence.

The effect of this provision is to exclude acts immediately surrounding the commission or investigation of the offence from the statutory definition of bad character. For example it would be proper for the prosecution to adduce evidence that a vehicle used as a getaway car after a break-in was stolen. Such evidence may be admissible 'without more ado': *Watson* [2006] EWCA Crim 1472 [19]. In *Tirnaveau* [2007] EWCA Crim 1239 Thomas L.J. [23] held 'the exclusion must be related to evidence where there is some nexus in time between the offence with which the defendant is charged and the evidence of misconduct which the prosecution seek to adduce'. It is, he said, 'a fact-specific exercise'. That nexus was absent in *Saleem* [2007] EWCA Crim 1923. The prosecution had wished to admit evidence the defendant had written violent rap lyrics three months before being involved in violent assault in order to prove he had planned the attack.

Misconduct is defined in s.112(1) as the 'commission of an offence or other reprehensible behaviour'. 'Offence' does not mean the same as conviction; 'other reprehensible behaviour' replaced the Law Commission's draft (Evidence of Bad Character in Criminal Proceedings (Law Commission No. 273 2001)) which was conduct that 'might be viewed with disapproval by a reasonable person'. The Government considered the draft too vague. 'Other reprehensible behaviour' is, apparently, much more certain. In *Renda* [2005] EWCA Crim 2826 the court stated there must be some element of culpability or blameworthiness before conduct could be reprehensible. *Munday*, ('What Constitutes "Other Reprehensible Behaviour" 2003?' [2005] Crim. L.R. 24, 35) argues that the meaning of reprehensible behaviour is a question of law for the judge. It is suggested that the courts will need to be able to demonstrate the relevance of admitting evidence of this type because of the duty under s.110 to state in open court the reason for 'a ruling on whether an item of evidence is evidence of a person's bad character'.

In *Osbourne* [2007] EWCA Crim 481 it was held that evidence that the defendant became verbally aggressive if he failed to take medication in respect of his schizophrenia could not be viewed as reprehensible behaviour on a charge of murder. Is this outside the 'culpability / blameworthiness' test in *Renda*?

9.4.2.2 **Admissibility and use of bad character evidence**

The statutory basis for admission of evidence of bad character of non-defendants is provided by s.100. This is covered at para.9.5. Section 101(1) provides seven 'gateways' of admissibility of bad character of the defendant. The detail on the gateways is contained in ss.102–106. In *Highton* [2005] EWCA Crim 1985 the Court of Appeal (per Lord Woolf) held 'a distinction must be drawn between *admissibility* of evidence of bad character, which depends on getting it through one of the gateways, and the *use* to which it may be put once it is admitted.' (original emphasis).

Lord Woolf asserted that once it is admitted, evidence of bad character can be put to any use to which it is relevant. He accepted that relevance may be limited by the terms of the gateway as in s.101(1)(d) but otherwise it could go to either or both a propensity to commit offences or to be untruthful. This view was strongly endorsed by Lord Phillips C.J. in *Campbell* a case involving gateway (d). We will postpone further consideration of this until we reach the gateway in question. We are now going to examine the gateways individually.

9.4.2.3 **The statutory gateways**

Paragraph (a) All parties to the proceedings agree to the evidence being admissible

In *Hanson* [2005] EWCA Crim 824 Rose L.J. [17] said 'we would expect the relevant circumstances of previous convictions to be capable of agreement, and that, subject to the trial judge's ruling on admissibility, they will be put before the jury by way of admission'. Paragraph (a) opens the door for this. There is overlap with gateway (b) which we consider immediately.

Paragraph (b) The evidence is adduced by the defendant himself or is given in answer to a question asked by him in cross-examination and intended to elicit it

A defendant might do this for a number of reasons. For example, there are occasions when a defendant seeks to alibi himself by reference to conduct which is reprehensible. In *Jones v DPP* [1962] 46 Cr. App. R. 129 the defendant advanced an unsupported alibi that, at the time of a murder, he had been with an unnamed prostitute. Alternatively he may be advised to 'front' his previous convictions rather than have them 'dragged out' of him by the prosecution in cross-examination. Again, a defendant might prefer to prevent the jury speculating about his character by being explicit about it. (He may be happier to be *known* to be a handler of stolen goods rather than *believed* to be a child-molester.)

The words 'and intended to elicit it' make it clear that the subsection does not apply unless the defendant intended the disclosure. The common law authorities in respect of irregular disclosure of evidence of a defendant's bad character tended to require that the jury be discharged.

Paragraph (c) It is important explanatory evidence

At common law the prosecution was entitled to lead evidence as to the 'history' of the case although it did not qualify as SFE/EAE (see below). Murphy (p.145) describes it as 'passive background evidence'. Such evidence might shed some light on the relationship between the defendant and his victim. The leading case is *Pettman* [1985] (unreported). Purchas L.J. said:

> 'Where it is necessary to place before the jury evidence of part of a continual background of history relevant to the offence charged in the indictment and without the totality of which the account placed before the jury would be incomplete or incomprehensible, then the fact that the whole account involves including evidence establishing the commission of an offence with which the defendant is not charged is not of itself a ground for excluding the evidence.'

Under the Act the twin statutory tests in s.102 are (a) if without the evidence the court or jury would find it impossible or difficult properly to understand other evidence in the case; and (b) its value for understanding the case as a whole is substantial. (This is known as the 'enhanced test of relevance' and we shall encounter it on a number of occasions in this chapter). In *Phillips* [2003] Crim. L.R. 629 background evidence about the matrimonial relationship of the parties was held admissible on a charge of murder of his wife by the husband. On the other hand in *Dolan* [2003] EWCA Crim 1859 evidence that one of the parents had a history of violence towards inanimate objects was held inadmissible where both parents were charged with murder of their baby in circumstances where one or other or both of them must be responsible.

In *Diana Butler* [1999] Crim. L.R. 835 the Court of Appeal held that events some three years before the facts in issue were too remote to be covered by the 'history' principle. The court also said even if such evidence was admitted and showed the defendant in an unfavourable light, she was, where appropriate, nevertheless entitled to a full good character direction under *Vye* [1993] 97 Cr. App. R. 134 (see para.9.4.1).

The jury must be directed that while the evidence is admissible as history, it is not to be used as SFE/EAE (see below). In other words, it must not be used as evidence of guilt. Both the judge and the defence should be on their guard to ensure the prosecution is not allowed to bootleg inadmissible SFE/EAE under the guise of history: *Sawoniuk* [2000] 2 Cr. App. R. 220, 234, 236 per Lord Bingham C.J.

Paragraph (d) It is relevant to an important matter in issue between the defendant and the prosecution

This subsection is amplified by s.103(1) as follows:

'103 Matter in issue between the defendant and the prosecution

(1) For the purposes of s.101(1)(d) the matters in issue between the defendant and the prosecution include—
 (a) the question whether the defendant has a propensity to commit offences of the kind with which he is charged, except where his having such a propensity makes it no more likely that he is guilty of the offence;
 (b) the question whether the defendant has a propensity to be untruthful, except where it is not suggested that the defendant's case is untruthful in any respect'

We shall examine each of the subsections separately below. First there are some general observations.

Unlike in s.100 and s.101(1)(e) there is no requirement of enhanced relevance i.e. that the evidence shall have substantial value for understanding the case. While this might be seen as an open invitation to the prosecution to use such evidence freely there are some constraints.

First, under Pt 35 of the Criminal Procedure Rules 2005 (SI 2005/384) 'a party' (this covers a co-defendant as well as the prosecution) is supposed to give 14 days notice of their intention to adduce the evidence thereby giving the defendant the opportunity to dispute its admissibility (relevance) as part of the pre-trial case management procedures. Where the court concludes notice was deliberately not given in order to try to ambush the defendant at trial the judge may decline to admit the evidence in his discretion: *Tirnaveanu* [2007] EWCA Crim 1239.

Second, in *Hanson* [4] Rose L.J. referring to s.103 said:

> 'It is accordingly to be hoped that prosecution applications to adduce such evidence will not be made routinely simply because a defendant has previous convictions but will be based on the particular circumstances of each case.'

The opening words of the subsection are 'it is relevant'. The onus of showing relevance to either propensity or credibility is on the prosecution. If observed in practice these words represent a significant burden for the prosecution and a significant pre-condition to admission of evidence of bad character: *Hanson*.

Third s.101(3) and (4) afford some protection, as does s.103(3).

Propensity to commit offences—s.103(1(a)

In *Makin v Att-Gen for New South Wales* [1894] A.C. 57 the defendants were charged with the murder of a baby. In addition to mainly circumstantial evidence of guilt, the prosecution was allowed to prove the finding of the bodies of thirteen other babies in premises occupied by the defendants. The Privy Council accepted the additional evidence had been correctly admitted and that it went to the issue in the case i.e. the defendants' guilt. We now refer to this kind of evidence as showing the defendant as having 'a propensity to commit offences of the kind with which he is charged': s.101(1)(a).

In *Makin* Lord Herschell said (65):

> 'It is undoubtedly not competent for the prosecution to adduce evidence tending to show that the defendant has been guilty of criminal acts other than those covered by the indictment, for the purpose of leading to the conclusion that the defendant is a person likely from his criminal conduct or character to have committed the offence for which he is being tried.
>
> On the other hand, the mere fact that the evidence adduced tends to show the commission of other crimes does not render it inadmissible if it be relevant to an issue before the jury, and it may be so relevant if it bears upon the question whether the acts alleged to constitute the crime . . . were designed or accidental, or to rebut a defence which would otherwise be open to the defendant.'

This statement became known as the 'two parts of *Makin*'. The second part is, decisively, not an exception to the first. The first part re-stated a common law principle to the effect that evidence which showed no more than that the defendant was of bad character was inadmissible. The second part qualifies the first by permitting evidence of 'other crimes' provided such evidence was relevant. Evidence of the commission of other crimes is, of course, evidence of bad character.

A major problem

Though it became known as the classic formulation of the principle involved, subsequent courts interpreted it as though the second part permitted such evidence *only* to rebut defences open to the defendant. It took some time to remedy this misinterpretation which is now recognised as clearly wrong. Across the law of evidence relevance is a question of fact (though initially a question for the judge) and cannot be categorised in this way.

Issues arising from decision

- The additional evidence referred to in the second part of *Makin* became known as Similar Fact Evidence (SFE). More recently it has become known as Extraneous Act Evidence (EAE).
- As we have seen, the evidence went to the defendants' guilt.
- The evidence was lead by the prosecution as part of its case. Admissibility did not depend on whether the defendant gave evidence.
- Admissibility was based on relevance.
- His Lordship's reference in the second part to 'the commission of other crimes' needs to be treated with caution. As we shall see, this kind of evidence was not limited to conduct which was criminal in nature: *Butler* (1987) 84 Cr. App. R. 12.
- Admissibility is a question for the judge: *Hanson*.

The effect of subsequent decisions at common law

The courts recognised the prejudicial effect of such evidence but also its great potential for proof ('probative value'). They developed a formula of words for admission based on the 'probative value outweighing the prejudicial effect'. In *Boardman v DPP* [1975] A.C. 421 the House of Lords held that in order to overcome the prejudicial effect there had to be 'striking similarity' between the commission of the offence and the SFE/EAE—effectively an enhanced common law test of relevance. Whatever the virtue of raising the test of admissibility in this way, it was lowered in *DPP v P* [1991] 93 Cr. App. R. 267. The test remains therefore one of relevance to the facts in issue. The onus of showing it is on the party proposing its admission.

The effect of the CJA 2003

The admission of evidence of this type is now governed by the Criminal Justice Act 2003 ss.101(1)(d) and 103(1)(a) and (2)–(5).

In *Hanson* Rose L.J. said:

> 'Where propensity to commit the offence is relied upon there are . . . three questions to be considered:
>
> (i) Does the history of conviction(s) establish a propensity to commit offences of the kind charged?
> (ii) Does that propensity make it more likely that the defendant committed the offence?
> (iii) Is it unjust to rely on the conviction(s) of the same description or category; and, in any event, will the proceedings be unfair if they are admitted?'

The first step is for the court to decide whether the proposed evidence goes to propensity to commit offences or to be untruthful (see below) or possibly both. Having done that, the court must then identify the specific matter in issue between the parties to which, it is alleged, evidence of misconduct is relevant. The key phrase is 'except where his having such a propensity makes it no more likely that he is guilty of the offence'. If the defendant admits the facts but e.g. denies his acts caused the particular outcome in question, it is difficult to see how previous convictions for offences of a similar nature could be relevant.

The process of identifying the relevance of previous misconduct prevents (or at least should prevent) use of such evidence as a blunt weapon of prejudice with no or only limited probative value. For example, evidence of a previous conviction for an offence against the person should not per se be admissible in a current trial for an offence against the person. Some such offences can be committed negligently (manslaughter) or recklessly (OAPA 1861 s.20) and would not be relevant to a charge of attempted murder where the issue was whether the defendant intended to kill. In *Bullen* [2008] EWCA Crim 4 the defendant pleaded guilty to manslaughter thereby accepting responsibility for the actus reus of the crime. He continued to plead not guilty to murder denying, on the ground of drunkenness, he had the requisite specific intent. The question was whether the defendant's previous convictions of relatively low level violence were admissible to prove specific intent. The Court of Appeal held the previous convictions could not assist the jury on the sole issue before them—specific intent—and should not have been admitted.

The chart below indicates this process.

Figure 52—Relevance of Misconduct

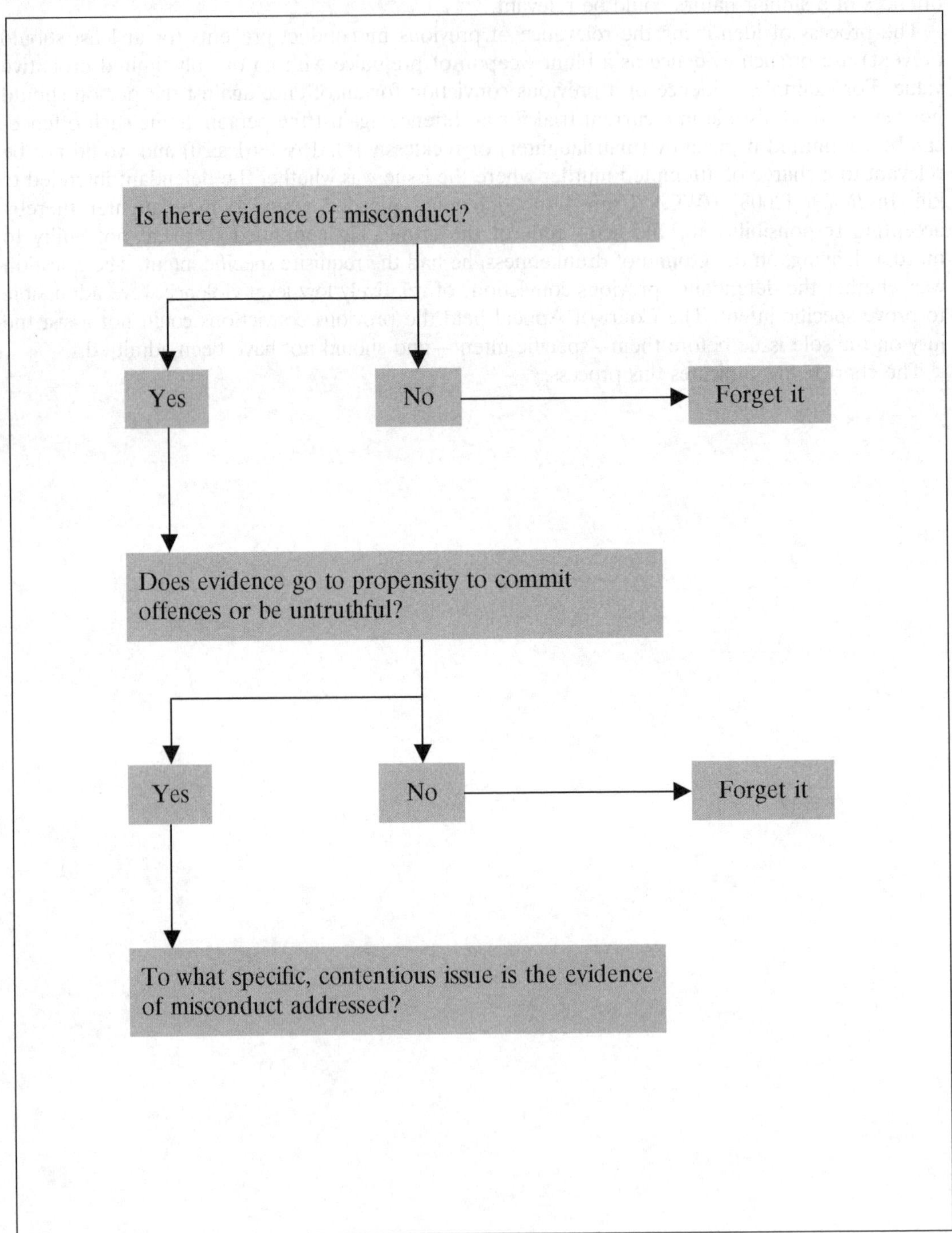

As we have seen, bad character is defined as 'misconduct' which is itself further defined as 'the commission of an offence or other reprehensible behaviour'. (ss.98 and 112 respectively). 'Offence' is not to be treated as the same as 'conviction'. The importance of this distinction should become clear as we consider s.103.

Section 103(2)–(5) amplifies how the prosecution may prove a defendant's 'propensity to commit offences of the kind with which he is charged' (s.101(1)(a)). It may (subs.(2)) 'without prejudice to any other way of doing so' be established by evidence showing that he has been convicted of:

(a) an offence of the same description; or

(b) an offence the same category as the one with which he is charged.

Two offences are of the same description when the written charge or indictment would be in the same terms: s.101(4)(a). Two separate categories have been specified in accordance with s.2(b) and 5 namely theft and sexual offences against those under the age of 16 years. They are specified in a Statutory Instrument SI 2004 No. 3346.

The effect of the words 'without prejudice to any other way of doing so'

These words operate to admit evidence of misconduct but in respect of which the defendant has not been convicted of an offence. Thus evidence of the following would seem to be admissible:

- previous acquittals: *Z* [2000] 2 Cr. App. R. 281; *Harrison* [2004] EWCA Crim 1792. These cases should not be taken to indicate that such evidence will always be admissible. There was overwhelming evidence of guilt in both cases the acquittals notwithstanding;
- an offence for which the defendant received a caution or which he asked to be taken into consideration: *Nicholson* (1948) 32 Cr. App. R. 98;
- other counts in today's indictment: *DPP v P* [1991] 93 Cr. App. R. 267. This is 'cross-admissibility' which we encountered earlier in this chapter;
- previous acts not charged at all: *Smith* (1916) 11 Cr. App. R. 229;
- possession of incriminating items or goods: *Wright* (1990) 90 Cr. App. R. 325 (though the decision here was to exclude);
- evidence of counts in today's indictment which the trial judge has stayed for abuse of process: *Smith (David)* [2005] EWCA Crim 3244.

Whether possession of gay literature by an adult (*Wright* above) would be regarded in the present day as 'reprehensible' is an open question. The same may be true in relation to some of the evidence admitted in *Butler*. The defendant was charged with rape of two women involving considerable sexual humiliation. Evidence of almost identical consensual sexual behaviour between the defendant and his former girlfriend was held admissible though whether it would today count as 'reprehensible behaviour' is open to debate.

In *Wallace* [2007] EWCA Crim 1760 it was held that where the defendant is charged with more than one offence in the same proceedings, evidence of other offences alleged against him amounts to evidence of bad character under the Act. In accordance with s.112(2) (which was at the heart of the decision) the prosecution should therefore be required to make an 'application for leave to admit' the other charges in accordance with s.101(3) (per Scott-Baker L.J. [44]).

What is the position if the prosecution wishes to prove behaviour which does not amount to 'misconduct' as defined in s.112 but which arguably shows the defendant in a bad light? It seems it remains admissible. In *Manister* [2005] EWCA Crim 2866 [76] the defendant (a man in his thirties) was charged with sexual offences against a girl aged 13 years. He had (five years previously) had a three-year relationship with a girl who was 16 years. The Court held that this was not evidence of statutory bad character because it did not amount to misconduct (neither an offence nor reprehensible). Kennedy L.J. said [95]:

> 'once it is decided that evidence of the appellant's sexual relationship with B did not amount to "evidence of bad character", the abolition of the common law rules governing the admissibility of "evidence of bad character" by section 99(1) did not apply. We have no doubt that evidence of the relationship was admissible at common law, in the particular circumstances of this case, because it was relevant to the issue of whether the appellant had a sexual interest in A. It was capable of demonstrating a sexual interest in early or mid-teenage girls, much younger than the appellant, and therefore bore on the truth of his case of a purely supportive, asexual interest in A. It was not in our judgment unfair to admit the evidence.'

Though no authority is cited for admissibility other than the 'common law' it would appear to be an application of the SFE/EAE principle. If so, although the common law rules relating to the admissibility of bad character evidence were expressly abolished by s.99(1) this kind of evidence remains admissible at common law. It follows that bad character now has two meanings—one under the Act (ss.98 & 112(1)) another at common law. None of the (albeit weak) statutory safeguards apply to admissibility at common law though presumably the 'prejudicial effect/probative value' test is still applicable.

Propensity to be untruthful—s.103(1)(b)

Not long after the decision in *Makin* Parliament passed the Criminal Evidence Act 1898. It made the defendant a competent witness for himself in criminal proceedings generally but its provisions engaged only if the defendant elected to give evidence. If he did, should he be freely exposed to cross-examination on his character (including any previous convictions)?

Answering that question in the negative, Parliament legislated a limited shield the effect of which was that the defendant could be cross-examined on his character only if he threw away the shield by e.g. making imputations about a prosecution witness or undermining the defence of a co-defendant. Even so, there was judicial discretion to disallow cross-examination where the prejudicial effect of the defendant's bad character outweighed its probative value: *Selvey v DPP* [1968] 52 Cr. App. R. 443. Admissibility of the defendant's bad character—usually but not exclusively his previous convictions—was a matter of law.

Although cross-examination of the defendant (if permitted) under the CEA involved evidence of bad character, the courts held the evidence went only to 'credibility'—a term we encountered above in relation to the first limb of *Vye*. To repeat, credibility is about whether, in the light of his bad character, the jury should believe the defendant in relation to any pre-trial statements or his evidence in the case. Unlike SFE/EAE, this evidence did not go towards guilt and the jury had to be warned in terms. The judicial warning in such terms became known as the 'standard direction': *Watts* (1983) 77 Cr. App. R. 126.

There were problems with this approach particularly where the defendant's previous convictions were for the same or very similar offences as the offence for which he now stood trial but where the evidence was not admissible as SFE/EAE. The standard direction may well have stretched the credulity of the jury when they were told such evidence could not be used by them as proof of guilt. In *Watts* Lord Lane characterised the standard direction as a 'feat of intellectual acrobatics' and one 'practically impossible' to achieve. The problem remains even though admissibility has migrated to the CJA 2003 ss.101(1)(d) and 103(1)(b). In this migration 'credibility' has been replaced by 'a propensity to be untruthful': s.103(1)(b).

The meaning of 'untruthful'

In *Hanson* [13] Rose L.J. said the word 'untruthful' was a deliberate Parliamentary choice conveying a different meaning from 'dishonesty' and:

> 'reflecting a defendant's account of his behaviour, or lies told when committing an offence. Previous convictions, whether for offences of dishonesty or otherwise, are therefore only likely to be capable of showing a propensity to be untruthful where . . . truthfulness is an issue and . . . either there was a plea of not guilty and the defendant gave an account, on arrest, in interview, or in evidence, which the jury must have disbelieved, or the way in which the offence was committed shows a propensity for untruthfulness, for example, by the making of false representations.'

As we have seen s.103 gives some indication of what is involved in the phrase 'propensity to commit offences of the kind with which he is charged'. The contrast with the phrase 'propensity to be untruthful' could hardly be more clear—for apart from the words 'except where it is not suggested that the defendant's case is untruthful in any respect' there is no explanation of what is intended. Nor are there any express safeguards concerning 'untruthfulness' in the Act. It is regrettable that there is no equivalent in s.103 to s.105(6) which provides that evidence to correct a false impression is admissible 'only if it goes no further than is necessary to correct the false impression'.

While in *Hanson* Rose L.J. [18] emphasised that the judge should warn the jury not to place undue reliance on convictions—in particular that the jury should not conclude the defendant is guilty or untruthful merely because he has convictions—the width of the subsection together with lack of safeguards creates an obvious risk of prejudice to the defendant. This is compounded if we consider the assumption, as the statute and case law seem to do, that a finding of 'guilty' on a 'not guilty' plea always justifies treating the defendant as untruthful. People plead not guilty for a number of reasons and the assumption in question is highly questionable. Should we assume that a defendant who has always previously pleaded 'guilty' but today pleads 'not guilty' is consequently truthful? To do so would be nonsensical but such nonsense is at the heart of this part of the law.

It was envisaged that a limited range of convictions such as those for perjury or obtaining by deception would be admitted under s.103(1(b). This is because only such offences would be capable of satisfying the test of relevance to an *important* matter in issue between the prosecution and the defendant: *Campbell* per Lord Phillips C.J. [30]. Unfortunately his Lordship proceeded [35] to blur the distinction between 'dishonesty' and 'untruthfulness' so clearly articulated by Rose L.J. in *Hanson*. Campbell had two convictions for offences of violence against women (he had pleaded guilty on both occasions) and was charged with similar offences. His bad character was admitted under s.101(1)(d) so the only relevance of the convictions can have been to a propensity to commit offences. Any decision by the jury that Campbell had a propensity to be untruthful must be a *consequence* of finding him guilty rather than a reason for it. Lord Phillip's judgment seems to ignore this crucial reasoning.

Proof of convictions

The prosecution can rely on a statement from a police officer with regard to the defendant's convictions as held on the Police National Computer whether they are adduced under s.103(1)(a) or (b). The printout is admissible under s.117 with regard to such matters as date, venue, trial, offences charged etc. There is no rule that background details of the defendant's convictions must be proved or even available in every case (*Lamaletie, Royce* [2008] EWCA Crim 314) though it was regarded by the Court of Appeal in that case as 'good practice'. However, if the prosecution wishes to rely on the background facts of the convictions then it must be in a position to prove them either by a statement from the complainant or calling the complainant to give direct evidence of what happened: *Humphris* [2005] EWCA Crim 2030.

Figure 53—Summary of issues relating to section 101(1)(d) and 103

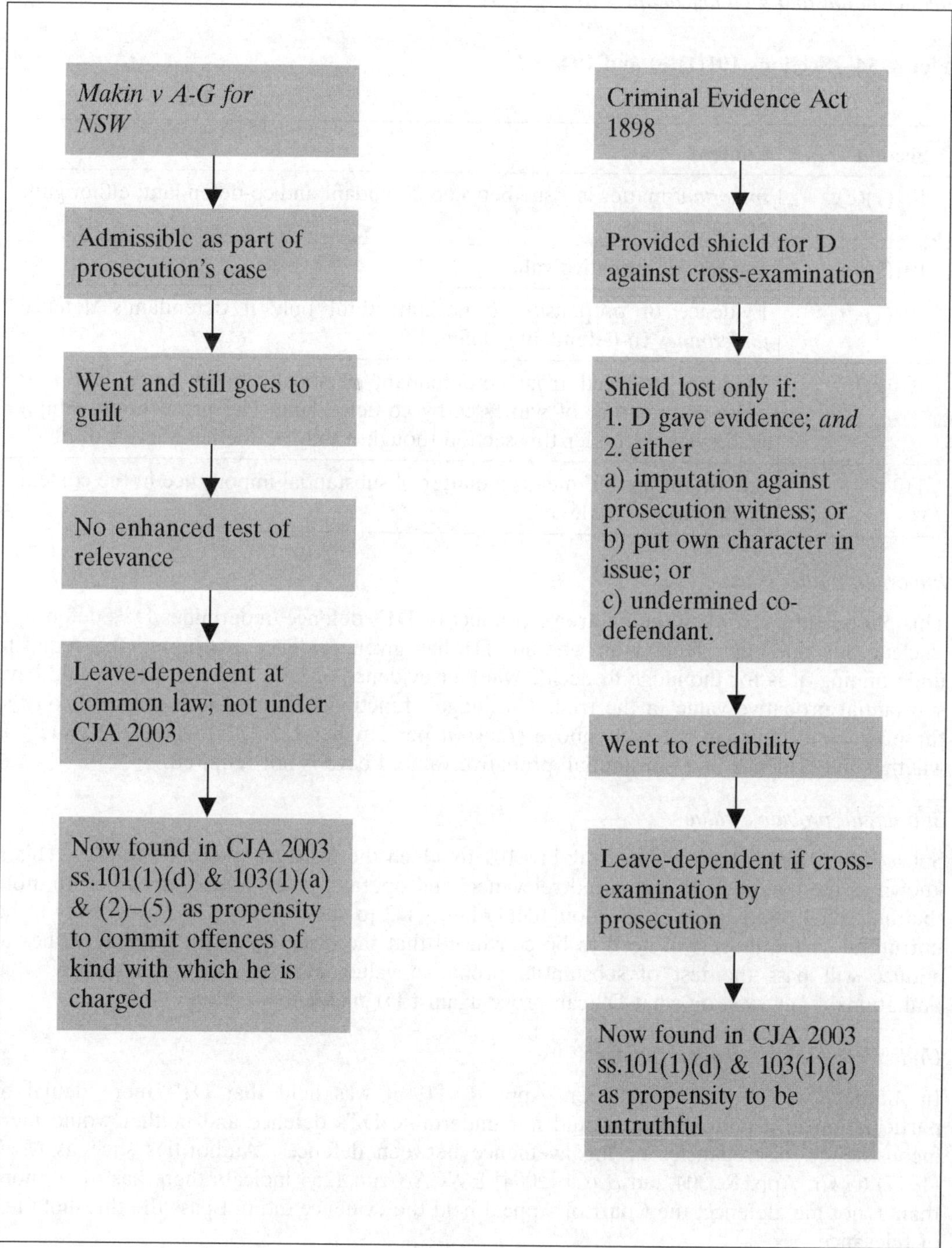

Paragraph (e) It has substantial probative value in relation to an important matter in issue between the defendant and a co-defendant

Figure 54—Sections 101(1)(e) and 104

Section	Content
101(1)(e)	*Important* matter in issue between defendant and co-defendant; either guilt or truthfulness.
101(1)(e)	*Substantial* probative value.
104(1)	Evidence of propensity to be untruthful only if defendant's defence *undermines* co-defendant's defence.
104(2)	Evidence adduced from co-defendant personally or by examination or cross-examination of witnesses by co-defendant. The prosecution cannot lead evidence under this section though it may be the beneficiary of it.
112	'important matter' means a matter of substantial importance in the context of the case as a whole.

Important matter is issue

This phrase refers to when the nature or conduct of D1's defence undermines D2's defence. It is clear this does not depend on whether D1 has given evidence. Assuming the requisite undermining, it is for the judge to decide whether evidence of D1's bad character would have substantial probative value in the trial. The judge's function is limited to a judgment on the three issues in italics in the table above (*Lawson* per Hughes L.J. [31]) where the issue was whether the evidence had 'substantial' probative value. Leave is not required.

Substantial probative value

Subsection (1)(e) is the only gateway in s.101 to which the word 'substantial' attaches. This is known as the condition of 'enhanced relevance' and operates to exclude evidence of no more than marginal or trivial value. Section 104(1) limits D2 to showing D1 has a propensity to be untruthful so the judge will need to be convinced that the evidence which D2 now wishes to adduce will pass the test of substantial probative value. We shall consider shortly what limitations if any exist on what D2 can prove against D1 under the section.

Undermine the co-defendant's defence

In *Murdoch v Taylor* [1965] 49 Cr. App. R. 119 it was held that D1's mere denial of participation in a joint venture would not undermine D2's defence and neither would mere inconsistency, discrepancies or inconvenience between defences. Authorities such as *Neale* (1977) 65 Cr. App. R. 304 and *B (C)* [2004] EWCA Crim 1254 indicate there has to be more than a 'not me' defence; the Court of Appeal held the evidence did not pass the threshold test of relevance.

While a hostile intent is not necessary, the higher than 'not me' threshold is reached when D1's evidence makes it more likely that D2 will be convicted. In *B* (above) Rix L.J. took the view that some combination of joint charges (*not* merely joint trials) either with or without cut-throat defences ('it was one of us but it wasn't me so it must be you' (see Ch.10, para.10.3.1)) is required before evidence of D1's bad character is admissible: *Davis* [1974] 60 Cr. App. R. 157; *Randall* [2003] EWCA Crim 436. But two words of warning. First, undermining does not depend on cut-throat defences—defendants may run parallel defences which can result in the acquittal of both of them. Second, *Randall* and some other pre-CJA 2003 cases held that D1's bad character might go not merely to credibility but also to guilt. As we shall see shortly this is no longer the case.

Has a propensity to be untruthful

The phrase 'has a propensity to be untruthful' indicates that evidence of D1's bad character admitted under s.104 can go only to credibility, not to guilt. The phrase appears in both ss.103(1)(b) and 104(1). Should it bear the same meaning in the sense of the width of permissible evidence? In *Lawson* Hughes L.J. [35] said there was a different framework of rules for each section. Citing *Hanson*, his Lordship implied [33] that evidence admitted under s.103(1)(b) (on a prosecution application) carried the risk that the jury might use it as going to 'propensity to offend and thus directly to guilt'. While acknowledging this risk also existed under s.104 his Lordship said [34]:

> 'it remains . . . wholly rational that the degree of caution which is applied to a Crown application against a defendant who is on trial when considering relevance or discretion should not be applied when what is at stake is a defendant's right to deploy relevant material to defend himself against a criminal charge. A defendant who is defending himself against the evidence of a person whose history of criminal behaviour or other misconduct is such as to be capable of showing him to be unscrupulous and/or otherwise unreliable should be enabled to present that history before the jury for its evaluation of the evidence of the witness. Such suggested unreliability may be capable of being shown by conduct *which does not involve an offence of untruthfulness*; it may be capable of being shown by widely differing conduct, ranging from large scale drug- or people-trafficking via housebreaking to criminal violence' (emphasis supplied).

This statement represents a substantial widening of evidence admissible to demonstrate D1's propensity to be untruthful as compared to prosecution evidence to prove the same issue under s.101(1)(d). As we saw above when considering s.103(1)(b) it was envisaged that only a limited range of offences would be admissible for the prosecution. The widening is recognition that one defendant must be allowed to present all relevant evidence in pursuing his defence and that preventing him from doing so runs the risk of violating art.6 of the ECHR. Nevertheless the references in the extract to 'unreliable' and 'unscrupulous' indicate the limitation to credibility and not an extension to guilt.

Paragraph (f) It is evidence to correct a false impression given by the defendant

We have seen that the common law allowed the defendant to prove his good character—it was known as 'putting his (good) character in issue'. He was, and remains, entitled to *Vye* directions in appropriate circumstances. The CJA 2003 does not use the language of 'good character' but does, in effect, allow the prosecution to rebut any such claim or implication when a defendant has created a 'false impression'.

False impression

Under s.105(1)(a):

> 'The defendant gives a false impression if he is responsible for the making of an express or implied assertion which is apt to give the court or jury a false or misleading impression about the defendant.'

If what the defendant says (or permits to be said on his behalf) is clearly untrue then it is false. However, it may also come within s.105 if, notwithstanding that the assertion is true, it is apt to mislead. Suppose the defendant asserts he is married and in regular employment (*Stronach* [1988] Crim. L.R. 48) and suppose this also to be true. He has convictions for theft. The impression from his assertion is that he is of good character (and therefore less likely to have committed the offence) when he is not. It is therefore a misleading impression. Evidence of bad character in rebuttal would affect the credibility of his evidence but does not and cannot rebut the truth of the assertion.

The impression can be asserted from conduct (subs.(4)). This overturns the decision in *Robinson* [2001] Crim. L.R. 478 where the defendant gave evidence while holding a copy of the Bible, 'gesticulating' with it. The Court of Appeal held his conduct did not amount to a claim of good character. 'Conduct' includes appearance or dress (ss.4 and 5) so appearing in court in a regimental or MCC tie and blazer (*http://content-usa.cricinfo.com/ci/content/image/index.html?object=207428;year=2006;month=5*, accessed March 31, 2008.) might well trigger the subsection.

When does the defendant create a false (or misleading) impression?

The impression may be made at any time from and including questioning under caution to the close of the defence. It does not depend on whether the defendant gives evidence—it could be made by his lawyer on his behalf. The defendant is responsible for the assertion unless (subs.(3)) he either withdraws it or disassociates himself from it. The Act does not specify a particular method for withdrawal and it has been held that he will not be treated as having withdrawn it if he is forced to admit the assertion is untrue under cross-examination: *Renda*.

Rebuttal evidence

Section 105(6) provides that such evidence should go 'no further than is necessary to correct the false impression'. This amounts to statutory reversal of the common law rule that the defendant's character is indivisible. That rule permitted (in the present context) admission of evidence of any aspect of the defendant's bad character in rebuttal of a claim to good character: *Winfield* [1939] 27 Cr. App. R. 139. The defendant was charged with indecent assault on a woman and called two female witnesses to testify to his good character in their dealings with him. It was held that his convictions for dishonesty were properly put to him under the indivisibility rule. Under the statute, rebuttal is fact-specific.

Paragraph (g) The defendant has made an attack on another person's character

General observation

At common law and under the CEA the prosecution was allowed to show the defendant's bad character where he made 'imputations' against prosecution witnesses including the deceased victim. It was known as 'tit for tat' and, subject to leave, allowed the jury to know the character of the person making allegations about another. The evidence went only to credibility (now called a propensity to be untruthful) and never to guilt.

The case of *Highton* has relevance both to para.(g) as well as to the function of the gateways generally. With regard to the narrower issue Lord Woolf said [9] that evidence admitted under gateway (g) could also go to the defendant's propensity to commit offences of the kind with which he is charged in the same way as can evidence admitted under gateway (d)—in other words to the issue. This view is supported by Lord Phillips C.J. in *Campbell* [26] where it is clearly obiter. *Munday* ([2006] Crim. L.R. 300) argues that Lord Woolf is wrong and the Act has made no change to the use to which evidence admitted under gateway (g) can be put. One of Munday's arguments (op cit p.309) is as follows. Under gateway (d) the prosecution can adduce evidence of the defendant's propensity to commit offences of the same kind or to be untruthful *only* if it is relevant to an important issue in the proceedings. If evidence of bad character admitted under gateway (g) can go to guilt as Lords Woolf and Phillips maintain, then it would not have to pass the 'important matter in issue test' which is the basis of gateway (d). So why was gateway (d) intentionally structured in this restrictive way if the prosecution can barge the door down provided the court decides the defendant has made an attack on another person's character—hardly the most demanding task to be encountered by prosecutors? This leads us to the wider issue in *Highton*.

The scheme of s.101(1) is clearly to provide a structure for admissibility of evidence of the defendant's bad character. The judgments in *Highton* and *Campbell* seem intent on denying the legitimacy of the statutory scheme. The judgment of Lord Phillips in *Campbell* is perhaps the more flagrant sample of this. As we saw above, Campbell had two previous convictions for similar offences. Lord Phillips held that provided they could be admitted under s.101(1)(d) and s.103(1)(a) as going to show a propensity to commit offences of the type in question, they could also go to the issue of untruthfulness under s.103(1)(b) provided they were relevant. As with the relationship between gateways (d) and (g) explored in the paragraph above, we might well ask why Parliament legislated the detailed scheme in question and whether, if his Lordship is correct, what is the point of s.103(1)(b) now?

Sections 101(1)(g) and 106 engage when any of the following occur:

- s.106(1)(a): the defendant adduces evidence 'attacking another's character'. It is not limited to prosecution witnesses or the deceased victim or, it would appear, to anyone else. It might include a co-defendant giving the prosecution the opportunity to introduce evidence of bad character; or
- s.106(1)(b): questions intended are or likely to elicit such evidence are asked in cross-examination; or
- s.106(1)(c): evidence is given in court of an imputation made by the defendant either (i) when questioned under caution or (ii) charged.

The words 'or are likely' in subs.(1)(b) represent danger for the defendant when cross-examining witnesses. It is not merely questions intended as an attack on another's character which risk a reprisal raid by the prosecution. Further danger lurks for a suspect who, possibly in the absence of legal advice, makes allegations against other persons while being interviewed under caution: subs.(1)(c).

'Character' and 'attack'

Character bears the same meaning here as in s.98 as amplified by s.112(1) and an 'imputation' is an assertion to that effect. Common law decisions as to what amounted to an imputation were inconsistent and many were often marginal. In *Hanson* the Court of Appeal held [14] they would continue to apply unless they were incompatible with the Act. In total contradiction Lord Phillips in *Campbell*, speaking generally about evidence of bad character said [24]: 'Decisions in this field before the (Act) . . . are unhelpful and should not be cited'.

An 'attack' is an imputation that another person has committed an offence—whether or not the offence charged against the defendant—or has behaved or is disposed to behave in a reprehensible (see para.9.4.2.1) way. We are now going to look at some specific instances under the pre-2003 law to see what amounted to an imputation.

The rape cases

Rape cases were treated as a special category because the 'defence' is usually consent and if the defendant were prevented from questioning the complainant freely about the circumstances of the alleged offence, he would be inhibited from making out a case. In *Turner* [1944] 30 Cr. App. R. 9 the defence was consent and in examination in chief the defendant said that the victim had committed an act of gross indecency on him. It was held that cross-examination to show the defendant had a conviction for assault with intent to ravish was improper. A 'defence' of consent was no more than a denial that the prosecution had established one of the specific legal burdens. The principle in *Turner* was approved in *Selvey v DPP* [1968] 52 Cr. App. R. 443 and should remain good law.

Caution is needed, nevertheless, with denial of an element of the offence which can amount to an imputation. In *Stone* [2001] EWCA Crim 2379 the defendant said he acted in self-defence against an unprovoked knife attack by the prosecution witness. The Court of Appeal upheld the judge that the defendant's claim that the victim had made such an attack went beyond mere denial and amounted to an imputation. Cross-examination on his convictions for violence was therefore proper. This may seem no different from consent in rape and, in truth, it probably is not. Rightly or otherwise, rape cases are treated as a special category.

Questions to the police

A rough distinction existed between suggestions of non-adherence to procedures such as the PACE Codes of Practice (not an imputation) and questions to discredit a particular officer (imputation). So a suggestion that an identification procedure was not held in accordance with the Code D should in principle be treated differently from statements or questions tending to discredit individual officers e.g. alleging that a confession was dictated by one police officer to another: *Clark* [1955] 39 Cr. App. R. 120. The key was the substance of the question or allegation rather than the form of words used. 'Mistake' might be a euphemism for 'lie' and 'lie' might be no more than an indignant denial of guilt. In this context, a suggestion that the witness has 'misremembered' may be useful!

'I had to'

It did not matter that it was a *necessary* part of the defence to make an imputation: *Hudson* [1912] 7 Cr. App. R. 256. The defendant was charged with stealing a cheque book in a pub. Prosecution witnesses were cross-examined to the effect that they had stolen it and put it in the defendant's pocket. It was held that cross-examination of the defendant on his own previous conviction was not improper. In any event, counsel had not objected to cross-examination at trial and, while not conclusive, that has a strong bearing on whether the defendant should be allowed to raise the issue on appeal.

Plea of not guilty, denial of guilt

A formal plea of not guilty or an in-trial denial of guilt or an assertion of innocence even if in strong terms was not an imputation. Any other view would have resulted in almost automatic disclosure of bad character. In *Rouse* [1904] 1 K.B. 184 the defendant was asked whether he had made a statement to which a witness had sworn. He replied, 'No, it is a lie and he is a liar'. It was held that this was no more than an emphatic denial of guilt. Nevertheless there were limits. In *Rappolt* (1911) 6 Cr. App. R. 156 the defendant said a witness was such a horrible liar that even his own brother would not speak to him. This was upheld as a general attack on the witness's character which justified cross-examination.

Might the words used in *Rouse* now be regarded as an allegation of reprehensible behaviour which would lead to admissibility of evidence of the defendant's character?

You were in it too!

Suggestions to a witness of complicity in the crime alleged against the defendant or of some other offence would clearly amount to an imputation.

In *Wainwright* [1998] Crim. L.R. 665 it was argued that since counsel for both sides agreed the bad character of the (deceased) prosecution witness there had been no imputation. The argument might be summarised as: 'no dispute—no imputation'. The Court of Appeal rejected the argument—a decision described by Murphy (p.164) as 'particularly outrageous'. The position was partly ameliorated by the Court of Appeal in *Taylor, Goodman* [1999] 2 Cr. App. R. 163. The previous convictions of a prosecution accomplice witness should, unless the defendant specifically asks otherwise, be disclosed to the jury from the outset. This avoids the defendant having to do it in cross-examination of the accomplice. A defendant's convictions may, of course, be admissible under s.101(1)(d) anyway.

The absent prosecution witness

A person whose evidence is given pursuant to ss.114–117 of the CJA 2003 (absence or fear) is still a witness for these purposes. It follows that an imputation on the character of an absent witness may still open the defendant to having his bad character proved under this subsection: *Miller* [1997] Crim. L.R. 217. Although the case concerned a witness's evidence in documentary form (previous legislation), it would apply equally to oral hearsay under the Act of 2003.

In *Britzmann & Hall* [1983] 76 Cr. App. R. 134 it was held that the prosecution should not rely on cross-examination if the case against the defendant is overwhelming. We have seen in extracts from *Hanson* that Rose L.J. seems to anticipate a similar position. Why should the prosecution refrain from seeking to admit evidence on which it is entitled to rely?

And finally . . .

Since the section is limited to evidence adduced by the prosecution it cannot be used by a co-defendant. This is important because unlike s.101(1)(e) it is not necessary for the evidence to have 'substantial' probative value. The discretion to exclude on grounds of fairness under s.101(3) applies expressly to this area. In practice the discretion might arise where the prosecution wishes to admit evidence of the defendant's bad character because of an imputation he made while being questioned under caution by the police. In *Nelson* [2006] EWCA Crim 3412 the Court of Appeal held that subs.(1)(g) should not normally be triggered where such imputation was made against a non-victim non-witness. The Court also held that the judge (and, surely, the defence?) should be vigilant to ensure that evidence of the allegations had been properly before the jury in the first place. It is 'improper' for the prosecution to rely on evidence of such imputations—especially where they are of marginal, if any, relevance—simply as a basis for satisfying gateway (g).

9.4.2.4 **Exclusion of evidence of bad character**

As we have seen (para.7.2.1), there was power at common law to exclude evidence of a prejudicial nature (*Sang* [1979] 69 Cr. App. R. 282) though the ambit of the decision was disputed. It is generally considered that s.82(3) of the PACE preserved that power while s.78(1) of the same Act both extended the scope of the power while limiting it to evidence on which the prosecution proposes to rely.

It follows that s.78(1) should, in principle, be applicable to any of the gateways under s.101(1) of the CJA 2003 where the prosecution is seeking admission of evidence of bad character. On the other hand while s.126(2) expressly preserves the application of s.78(1) with regard to the hearsay provisions of the Act (Pt 11, Ch.2) it does not do so in relation to the bad character provisions (Pt 11 Ch.1). Whether this anything more than inept drafting remains to be seen.

Further, s.101(3) and (4) of the Act apply expressly but only to gateways (d) and (g) and it is arguable that s.78(1) is therefore impliedly excluded from such gateways. Since the wording of s.101(1)(3) and s.78(1) is virtually identical it may not matter if this argument is correct though it is worth noting that subs.(3) is mandatory when the court reaches a decision on the adverse effect of the admission of the evidence ('must not'). Section 78(1) is permissive ('may refuse'). In *Tirnaveanu* Thomas L.J. [28] described this as 'a distinction without a difference' confirming the power as identical.

On the other hand, the duty to exclude under subss.(3) and (4) arises only on an application by the defendant whereas the power under s.78(1) requires general vigilance by the court and is not application-dependent. It is also worth noting that while s.78(1) does not apply (s.78(3)) to proceedings before a magistrates' court inquiring into an offence as examining justices there is no similar exclusion in relation to of s.101(1)(3) or (4). For the time being we cannot say whether s.78(1) applies across all of the gateways.

There is a narrow point of exclusion in s.103(3). A court is required to exclude evidence of a propensity to commit offences of the kind charged (*not* a propensity to be untruthful) if satisfied that by reason of the length of time since the previous conviction 'or for any other reason' that it would be unjust to admit it. In contrast to s.101(3) the power in s.103(3) is not expressed to be defendant application-dependent. You will recall that in *Highton* Lord Woolf held evidence admitted under gateway (g) can be relevant not only credibility but also to the issue. If this is correct, it would mean the courts' duty under s.103(3) with regard to evidence going to the issue would not engage if it had been admitted under gateway (g). This cannot have been intended and is another reason to doubt this part of the judgment of Lord Woolf in *Highton*.

Whether art.6 of the ECHR has any application to exclusion is unclear. In *Musone* [2007] EWCA Crim 1237 the Court of Appeal held there was no power under gateway (e) to use art.6 if the requirements of the gateway (in particular 'substantial probative value') were fulfilled. It is arguable that this approach is applicable to all the gateways.

Figure 55—Discretionary exclusion of evidence of bad character

Power to exclude evidence of bad character	**PACE s.82(3)**	**PACE s.78(1)**	**CJA S.101(3) & (4) on D's application**	**CJA s.103(3) whether or not on D's application**	**ECHR Article 6**
Common law	Yes	Concurrent with s.82(3)	n/a	n/a	No: *Musone* (above)
CJA s.101(1)(a)	Yes	Concurrent with s.82(3)	n/a	n/a	As above
s.101(1)(b)	Yes	Concurrent with s.82(3)	n/a	n/a	As above
s.101(1)(c)	Yes	Concurrent with s.82(3)	n/a	n/a	As above
s.101(1)(d)	Yes	Possibly not	Yes	Yes but only re: s.103(1)(a) & (2)	As above
s.101(1)(e)	Yes	No	n/a	n/a	As above
s.101(1)(f)	Yes	Yes	n/a	n/a	As above
s.101(1)(g)	Yes	Possibly not	Yes	n/a	As above

9.4.2.5 **Triggers**

As we have seen the defendant was immune from having his previous convictions proved against him for the purpose of undermining his credibility unless he both:

- lost his shield under the Act of 1898; and
- gave evidence.

The table below shows which of the statutory gateways is triggered by the defendant doing something (whether by giving evidence in person or not).

Figure 56—Statutory gateways triggered by the defendant

Paragraph	Yes or No
(a) all parties to the proceedings agree to the evidence being admissible	Yes
(b) the evidence is adduced by the defendant himself or is given in answer to a question asked by him in cross-examination and intended to elicit it	Yes
(c) it is important explanatory evidence	No
(d) it is relevant to an important matter in issue between the defendant and the prosecution	No
(e) it has substantial probative value in relation to an important matter in issue between the defendant and a co-defendant	No
(f) it is evidence to correct a false impression given by the defendant	Yes
(g) the defendant has made an attack on another person's character	Yes

9.5 Bad character of witnesses other than the defendant

At common law cross-examination of non-defendant witnesses as to their character was something of a free for all. As we saw in Ch.2, para.2.8 under the CJA 2003 ss.98 & 100 this area is much more tightly circumscribed. Section 100(1) is essentially exclusionary permitting evidence of the bad character of a non-defendant 'if and only if . . .

(a) it is important explanatory evidence,
(b) it has substantial probative value in relation to a matter which

 (i) is a matter in issue in the proceedings, and
 (ii) is of substantial importance in the context of the case as a whole

or
(c) all parties to the proceedings agree to the evidence being admissible.'

Detail on the subsections—subsection (1)

The three subsections are clearly alternatives. We dealt with the meaning of subs.(1)(a) when we covered 101(1)(c). Subsection (c) is self-explanatory. Subsection (1)(b) deals with the situation when the character of a non-defendant has probative value in the case against the defendant. It is clear that it covers both witnesses and non-witnesses and might even cover the character of a person whom a party would not generally be able to call to give evidence: *Blastland* [1985] 3 W.L.R. 345.

The wording of subs.(1)(b) has something in common with s.101(1)(d), but more closely resembles that of s.101(1)(e). Protection for non-defendant witnesses is, however, much enhanced first because admission of such evidence under both subs.(1)(a) and (b) is leave-dependent; and, secondly, because of the conditions in subs.(3), which we will cover shortly.

It is clear that subs.(1)(b) would cover issues going to guilt. In *S (Andrew)* [2006] EWCA Crim 1303 it was held that the phrase 'is a matter in issue in the proceedings' in s.100(1)(b)(i) includes the creditworthiness of the non-defendant witness. This construction of 'matter in issue' is wider than that we saw in Ch.2, para.2.8.2 (where we used the phrase 'facts in issue') but is essential:

> 'Since otherwise it would never be possible to cross-examine a witness as to his previous convictions where the purpose of doing so was to demonstrate that the witness was unworthy of belief; but there are inevitably cases in which justice requires such a course to be taken.' (per Laws L.J. [7]).

His Lordship proceeded to amplify 'unworthy of belief' to include, by way of example, whether a 'witness is especially prone to forgetfulness by reason of accident or disease'. In this context, therefore, 'matter in issue' covers all three areas we considered in Ch.2, para.2.8.2—facts in issue; matters of credit (credibility); accuracy or reliability of the witness.

Detail on the subsections—subsection (3)

The subsection lists (non-exhaustively) the factors which the court must consider when assessing the probative value of evidence to be admitted under s.100(1)(b). It is constructed so that subs.(3)(a) and (b) (nature, number and time of events) apply to all cases. Paragraphs (c) and (d) have some commonality but are aimed at differing circumstances. The commonality is that they each specify 'misconduct' which is covered by the standard definition in s.112(1) as 'the commission of an offence or other reprehensible behaviour'.

Subsection (3)(c) covers the situation where the 'person's misconduct has probative value by reason of that and other alleged misconduct'. An example would be that a police officer had previously falsified confessions and persuaded defence witnesses not to give evidence. The officer's misconduct might be thought to have probative value though that value will also need to be 'substantial'.

Subsection (3)(d) deals with the situation where:

(i) there is evidence of another person's misconduct; and

(ii) the defence suggests that the 'person' whose misconduct is in issue is responsible for the misconduct charged; and

(iii) there is a dispute as to the identity of the person charged with the misconduct.

The bad character evidence must show or tend to show that the same person was responsible each time.

Section 112(3)

The section provides (inter alia) that nothing in the Chapter affects the exclusion of evidence under:

- the rule which prevents a party from impeaching his own witness (see Ch.2, para.2.2.12.1); or
- s.41 of the YJCEA 1999 (see above Ch.2, para.2.12.2.1).

9.6 Miscellaneous

9.6.1 Section 108

The effect of the section is that if the defendant is over 21 years, evidence of conviction when under 14 years for an offence is inadmissible unless both offences are indictable only and the court finds it is in the interests of justice to admit the evidence.

9.6.2 Section 109

Any reference to relevance or probative value of evidence in the chapter (ss.98–113) are on the assumption that the evidence is true (subs.(1)) but the court need not assume it to be true if no court or jury could reasonably believe it to be true (subs.(2)).

9.6.3 Section 110

The section applies when a court decides on trial on indictment:

- *either* on whether an item of evidence amounts to evidence of character under the Act;
- *or* whether to admit evidence of bad character;
- *or* whether evidence is contaminated within s.107 (see para.9.6.4)

the reason(s) for the decision must be given in open court (absent the jury).

9.6.4 Collusion and contamination

The common law developed rules to cover collusion—a concept described by Lord Taylor in *Ryder* (1994) 98 Cr. App. R. 242 as 'deliberate or unconscious influence by one witness on another.' (The Criminal Law Review Commentary [1993] Crim. L.R. 601 contains an interesting piece of speculation about 'unconscious influence'). An allegation of collusion often arises in the context of sexual offences and cross-admissibility under the SFE/EAE principle.

The leading common law case is *H (Evidence Corroboration)* [1995] 2 Cr. App. R. 437 where the House of Lords summarised the correct approach when such an allegation is made. The judge should approach admissibility on the basis that the evidence in question is truthful and accurate. This is aimed at avoiding the judge being drawn into the jury's area. If, having admitted the evidence, it becomes apparent that no reasonable jury could act on it as being free from collusion, the judge should instruct the jury to disregard it. What amounts to a serious collusion risk is, therefore, a question of law for the judge.

If the collusion risk remains but is below the threshold when the jury is directed to disregard the evidence the judge must warn the jury about the risk and leave it to them to decide the value of the evidence.

The word 'contamination' is found in s.107 of the Criminal Justice Act 2003. On a trial before judge and jury, where evidence of bad character has been admitted under s.101(c)–(g) (only) the court can stop a trial at any time after the close of the prosecution case if it is satisfied that the evidence of 'a person' is contaminated and where that evidence is sufficiently important that a conviction would be unsafe. Section 107(5)(a) covers conspiracy and collusion between the person and others while subs.(b) covers what is known as 'innocent contamination'. This occurs where the person becomes aware either directly or indirectly of an allegation by another against the defendant (as, e.g. where two or more witnesses are inexpertly questioned by the same investigative team: *Fahy* [2002] EWCA Crim 525). The section is not based on discretion. Once the judge is satisfied that important evidence is contaminated, he must direct either an acquittal or a re-trial: *Card* [2006] EWCA Crim 1079. If the contamination is not of that level, a direction in accordance with *H* should be given.

9.7 Summary

(a) The chapter has been concerned with good and bad character of the defendant and witnesses.

(b) In practice the admissibility of evidence of bad character is governed by the CJA 2003. Proof of bad character often takes the form of evidence of previous convictions but the CJA refers to misconduct and this is wider than convictions. In apparent contradiction of meaning 'misconduct' includes previous acquittals.

(c) Where the defendant is of good character he will normally be given the benefit of the two-limbed common law direction in *Vye*.

(d) Section 101(1) of the CJA 2003 contains sevengateways through which evidence of the defendant's bad character must pass.

(e) Once it passes one of the gateways the use to which the evidence is put is mainly governed by the common law though some of the gateways prima facie limit the way in which such evidence *ought* to be used.

(f) Although the provisions of s.101 represent a big change in the rules as to admissibility of the defendant's character, the decision in *Hanson* places clear limits on when the prosecution should be allowed to lead evidence of previous convictions. Maverick decisions such as *Highton* (in part) and *Campbell* (almost totally) should be treated with caution.

9.8 Further Reading

'Bad Character Evidence'. *http://sfo.gov.uk/operationalhandbook/1163172867509.html* (accessed March 28, 2008)

Bostock, 'The Effect on Juries of Hearing About the Defendant's Previous Criminal Record' [2000] Crim. L.R. 734

Mirfield, 'Character, credibility and truthfulness' [2008] 124 L.Q.R. 1

Munday, 'What Constitutes "Other Reprehensible Behaviour" under the Bad Character Provisions of the CJA 2003?' [2005] Crim. L.R. 24.

Munday, 'Bad Character Rules & Riddles: "Explanatory Notes" and the True Meanings of s.103(1) of the CJA 2003' [2005] Crim. L.R. 337

Munday, 'Cut Throat Defences and "The Propensity to be Untruthful" under s.104 of the CJA 2003' [2005] Crim. L.R. 624

Munday, 'The purpose of Gateway (g): Yet another Problematic of the CJA 2003' [2006] Crim. L.R. 300

Redmayne, 'The relevance of Bad Character' [2002] C.L.J. 684

Tapper, 'The CJA 2003 (3): Evidence of Bad Character' [2004] Crim. L.R. 533

The Law Commission, 'Evidence of Bad Character in Criminal Proceedings' (Law Commission No. 273) 2001.

Thornton, 'The Prejudiced Defendant: Unfairness Suffered by a Defendant in a Joint Trial' [2003] Crim. L.R. 433.

10 Corroboration, Suspect and Other Fallible Evidence

10.1 Introduction

This chapter is concerned with two situations in criminal proceedings. The first is where, by statute, corroborative evidence is required. This is covered in para.10.2. The second is where, for a variety of reasons, the courts have decreed that some additional evidence is required as a matter of practice, and that a warning should be given to the jury as to whether, and if so, they can proceed in its absence. This is covered in para.10.3. Legal rules which are prescriptive (or restrictive) about the weight to be given to evidence are unusual in common law criminal justice systems and might be thought to conflict with a basic common law principle of 'free proof' under which the jury assesses the credibility of evidence without instruction as to how it can be used.

10.2 Corroboration required by statute

10.2.1 The meaning of corroboration

In ordinary speech, there is nothing technical about the idea of corroboration—it simply means additional facts or opinion in support of some other facts or opinion. In criminal proceedings, however, 'corroboration' has a technical meaning. The law requires first some additional evidence which often, but by no means always, takes the form of a second testifying witness (W2). The corroborative evidence makes it more likely that the evidence of the witness to be corroborated (W1) is true and that it is reasonably safe to act on it.

The phrase 'evidence of W1 is true' has two distinct elements. First, W1's evidence must be verified (supported) by W2; second it must implicate the defendant—it must connect him to the offence. In *Baskerville* (1916) 12 Cr. App. R. 81 the defendant was charged with indecent assault of two boys, W1 and W2, who were accomplices. The trial judge held that a letter arranging to meet the boys and containing a ten shilling note (paper equivalent of the 50p coin) was capable of corroborating the boys' evidence that it was the defendant who had committed the offence. The appeal held that both elements (support and implicate) were required.

While the case holds that the double formula was a strict requirement of corroboration, Lord Reading said the nature of the corroborative evidence will vary according to the particular circumstances of the offence and declined to formulate anything approaching a rule as to the *kind* of evidence which could be corroborative.

10.2.2 No general corroboration requirement at common law

For many years English law had no general corroboration requirement—English courts could convict a man on the sole testimony of one witness, a situation which generally holds today. There were exceptions which tended to focus on two main areas: evidence of complainants in sexual offences and evidence of accomplices as a prosecution witness. For a number of reasons the CJPOA 1994 s.32 abolished the corroboration requirement in the two main areas. There is now almost nothing left of corroboration in its technical sense as a mandatory requirement of the law of evidence, i.e. where the judge *must* warn the jury of the need to find additional evidence implicating the defendant before they can convict. We will now deal with these areas.

10.2.3 Corroboration required as a matter of law (statute)

10.2.3.1 Perjury

Under the Perjury Act 1911 s.13 no one is to be convicted of perjury, procuring (suborning) perjury, or an offence akin to perjury on the sole evidence of one witness as to the falsity of any statement alleged to be false.

Corroboration is required in respect of the fact that the statement was false and not whether the defendant believed it was true or false: *O'Connor* [1980] Crim. L.R. 43. The corroborative evidence may take any form—a letter suborning another to commit perjury would be sufficient. It is insufficient to show the defendant made contradictory statements on oath unless it is proved (and corroborated) which of the statements is false. It may be clear that the defendant has committed perjury on one occasion but it may not be possible to establish which. If so he must be acquitted.

10.2.3.2 Road traffic

Under the Road Traffic Regulation Act 1984 s.89(2) a person cannot be convicted of driving above the maximum or below the minimum speed limit (contrary to s.89(1)) on the evidence of W1 unless W1's opinion is corroborated by the evidence of W2. This has nothing to do with speed recorders which register facts not opinions.

10.2.3.3 Treason Act 1795

Under s.1 a person may not be convicted of compassing the death or restraint of the monarch except on the evidence of two credible witnesses.

10.2.4 Conclusion

If there is no corroborative evidence in the specified circumstances the defendant cannot be convicted. Any 'conviction' will be quashed. However, if corroboration was present but the judge failed to warn the jury on the need for corroboration, the conviction will not necessarily be unsafe.

Figure 57—Summary table

Corroboration required by statute	Perjury Act 1911	Road Traffic Regulation Act 1984	Treason Act 1795
1. Support 2. Implicate	As to falsity	As to opinion	Plotting death or restraint

10.3 Additional evidence required as a matter of practice

10.3.1 Witnesses with a motive to misrepresent

The trial judge must warn the jury about the dangers of convicting the defendant on the evidence of a witness with a motive or potential to misrepresent facts as a consequence of prior events or relationships.

Who might this cover?

It could cover any relationship. Here are a few examples:

- a handler of stolen goods giving evidence as a prosecution witness at the trial of a person alleged to have stolen the goods. This was one of the occasions when the full corroboration warning was mandatory at common law;
- an agent provocateur or informant;
- a prostitute giving evidence at the trial of her pimp;
- a disgruntled ex-employee giving evidence at the trial of his former employer;
- a neighbour giving evidence when there is bad feeling between him and his neighbour;
- a witness who has asked for a reward: *Rasheed*, *The Times*, May 20, 1994, where it was held that a request for a reward by a witness might have a bearing on their motives for coming forward to give evidence. It must always be disclosed to the defence;
- a witness who has been offered an immunity of some type by the police or prosecuting authorities;
- a person remanded in custody giving evidence of an alleged 'cell confession' by another person also in custody. Such a person's antecedents and character should be fully researched by the prosecution which is under a duty to disclose such matters to the defence: *Hickey* (1997) (Unreported); *Benedetto v R., Labrador v R.* [2003] 1 W.L.R. 1545.

In practice, the most problematic area is co-defendant (D2) giving evidence on his own behalf at the joint trial of himself and D1 or where an accomplice gives evidence as a prosecution witness

(AW). There is a clear motive for D2 or AW to minimise his role in the offence while highlighting that of D1.

Cut throat defences

Suppose D1 has produced alibi evidence. D2 gives evidence that D1 was the planner, procurer and main actor in the offence. This is an example of a cut-throat defence which may be full or modified. It is full where D2 says D1 alone is responsible for the outcome and is modified where D2 accepts some blame for the outcome while placing most of it on D1. *Jones, Jenkins* [2003] EWCA Crim 1966 is an example of a full cut-throat defence by Jenkins who said he had not hit the deceased. Jones said that both he and Jenkins had hit the deceased so his was a modified cut-throat. Auld L.J. regarded both appellants as running modified cut-throat defences but it is open to question whether he is correct.

In *Cheema* (1994) 98 Cr. App. R. 195 Lord Taylor said that most instances could be covered by a standard warning to treat such evidence with care because of the self-serving motive. Occasionally, the judge should warn of the need to look for corroboration (and what evidence would suffice) if the attack by a co-defendant had been particularly severe. In *Jones, Jenkins* it was held that a cut throat defence—whether full or modified—should *normally* give rise to a warning that a co-defendant had an interest of his own to serve. To the extent that *Burrows* [2000] Crim. L.R. 48 was to the contrary it should not be followed. The warning is particularly important where as in *Jones, Jenkins* one of the defendants is silent at interview and is therefore in a position to tailor his evidence to fit the facts.

In *Jones, Jenkins*; Auld L.J. said there were four points.

> 'That a judge, when dealing with the case against and defence of each co-defendant, might consider . . . to put to the jury—points that would not offend any sense of justice and certainly would not cast the judge in the light of one who has formed an adverse view against either or both co-defendants'.

The four points are:

1. The jury should consider the case for and against each defendant separately.
2. The jury should decide the case on all the evidence, including the evidence of each defendant's co-defendant.
3. When considering the evidence of co-defendants, the jury should bear in mind that he may have an interest to serve or, as it is often put, an axe to grind.
4. The jury should assess the evidence of co-defendants in the same way as that of the evidence of any other witness in the case.

Jones, Jenkins was critically considered in *Petkar, Farquhar* [2003] EWCA 2668. On behalf of the Court of Appeal Rix L.J. said that 'we would venture our concerns in this way'. He suggested, first, that a warning might serve to devalue the evidence of the defendant and co-defendant in the eyes of the jury. His Lordship felt this was more of a problem than the judge possibly appearing to have formed an adverse view about one of the parties. His second concern was whether the third and fourth 'limbs' of the suggested *Jones; Jenkins* direction lay easily together. It is vital to distinguish what a co-defendant says in his own defence from anything he says which incriminates the defendant. In *Jones, Jenkins*, the latter said that he had not hit the deceased at all but he did not suggest that Jones had. To the extent that Jenkins incriminated Jones at all it was by his admission that the victim had received serious injuries but that was hardly contentious.

The judge's duty

By virtue of the CJPOA 1994 s.32(1):

> 'Any requirement whereby at a trial on indictment it is obligatory for the court to give the jury a warning about convicting the accused on the uncorroborated evidence of a person merely because that person is (a) an alleged accomplice of the accused, or (b) where the offence charged is a sexual offence, the person in respect of whom it is alleged to have been committed, is hereby abrogated'.

In *Makanjuola, Easton* [1995] 3 All E.R. 730 the appellants were convicted of indecent assault on the uncorroborated testimony of the complainants. There were two main arguments. The first was that the judge should still warn the jury about convicting on the uncorroborated evidence of a complainant in a sexual offence. Lord Taylor C.J. said the effect of this would be that Parliament would have legislated 'in vain'. While it is clear the judge might warn in such circumstances in a particular case, the use of the word 'merely' in the section was intended to abrogate such need on a day-to-day basis.

The second argument was that if the judge did decide to warn, the warning should be what was known as the full corroboration warning which involved the judge directing the jury that it was 'dangerous' to convict without supporting evidence which also implicated the defendant: *Baskerville*. His Lordship rejected this in forthright language styling it an attempt to re-impose the old strait-jacket of corroboration and saying that attempts to do so 'are strongly to be deprecated'.

The importance of *Makanjuola* is its two-stage approach. First, before a warning is given, there must be some evidential basis for that warning i.e. some evidence which suggests the witness is unreliable. The judge's perception must be evidentially grounded, in other words, it must be based on something more than an allegation by counsel that a witness had some ulterior motive. Counsel should be involved in the process as to whether to warn. On the facts, there was no evidential basis for supposing either complainant to be unreliable. In *Walker* [1996] Crim. L.R. 742 the complainant in a rape prosecution followed her complaint with a retraction which she subsequently in turn retracted, the net effect being to leave her complaint intact. The Court of Appeal quashed the conviction. The retraction and subsequent withdrawal were, on these facts, an evidential basis calling for a judicial warning to the jury following discussion with counsel. The facts 'cried out' for a warning (per Ebsworth J.).

In *Dawes* [2007] EWCA Crim 1165 a co-defendant who was an accomplice did not implicate the defendant in interviews with the police but at trial gave evidence which did incriminate him. Such behaviour was held to be sufficient evidential basis for a warning.

The second step is to decide on the terms of any warning and this should be tailored to the evidential risk which the judge apprehends. Sometimes the warning will be very strong, even to the point of including a phrase such as 'there may be dangers in convicting on the evidence of

Jones alone'. Other cases will justify pointing out to the jury any motive for misrepresentation but in less dramatic language: 'you should consider Jones's evidence with care'. Where the judge considers evidence exists capable of supporting 'suspect' evidence then he must identify it to the jury. The judge must also identify any evidence which cannot in law be supportive.

10.3.2 Visual identification—the *Turnbull* guidelines

The case of *Turnbull* (1976) 63 Cr. App. R. 132 is concerned with disputed visual identification of the defendant, when such evidence is admissible, whether the jury should be warned about the identification and, if so, in what terms. We start by considering the distinction drawn by Lord Widgery C.J. between poor and good quality identification. As to the former he said:

> 'When, in the judgment of the trial judge, the quality of the identifying evidence is poor, as for example when it depends solely on a fleeting glance or on a longer observation made in difficult conditions . . . the judge should . . . withdraw the case from the jury and direct an acquittal unless there is other evidence which goes to support the correctness of the identification . . . to make the jury sure that there has been no mistaken identification: for example, X sees the accused snatch a woman's handbag; he gets only a fleeting glance of the thief's face as he runs off but he does see him entering a nearby house. Later he picks out the accused on an identity parade. If there was no more evidence than this, the poor quality of the identification would require the judge to withdraw the case from the jury; but this would not be so if there was evidence that the house into which the accused was alleged by X to have run was his father's. Another example of supporting evidence . . . is to be found in *R. v Long* (1973) 57 Cr. App. Rep. 871. The accused, who was charged with robbery, had been identified by three witnesses in different places on different occasions but each had only a momentary opportunity for observation. Immediately after the robbery the accused had left his home and could not be found by the police. When later he was seen by them he claimed to know who had done the robbery and offered to help to find the robbers. At his trial he put forward an alibi which the jury rejected. It was an odd coincidence that the witnesses should have identified a man who had behaved in this way. In our judgment odd coincidences can, if unexplained, be supporting evidence.'

The case must be withdrawn if the quality of the evidence is poor and unsupported. Assuming the case is left to the jury, his Lordship said:

> 'First, whenever the case against an accused depends wholly or substantially on the correctness of one or more identifications of the accused which the defence alleges to be mistaken, the judge should warn the jury of the special need for caution before convicting the accused in reliance on the correctness of the identification or identifications. In addition he should instruct them as to the reason for the need for such a warning and should make some reference to the possibility that a mistaken witness can be a convincing one and that a number of such witnesses can all be mistaken. Provided this is done in clear terms the judge need not use any particular form of words.'

Figure 58—*Turnbull* guidelines of visual identification

Turnbull (1976)	Poor quality ID	Good quality ID
	Withdraw case from jury unless good supporting evidence: *Long*.	Warnings. 1. Special need for caution; *and* 2. reason for caution: court's experience of mistaken ID; *and* 3. convincing witness(es) can be mistaken.

What is 'good quality'?

It is good when 'for example the identification is made after a long period of observation, or in satisfactory conditions by a relative, a neighbour, a close friend a workmate and the like . . .' (per Lord Widery in *Turnbull*). It is 'not appropriate' to hold a voir dire for the purpose of establishing the facts on which the quality of any identification evidence is based: *Flemming* (1988) 86 Cr. App. R. 32.

Key elements for the judge

Even if the quality of the identification is good, the judge must nevertheless warn of the dangers of relying on it; *and* say that a convincing witness can be mistaken; *and* mention the courts' experience of wrongful convictions based on such evidence. Failure to emphasise all (note '*and*') limbs of the above can result in quashing of a conviction: *Hunjan* (1978) 68 Cr. App. R. 99; *Reid v R.* (1990) 90 Cr. App. R. 121; *Bentley* [1991] Crim. L.R. 620. The reason for the word 'must' is according to Lord Mustill in *Daley v R.* [1993] 98 Cr. App. R. 447 that experience has shown that such evidence has a very slender base, that it is unreliable, and insufficient to found a conviction.

It may also be necessary to warn that there have been miscarriages where two or more witnesses had made a positive identification: *Pattinson* [1996] 1 Cr. App. Rep. 51.

The guidelines apply to virtually all cases involving visual identification and are not limited to what are sometimes known as the 'fleeting glimpse' situation.

'The defendant alleges to be mistaken'

If the defendant concedes presence at the crime but denies any participation in the events, the case does not involve a mistaken identification: *Slater* [1995] 1 Cr. App. R. 584. It follows that a *Turnbull* warning is not required, far less is it mandatory. A slight variation of the facts as e.g. where there was a mêlée and the issue arises as to who did what should give rise to the warning: *Thornton* [1995] 1 Cr. App. R. 578.

The defence alleges lack of credibility rather than mistake

Where the case involves visual identification the 'strong general rule' requiring a warning remains even if the major thrust of cross-examination is to show that the witness is not credible, as where it is sought to show that he is a liar rather than mistaken: *Beckford v R* [1993] 97 Cr. App. R. 409

per Lord Lowry (415). If the jury decides that the witness is in fact credible it would follow that they should have been given a *Turnbull* warning.

The Court of Appeal has recognised, however, that if the sole issue is the witness's veracity the warning is not merely unnecessary but its inclusion would probably merely confuse the jury: *Courtnell* [1990] Crim. L.R. 115; *Cape* [1996] 1 Cr. App. R. 191. In the latter case two of the defendants alleged the witness was lying because of a grudge.

Identification, recognition and description

We recognise someone we know and identify persons we do not. The *Turnbull* guidelines cover both: *Beckford v R.* (1993) 97 Cr. App. R. 409. In *Turnbull* Lord Widgery said:

> 'Recognition may be more reliable than identification of a stranger; but even when the witness is purporting to recognise someone whom he knows, the jury should be reminded that mistakes in recognition of close relatives and friends are sometimes made.'

There might be circumstances where the parties are so well known to each other that a *Turnbull* warning would be unnecessary (*Shand v R.* [1996] 2 Cr. App. R. 204) but they would be highly unusual.

Suppose a witness says the person she saw was male, was about 1.7 metres tall, of slim build with long blond hair and a noticeable tattoo on is left forearm. Does this amount to 'visual identification'? The answer is almost certainly 'no'. In *Gayle* [1999] 2 Cr. App. R. 130 (the case involved whether an identification procedure was required at a police station) a school caretaker described the build and clothes of a man he saw but whose face he had not seen. The Court of Appeal held that there had been no identification.

Supporting evidence

It is the judge's duty to tell the jury of any evidence which can, as well as that which cannot, in law support the identification: *Stanton* [2004] EWCA Crim 490. In *Freemantle v R.* [1994] 1 W.L.R. 1437 the witness commented to the defendant at the scene that the latter had been recognised, whereupon the defendant replied with a low level obscenity which was treated as an acknowledgement of the accusation. This helped further to strengthen otherwise good quality visual identification.

In *Castle* [1989] Crim. L.R. 567 disputed identification of the defendant as having been involved in a crime was held to be supported by the evidence that the witness correctly identified *another* participant who pleaded guilty to the offence.

Suppose it is suggested the defendant has told lies and they could support disputed visual identification. Lies might do this but, because people lie for many reasons, the jury must be instructed in accordance with the Court of Appeal's guidelines in *Lucas* [1981] 73 Cr. App. R. 159,163. We covered this issue in detail in Ch.8, para.8.2.5, and reference should now be made to that section. In *Mills* [1995] 1 W.L.R. 511 Lord Steyn said the jury must be warned that rejection of an alibi defence does not of itself support poor quality identification evidence, though this warning is not necessary if the only evidence of the alibi is unsworn: *DPP v Walker* [1974] 1 W.L.R. 1090. Only if the jury is satisfied that the sole explanation for a fabricated alibi is the attempt to deceive them, should they use their disbelief to support identification evidence and they must be expressly warned to this effect: *Pemberton* (1994) 99 Cr. App. R. 228. This is a particular application of the *Lucas* direction.

Summarising the evidence

Pattinson holds that while there is no mandatory requirement to summarise the identification evidence, any summary that is given must be of both sides. It is unnecessary to rehearse defence counsel's arguments but the judge must tell the jury of any weaknesses in the identification evidence and ask them to consider the cumulative effects of such weaknesses on the identification evidence as a whole: *Fergus* (1994) 98 Cr. App. R. 313. This includes *all* stages of the identification process and is a specific obligation on the judge even in the shortest cases involving identification evidence: *Stanton*. It is insufficient to draw the jury's attention to what counsel has said about identification—the judge must summarise the evidence for the jury himself.

The wording of the direction

In *Mills* Lord Steyn said that *Turnbull* is 'not a statute' and that a judge has broad discretion to express himself in his own way when directing on identification. He must comply with the 'sense and spirit' of *Turnbull*. The judge must nevertheless ensure that all three parts of the warning (linked by 'and') are complied with.

Figure 59—*Turnbull* flow chart

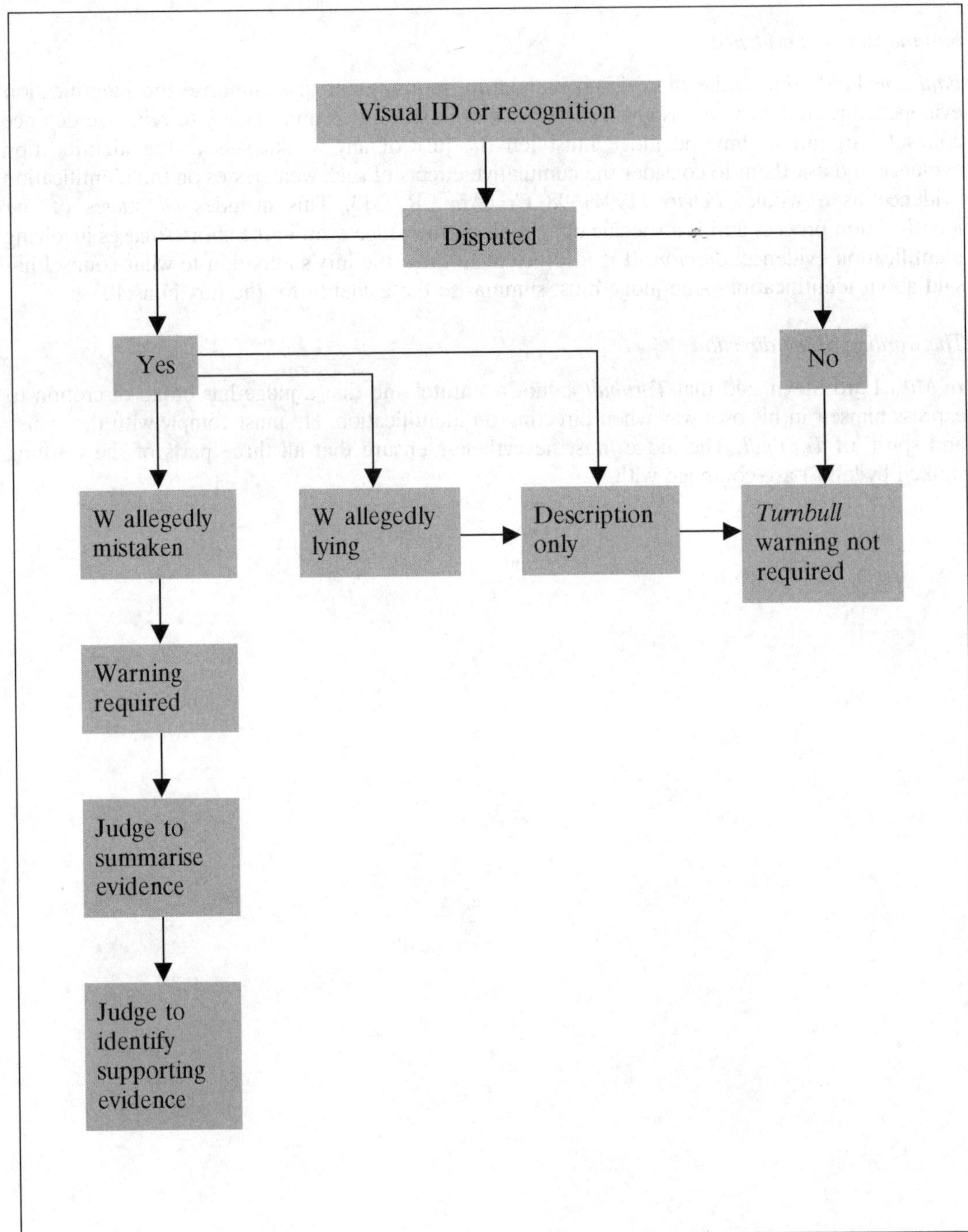

10.3.3 Voice recognition

In *Hersey* [1998] Crim. L.R. 281 the Court of Appeal held the jury should be warned about relying on voice recognition suggesting a procedure parallel to *Turnbull* tailored to the issues of voice identification or recognition would be generally appropriate. In *Roberts* [2000] Crim. L.R. 183 the same court suggested that voice identification was more problematic than visual identification (a view supported by academic research) and mandated a warning even more stringent than the *Turnbull* direction. In *Chenia* [2003] 2 Cr. App. R. 6 the Court of Appeal quashed convictions where, inter alia, the jury had been 'required' to become their own voice expert in the sense of comparing one voice with another by comparing the characteristics of each.

The problems were addressed by the Northern Irish Court of Appeal in *O'Doherty* [2003] 1 Cr. App. R. 5 which held that both auditory phonetic analysis (dialect/accent) and quantitative acoustic analysis (the individual's vocal tract, mouth and throat) should be the subject of expert evidence. If the evidence of voice recognition was relied on by the prosecution the jury should be allowed to listen to a tape-recording of the defendant's voice—if he had given evidence. The tape could help the jury to evaluate the expert evidence but they should also be warned about relying on their own untrained ears.

10.4 Summary

(a) There are limited circumstances where corroboration in a formal and technical sense is still required as a matter of law.

(b) There are plenty of circumstances when we might suspect that a witness has a motive of their own to serve. The court will then give a warning of the problems tailored to the facts.

(c) The *Turnbull* direction is almost statutory in its application and, if applicable, must be given in its entirety.

10.5 Further Reading

Birch, 'Corroboration: Goodbye To All That?' [1995] Crim. L.R. 524
Dein, 'Non Tape recorded Cell Confession Evidence—On Trial' [2002] Crim. L.R. 630
Ormerod, 'Sounds Familiar?—Voice Identification Evidence' [2001] Crim. L.R. 595
Roberts, 'The perils and possibilities of qualified identification: *R. v George*' (2003) 7E. & P. 130

INDEX

LEGAL TAXONOMY
FROM SWEET & MAXWELL

This index has been prepared using Sweet and Maxwell's Legal Taxonomy. Main index entries conform to keywords provided by the Legal Taxonomy except where references to specific documents or non-standard terms (denoted by quotation marks) have been included. These keywords provide a means of identifying similar concepts in other Sweet & Maxwell publications and online services to which keywords from the Legal Taxonomy have been applied. Readers may find some minor differences between terms used in the text and those which appear in the index. Suggestions to *taxonomy@sweetandmaxwell.co.uk*.

(All references are to paragraph number)